"Unforgettable. A blend of history, family saga, and family questions, [Freeman's] book proves to be a winning and moving success."

—*Richmond Times-Dispatch*

"A captivating tour de force."

—*San Antonio Express-News*

"*The Jersey Brothers* brings welcome comparisons to Laura Hildebrand's *Unbroken* . . . both masterfully written stories of endurance and sacrifice that tell bigger truths than the experience of individuals during wartime."

—*Naval History*

"A spellbinding cliffhanger."

—*New Jersey Monthly*

"As engaging and readable as a fine novel."

Minneapolis Star Tribune

"A rare look into the deepest personal emotions of a family of America's Greatest Generation."

—*The Dallas Morning News*

"Freeman's riveting account . . . proves that the well of compelling war narratives has nowhere near run dry."

—*Business Insider*

"A touching, suspenseful, and deeply troubling story of one family's patriotic devotion and betrayal."

—*Kirkus Reviews* (starred review)

"This book is so much more than a summer read, it should be a required one."

—*Pittsburgh Post-Gazette*

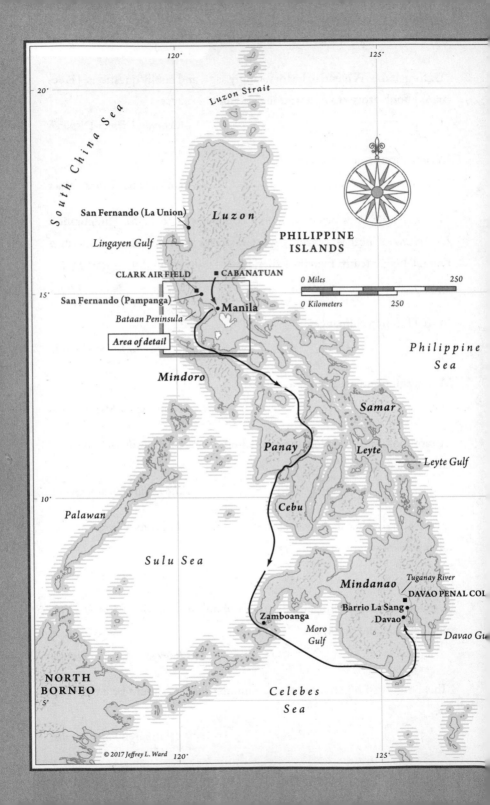

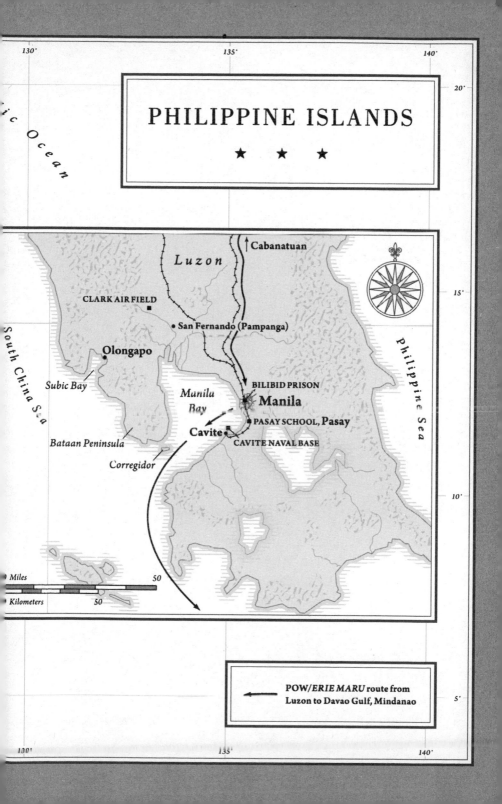

THE

JERSEY
BROTHERS

A Missing Naval Officer in the Pacific and
His Family's Quest to Bring Him Home

★ ★ ★

SALLY MOTT FREEMAN

SIMON & SCHUSTER PAPERBACKS

New York London Toronto Sydney New Delhi

Simon & Schuster Paperbacks
An Imprint of Simon & Schuster, Inc.
1230 Avenue of the Americas
New York, NY 10020

First Simon & Schuster trade paperback edition May 2018

SIMON & SCHUSTER PAPERBACKS and colophon are registered trademarks of Simon & Schuster, Inc.

For information about special discounts for bulk purchases, please contact Simon & Schuster Special Sales at 1-866-506-1949 or business@simonandschuster.com.

The Simon & Schuster Speakers Bureau can bring authors to your live event. For more information or to book an event, contact the Simon & Schuster Speakers Bureau at 1-866-248-3049 or visit our website at www.simonspeakers.com.

Interior design by Ruth Lee-Mui

Manufactured in the United States of America

10   9   8   7   6   5   4   3   2

Library of Congress Cataloging-in-Publication Data is available.

ISBN 978-1-5011-0414-5
ISBN 978-1-5011-0416-9 (pbk)
ISBN 978-1-5011-0417-6 (ebook)

Dedicated with love

to the First Siblings,

Adam Sutherland Mott and Jeannette Mott Fritz

Contents

On New Year's Eve of 1941, the American and Filipino army wounded at Manila's Sternberg Hospital were rushed from their wards to an awaiting hospital ship, the last vessel to depart Manila before it fell to the Japanese. Looking on in disbelief, navy nurse Bertha Evans asked, "What about the navy patients? What's supposed to happen to them?"

Preface

I have a clear memory of that moment when our innocence was fractured, perhaps because it was in such contrast to our blissful cousin-play. It was a midsummer night in the 1960s, and we were playing badminton on the south lawn of Lilac Hedges, our grandmother's home in New Jersey. The highlight of those summer visits was seeing our cousin there, whom we adored and rarely saw otherwise. I know it was dusk because that was when the bats started dive-bombing the birdie, our favorite part of the evening.

The adults—my father, mother, aunt, and grandmother—were having their cocktails on the front porch. Suddenly we heard Aunt Rosemary's voice rise up over the rest, after which she burst into tears. Then we heard a glass break, which is when we stopped our play, got dead quiet, and strained our ears. When I say *break*, I don't mean fall-off-the-table break; I mean throw-against-the-wall break. Then we heard our mother try to say something, and then *she* started crying.

My father was an admiral, and at the time serving as the navy's judge advocate general (JAG). He usually held the attention of the people around him—at work and at home. But his attempts to restore calm were in vain that evening, as apparently were my mother's attempts to assist him. We couldn't hear much, but without a doubt, the ever-charged topic was our mysterious Uncle Barton, a naval ensign who had been wounded and taken prisoner by the Japanese long before any of us was born.

We kids had never met Uncle Barton, but my siblings, cousin, and I all knew what he looked like. There were photos of him on every wall of every room at Lilac Hedges. You would hardly have known that our grandmother had three other children. I especially remember Barton's imposing oil portrait on the facing wall at the turn near the top of the front stairs. I was sure his smiling green eyes followed my every step as I walked up. We joked that he was winking at us, but whenever I reached that landing, I took those last two steps in a leap of terror, as though fleeing a ghost.

We left Lilac Hedges abruptly the next morning for the drive back to Washington, DC. A flimsy explanation for the early departure was offered as four glum kids took turns hugging our cousin, promising him unconvincingly that we'd be back, and then piling into our old Chevy wagon. I don't remember what reason was offered, just that none of us believed it.

One thing was certain: there was always tension when this Uncle Barton's name came up. Each time, I felt a familiar tingling at the back of my neck and then braced myself. *Here we go again.* What was going on here? As children, and then teens, and then young adults, we analyzed every syllable whenever the topic sprang from its dark corner, hoping to elicit conclusive details. But the mystery persisted long into our adulthood. Speculation on what had happened to him—and when—became a sort of a parlor game for us, and it never ended satisfactorily.

When I set out to unravel this family mystery, my objective was to uncover the facts that led to the anguished outburst that night—and which ended our traditional summer visits to Lilac Hedges. I was determined to learn more about this Uncle Barton, but what I uncovered would have stunned the adults on that porch.

PART
ONE

1

★ ★ ★

APRIL 1942, LUZON,
THE PHILIPPINES

THEY HAD BEEN MARCHING at bayonet point when Barton Cross realized a fellow navy patient was dead. Neither Barton Cross nor Charles Armour—shouldering the other end of their friend's crude litter—slowed his pace, despite the dreadful truth that passed between them. They didn't dare stop. By this point in their imprisonment, they had learned that it was safer to proceed as silent pallbearers than call attention to themselves—risking a rifle butt in the rib, a bayonet in the back, or a shot in the head. Wordlessly, they moved in step with the grim prisoner procession through Manila's choking heat and rising red road dust.

Like Barton, the deceased had been wounded during the Japanese bombings of Cavite Navy Yard, the US naval installation near Manila. He was near death at the start of the march, but Barton and Charles had agreed not to let on if he were to die en route. They wanted to get him to a place where his name and death could be recorded. Hundreds before him had not been so lucky. As much as dying itself, all the prisoners feared being dumped into an unmarked grave, their fate forever untold.

Barton's own shrapnel wounds oozed with every step as he struggled under the corpse's sagging weight. The filthy, matted dressing had fallen away, exposing months-old gashes in his leg and foot that had never healed properly. Ahead of him, Charles stared at the road passing under his boots in a grim, trancelike state. His own wounds were deep, but invisible; it would do neither of them any good if Charles were to break down again.

Barton's gold watch had been taken from him when he was captured, but since then he had marked off the long days and nights on an old ten-peso bill. It had been just over a hundred days since he was taken prisoner from a hospital cot in Manila, the tip of a saber at his temple. As Barton worked to absorb the loss of yet another friend, he tried to make sense of all that had happened to him since those first moments as a prisoner of war.

IT SEEMED LIKE DAYS, not months, since Barton heard Don Bell's anxious voice over KZRH, Radio Manila, blaring from a nearby barrack. The carousing ensigns had returned to Cavite late the night before and were walking to the mess hall for Sunday-morning sausages and hotcakes. It was December 8 (December 7 in Hawaii). "Those dirty little bastards have struck Pearl Harbor!" Bell shouted between audible panting. "Reports remain sketchy, but there is no doubt! Oh my God!" Bell was actually crying, near hysteria. "Those yellow-bellied Japs hit our ships at anchor!"

The ensigns hurried on to the mess, which was in chaos over the news. All hands had been ordered to report to their commanding officers on the double. Captain Joel Newsom convened the crew of Barton's ship, submarine tender USS *Otus*, in the Yard's administrative building. Gathered, too, were the captains of submarines *Sculpin*, *Sealion*, *Salmon*, *Sailfish*, and *Seawolf*, all talking nervously among themselves and comparing notes on their clipboards. The room was abuzz with speculation but quieted instantly when Captain Newsom cleared his throat.

"Men, listen carefully. The following message was received from Admiral Hart this morning. 'To Asiatic Fleet . . . Urgent . . . Japan has commenced hostilities . . . the Pacific Fleet has been immobilized . . . govern yourselves accordingly.'" Admiral Thomas C. Hart was the Asiatic Fleet's commander in chief and the highest-ranking naval officer in the Philippines; they knew this meant they were likely the next target.

Captain Newsom proceeded to list a lengthy series of urgent tasks. They could come under attack at any time, and loading, camouflaging, and servicing the submarines were now time critical. Barton and *Otus*'s crew went straight to the docks following the briefing and ratcheted the work to a breakneck pace.

Later that same day, exactly nine hours after the decimation of the Pacific Fleet at Pearl Harbor, the Japanese began their assault on the Philippines. Their opening salvos went to the heart of the island's air defenses, which proved an easy mark. Despite Washington's urgent, repeated orders to General Douglas MacArthur—at the time the US Army Forces Commander in the Far East—to launch his planes and initiate air operations, beginning minutes after the start of the attack on Pearl Harbor, he did not respond. Nor did he ever issue the order. As a consequence, virtually every US plane at Luzon's primary airfields, Clark Field and Nichols Field, was bombed on the ground, wingtip to wingtip. The army's entire staple of bombers, their payloads full, was wiped out in a matter of hours.

The men at Cavite Naval Base reeled at the news. The loss was particularly alarming to the submariners, who relied heavily on army air reconnaissance to prevent enemy flyers from spotting them through some of the world's clearest coastal waters. With air protection gone, Admiral Hart was forced to change his strategy. For officers and crew of the USS *Otus*, one of the fleet's crucial submarine tenders, that meant preparing for immediate sortie into dangerous waters with the subs under their care. They would make for the relative safety of Darwin, Australia, and await further orders.

The slender Asiatic Fleet had a few vintage destroyers, but its signature strength was a large contingent of submarines—more than double that of the Pacific Fleet. Because of its miles of coastline, eddies, and deep harbors, the Philippines was deemed ideal for a submarine defense. The Asiatic Fleet's recent relocation from Shanghai to Manila was for the specific purpose of deterring a seaborne Japanese attack. The three tenders, *Otus*, *Holland*, and *Canopus*, were charged with keeping those subs, which required significant maintenance, action-ready and in uninterrupted service.

Inside the Yard, antiaircraft units were put on five-minute-alert cycles. Barton and his shipmates worked deep into the nights of December 8 and 9. First priority was to ensure that the subs were stocked, armed, and primed for launch. They filled *Otus*'s exposed fuel tanks with water to prevent incineration if hit and installed antiaircraft guns on her deck. Surplus machinery and ammunition were stored in casements and tunnels around the Yard, and as *Otus*'s paymaster, Barton rushed to secure the ship's funds and financial records.

At approximately 1100 hours on December 10, warning sirens pierced Cavite's soft tropical air. Following their wail came a stern broadcast over the Yard's loudspeakers: enemy formations were approaching from the northeast. Within minutes the assailants were visible—fifty-four planes in three tight Vs, the whole formation making one large V. The *Otus* crew looked up in surprise; they had never seen bombers fly so high.

Antiaircraft gunners squinted, aimed, and fired, but the planes were so far above the range of the 1918-vintage weapons that the shells burst in harmless black puffs less than halfway up to their targets. With air cover lost and only toylike antiaircraft guns for defense, the submarines had to get out to sea.

Two submarines with their hatches open lay astride *Otus*. Their crews were topside, scrambling to take on a last cache of supplies. Barton shouted to them to close their hatches and get under way as one enemy bomber after another opened its payload.

The first air group had barely cast a shadow on the east side of the Yard before ships, docks, men, and buildings started exploding in a line. The planes then flew at an almost leisurely pace to the other side of the Yard and discharged the rest of their payloads. The oil storage tanks erupted like geysers, and droplets of oily fire lit the surrounding ground. Corpses by the dozens flew into the air, their smoldering parts scattering down across the Yard.

The next air group set its sights on the congested center of the facility, where its bombs cut a glinting path of destruction. In minutes, fueling depots, machine houses, and storage facilities were ablaze, and plumes of black, choking smoke shot up across Cavite. That was the last thing Barton remembered before he too was struck down by branding-hot shrapnel. The explosion that snared him crippled *Scalion*, one of the two subs he'd been shouting at, and reduced the dock and pilings to splinters. When he awoke, he was lying on a stretcher in Cavite's base hospital intake area.

Men all around him were blackened from head to foot and lying in puddles of their own blood. Slashes of ripped khaki, soaked red, were all that remained of Barton's pant legs, and his shoes pooled with blood. Navy medics triaged among the wounded with surreal calm, applying tourniquets and giving morphine to some, and placing sheets over others.

By evening, the base hospital, named Canacao, was overwhelmed with casualties. Worse, since it was located next to a packed munitions depot, it was a prime future target. With air attacks expected to resume the next day, the facility had to be evacuated. By midnight, hospital staff had requisitioned a boat to move the Canacao patients across the bay to Manila's Sternberg Hospital.

IT SEEMED THAT ONLY bodies and body parts were left to be counted as the stretchered wounded were jostled in the smoky dark to Cavite's civilian docks. The stretcher bearers—an odd group of seventeen native musicians, none of whom Barton had seen before or since—struggled in the blackness to avoid stepping on some hideously burned arm or leg. Crews all around them gathered human remains to inter in bomb craters before the Japanese returned. The crews and stretcher bearers both had to sidestep frantic dogs, cats, chickens, and pigs tearing at the fallen flesh, already putrefying in the tropical heat. At the docks, a hastily appropriated pleasure cruiser named *Mary Anne* awaited.

The patients were quiet as the Filipino captain threw off *Mary Anne's* dock lines and steered toward Manila. The Cavite fireworks sliced up the night sky behind them, the Yard's molten carnage lighting the ghostly remains of the anchorage. Disoriented and morphine-dazed, the patients lay about the festively painted *Mary Anne*, muttering curses and such, making little sense. They periodically looked back at Cavite, shaking their heads. In front of them, Manila appeared relatively safe. They saw isolated columns of smoke over the city—but nothing like the conflagration at Cavite.

This was the night Barton met Ensign Charles Armour, who had been discharged from the USS *Louisville* at Cavite for "treatment" just weeks before. "Yeah, well, my timing's never been too good," Charles said in a dry Arkansas drawl. This was no time for laughing, but Barton was amused by Charles's quips in the midst of the madness all around them.

There was something strange about Charles that he couldn't pinpoint, though Barton felt grateful for the companionship under the circumstances. It was curious that his new friend was at Canacao in the first place. He had no obvious injuries.

At first light, the *Mary Anne* downshifted and drew up to the Manila pier. Corpsmen unloaded the patients in the spectral quiet and slipped them into waiting ambulances. It was about this time that Barton began to inquire what had happened to his shipmates. Dead? Wounded? And his ship? Sunk? But none of the medical staff knew that while he had been drifting in and out of consciousness at Canacao, *Otus* hastened out to sea after the *Sealion* blast, leaving Barton behind. With no time to spare, Captain Newsom had ordered an evasive zigzag toward Australia at flank speed.

By the time the navy patients got to Sternberg Hospital, Charles had fallen asleep. Barton's stretcher was placed along a wall off the entrance foyer, this time among a group of bleeding and weeping civilians, themselves waiting for treatment. One of the most seriously wounded, Ken Koenig, whom Barton also befriended on the *Mary Anne*, was taken to surgery right away. Ken's gurney disappeared through swinging doors, his attendants murmuring about blood loss and a weak pulse.

In retrospect, Barton realized that Sternberg had lulled him into a false sense of security. It was so orderly and lovely with its Spanish architecture, gardens, and large, gracious wards cooled by polished mahogany fans. On that first night, even in the chaos, he had believed that Sternberg, a US military hospital, was the first of many steps away from uncivil engagement. Supply Corps officers weren't supposed to be on the fighting front, were they? He hadn't even been issued a gun.

Barton's confidence ebbed as December wore on. He and his fellow navy patients listened nightly to KZRH as Don Bell somberly detailed the Manila-bound progress of tens of thousands of Japanese soldiers. Wave after wave of enemy troops had come ashore at Lingayen Gulf, 135 miles to the north. They were roaring toward the capital in trucks, on bicycles, and in marching columns, Bell reported in a tone so grave it required little interpretation.

On Christmas Eve, General MacArthur ordered a military evacuation of Manila and declared the Philippine capital an open city, meaning that all Allied defensive efforts had been abandoned there. The open city designation was intended to trigger the 1907 Hague Convention regulating land warfare that forbade attacks on undefended localities. But the designation was ignored by Japan, a Convention signatory; they continued to bomb Manila, including the city hall and other buildings close to the hospital.

By Christmas Day, MacArthur had completed his own retreat to the island fortress of Corregidor near the entrance of Manila Bay. The more than 70,000 American and Filipino troops had also evacuated—to either Corregidor or Luzon's Bataan Peninsula, which bordered the bay on one side and the South China Sea on the other. The evacuation was part of War Plan Orange-3, an emergency contingency plan developed before the war in the extremely unlikely event of a successful Japanese attack. WPO-3 also called for the prepositioning of a supply of food, fuel, medicine, and arms capable of sustaining the evacuated forces for a six-month defensive stand. This latter measure was not taken by General MacArthur.

By New Year's Eve, KZRH had gone off the air, and the sounds of sirens and frantic traffic exiting the city had faded. But the wounded at Sternberg had yet to be relocated to any safe haven. They were the only remaining US military contingent in Manila. Then the unimaginable took place.

Late on December 31, a brief but stunning order from MacArthur's Corregidor headquarters was delivered to the hospital: all army wounded were to be taken down to Pier 7 immediately. They were to be loaded onto a Red Cross ship, the SS *Mactan*, and transported to Australia. The ship must depart as soon as possible, it said, in order to evade Japanese forces, now hard by. Confused, nurses and doctors both responded to the order with the same question: "What about the navy patients?" MacArthur's order made no mention of the navy patients, the sentry said. Only the army patients.

As the senior-most military officer in the Philippines, MacArthur had the authority to include them, but unaccountably had not. Barton, Charles, and thirty other navy wounded at Sternberg Hospital now had no orders to anywhere, from anyone. Could their papers have been on the way, lost in the melee of civilian and military retreat? Could orders have failed to reach them due to blocked roads, cut power and phone lines? Or had this small navy contingent simply been forgotten?

The Filipino ambulance driver told the navy patients and skeletal Sternberg staff he would return for them if there was room aboard the *Mactan*.

They were encouraged, despite the nagging question of whether, absent specific orders, this constituted military disobedience.

Down at Pier 7, a total of 224 army wounded were loaded onto the Mactan—which had been hastily converted from an inter-island steamer into a hospital ship. Her dock lines were then hacked with a knife and tossed into the water. In the waning hours of 1941, amid pelting rain and high winds, the Mactan's Red Cross–painted funnel vanished into the mist. It was the last vessel to depart Manila before the city fell to the Japanese.

The navy patients had waited anxiously for the ambulance to return. Sternberg was darkened, and their ward was quiet as a tomb. Barton, Charles, Ken, and the others lay on their cots behind blackout curtains, listening, sifting through the noise of the pounding rain for sounds of a returning flatbed-truck-turned-ambulance.

Charles became increasingly agitated, and the other patients tried to placate him quietly. He had already been taken from their ward once, shortly after their arrival at Sternberg; he was reassigned to a mental ward with a diagnosis of manic-depressive psychosis. During his absence, Barton learned why Charles had been put off USS Louisville at Cavite. "Attempted suicide," reported the loose-lipped corpsman. "Japs can't do nothin' to him he ain't already tried to do to himself." When a somewhat withdrawn Charles rejoined his fellow patients, they took pains not to unravel him further.

The ward settled into an uncomfortable silence, but they knew they were trapped, and nobody slept. Over the years, Barton had developed an aptitude for getting out of tight spots—of which there had been many in his young life—but this time he came up empty-handed. As the night wore on, their sense of doom only intensified. When they heard loud banging on the hospital's front door and then what sounded like the door crashing on the foyer floor, they froze.

A nurse screamed. Dozens of footsteps, mingled with bursts of unintelligible Japanese, drew closer. They heard the double doors burst open and footsteps running up the first flight of stairs. Doors opened and slammed and glass shattered. Japanese soldiers chattered excitedly as they took the stairs by twos and threes.

The men lay stock-still. The footsteps were closer now—on *their* floor. The ward's wide doors finally swung open, slamming against the walls. Gripped with fear, their eyes closed, the navy patients lay helpless with fists clenched and hearts pounding, their bodies soaked with sweat.

OVER THE NEXT SEVERAL months, the patients were moved from one makeshift prison hold to another, none with even basic medical care, under steadily worsening conditions. Those that couldn't walk were carried. Ken, whose litter Barton and Charles had lifted through those long marches, did not survive. Every move of the prisoners began with their being paraded through the streets of Manila past a saddened citizenry. The macabre displays were intended to humiliate the captured Americans and brandish the new Japanese dominion over the Filipinos.

Their longest holding pen was at Santa Scholastica, a women's college seized by the Japanese to consolidate the navy wounded from Cavite that had been scattered around Manila for treatment. As the patients were being shuffled, meanwhile, the tens of thousands of soldiers and sailors on Bataan and Corregidor were putting up the fight of their lives against a Japanese onslaught. They were outnumbered, outgunned, and slowly starving on half rations, but they continued to hold out and inflict significant enemy casualties.

The longer Bataan and Corregidor held, however, the angrier the Japanese became over those casualties and their stalled seizure of the Philippines—and the worse it got for the navy patients. It was at Santa Scholastica that the patients and their medical attendants came to understand the depth of contempt the Japanese felt toward them.

They were viciously slapped, their food and medical supplies were confiscated, and they were forced to erect a vast stretch of barbed wire to cut them off from all but a tiny corner of the compound. Beds were removed, bathing curtailed sharply, and laundry facilities were declared off-limits. Perhaps worst of all, their precious supply of quinine, used to treat symptoms of rampant malaria—fever, chills, fatigue, vomiting—was seized.

As an officer, Barton was summoned repeatedly for questioning by a committee of Imperial military police, the Kempeitai. They inquired about the name and location of his ship and the submarines of the Asiatic Fleet, the number and layout of mines in the bays and harbors, and other surprisingly detailed questions. Barton replied that he had been wounded and unconscious early in the attack on Cavite and didn't know the answers.

But the interrogations continued. The Kempeitai eyed the navy patients and their medical staff warily, wondering why this single American contingent had stayed behind in Manila while all the others had evacuated to Bataan or Corregidor. The interrogators suspected that the group had been ordered to remain to conduct espionage and that the only thing their bandages concealed was their true identity as spies.

Barton offered little useful information because he had little, but he was also adept at appearing cooperative without being so. He was in the *Supply Corps*, he would tell the Kempeitai, suggesting a unique disinterest in warfare of any kind. The interrogations were a poignant reminder of others he had endured over time—at home, at the Citadel, and at the US Naval Academy—all of which had honed his ability to survive cross-examination without confessing much of anything. In fact Barton had built quite a reputation for his Huck Finn prowess at getting out of scrapes—and his success rate was nearly as high.

One set of facts was a concern, however: that Barton's two brothers *were* of meaningful rank, and, respectively, engaged in high-level naval combat and espionage. Would such a discovery by his interrogators make him a candidate for greater mistreatment, or worse, useful barter?

Benny and Bill—Barton's older brothers and lifelong protectors—were both Annapolis-minted officers. Biologically, they were half brothers, Barton being the only son of their mother Helen's second marriage. Benny, the oldest, was antiaircraft and gunnery officer on the carrier USS *Enterprise*, which was—or at least had been—stationed at Pearl Harbor. Barton had just visited Benny during his stopover at Pearl en route from New Jersey to Manila. That was barely three weeks before he was wounded. He'd had no contact with Benny since.

Bill, the middle brother, was a Naval Intelligence officer in Washington whose top secret work put him in regular contact with senior brass, not to mention with President Franklin Delano Roosevelt himself. Would Barton be guilty by association were the Japanese to make the connection?

BENNY AND BILL HAD been little boys when Barton, a premature baby, made his entry into the world in 1918. Whether or not it was due to his fragile early arrival, he could not recall a time when they had not looked out for him. If history was any guide, they were making every effort to find him now. In fact, Bill had pulled every imaginable string in Washington to help Barton get his officer's commission—no easy task, since Barton had bilged out of the Naval Academy after just two years. But Bill knew that his younger brother's subsequent business degree was just the expertise needed by incipient Supply Corps officers. And being the navy's business office, its mission was anything but dangerous, a winning card with their mother.

Helen's greatest fear had been that, without a commission, her youngest and favorite son would be drafted into the army and sent to God knows where. So she was most pleased with Bill's efforts. But the fleeting maternal approval ended when Barton's orders to the Philippines—over which Bill had zero influence—arrived. "Spitting distance from Japan!" lioness Helen groaned.

"She went on and on and on," Bill had vented to Benny. His brother simply listened, knowing a reply was not necessary. "She said, 'There you are, Billy, at Roosevelt's elbow. Can't you do something?'" Calling Bill by his affectionate childhood nickname always had its effect. On the other hand, her loathing of all things Franklin Roosevelt was a long-standing fact, and the possibility of the president's doing something that might please her was remote.

But reflexively, Bill and Benny sought to safeguard Barton when his orders came through. Bill arranged his accommodations at Manila's posh Army and Navy Club and they both contacted officer friends in Manila who promised to keep an eye on him. This had long been the family pattern: by cultivating their shared role as Barton's elders, they were assured their mother's sparing affection. If Benny and Bill were aware of the sad irony— that they always seemed to be seeking her attention and that Barton was always trying to break free of it—they kept it to themselves.

ONE THING WAS CERTAIN, Barton didn't want his brothers to pull strings and try to bail him out—not this time. He had *wanted* to go to the Philippines precisely for this reason: to break his family's stubborn tether. At twenty-three years old, surely he could now manage matters himself. That's exactly why he had asked one of the nurses at Sternberg to send a telegram to Lilac Hedges, the family keep in New Jersey, from Manila's Army and Navy Club on Christmas Eve—not from the hospital. He didn't want his family to know he'd been wounded and then try to pull strings and extract him like a child from the war zone.

"Quite well," he dictated. "Don't worry. Happy Xmas. Much love, Barton."

Nothing more.

The nurse expressed concern when Barton finished. Why wouldn't he give real information—quite possibly his last chance to do so? "Please," he'd said to her, "you don't know my mother. This is best for right now."

There was still a chance his luck would turn—that the promised rein- forcements were on their way to repel the Japanese incursion. Optimism that his captivity might still be short-lived propelled him from day to day. He would finally get a chance to live up to his family's expectations—on his own terms and under his own power. He clung to this hope despite his mangled condition and the increasingly harsh Japanese treatment.

By March 1942, some two hundred navy wounded from Cavite had been consolidated at Santa Scholastica, at which point they were told to prepare for another move. The place, their doctors were told, was a well-equipped convalescence hospital where they would finally receive badly needed medical care. But when their transport trucks came to a halt at a place called Pasay, fear again replaced hope. A single order was announced as they filed into an abandoned, low-slung building surrounded by tufting weeds: obey all orders or be executed. The peeling sign over the front door of their new accommodation read "Pasay School."

The onetime elementary school was a small, rectangular building with a tiny courtyard at its center. Fifty men were quartered in each sixteen-by-twenty-foot classroom, which teemed with rats, mosquitoes, and green-headed flies. The dwarfish compound was bordered by open latrine trenches swarming with feasting flies. The courtyard, once the school's playground, was so small that the burgeoning prison population could not move about. Adding to the tension of perpetual restraint, the air was sickly hot and humid, and mingling latrine stench and smoke rising from burning garbage hung thick in the air. There were no beds, plumbing, or sanitation at Pasay.

Under these conditions, and with waning optimism that the Allies were coming to their rescue, the patients weakened further and also began to yield to a growing sense of hopelessness. Not only did Pasay claim men from gangrenous wounds, disease, and starvation, but also from sheer despair.

Though he had lost some twenty pounds from his modest frame, Barton had still not lost faith. Things were plenty grim, but so far the Japanese hadn't ordered him to dig a massive tree stump out of frozen ground with a pickax for punishment and "an opportunity for reflection," as he had endured many times at Christ School in Arden, North Carolina. Nor had they beaten him with a broom until he bled while balancing on billiard balls holding up heavy furniture as two Annapolis second classmen had done during his plebe indoctrination. He would weather this just as he had those and other early trials: with a persistent combination of optimism and imperturbable humor.

Barton was less concerned about his own predicament than he was about Charles's precarious emotional state, which was exacerbated by Pasay's miserable confines. A dark switch seemed to have been thrown permanently. Charles had an outsized hatred toward his captors, for whom he had various names, nearly always preceded by "those goddamn," including slopeheads, nips, yelluhs, and worse. He could often be heard saying to nobody in particular, "I'll tell you what, those goddamn —— can just shut the fuck up. Can't understand 'em anyway." The slurs may have been meant for dark amusement, but there was a growing fear that Charles's demonstrated disinterest in preserving his own life could bring harm to others.

Even when he wasn't cursing, his badass southern boy strut back and forth across the tiny courtyard alone seemed capable of sparking an incident. It was a dangerous game. Barton was in constant fear that Charles might do something to place them all at risk. The savage slapping of patients who neglected to bow to passing guards especially enraged Charles, and he threatened privately to retaliate. So Barton focused on helping his friend contain his rage by both cajoling him and deploying creative tactics.

Tenko was the twice-daily prisoner roll call during which guards would count off the bowing prisoners in a process called *bango*. While walking together to *tenko* one evening, Barton suggested to Charles that they take a deep breath upon the guard's approach and exhale only after he had passed them. Refusing to breathe the same air fouled by the breath of their captors was an act of resistance and self-respect, but no slapping would result from it.

As the guard approached, counting prisoners and awaiting bows— *"Ichi, ni, san, shi, go, roku . . ."*—Charles and Barton drew their breaths and bowed deeply. When the guard had passed, continuing his count—*"hachi, kyuu, juu . . ."*—they raised their heads, exhaling slowly. With this, Barton coaxed a rare satisfied smile out of Charles. Their developing partnership helped distract Charles from his self-defeating propensities and both of them from gnawing hunger and fear.

Despite the vitiated air, they would venture into the courtyard to the "shower": a hose fastened to a large punctured tomato can poised over a wooden grate. Since the water was turned on only at certain times, groups of twenty men would disrobe en masse and take turns stepping under the shower head. They would then step back and make way for the next group to do the same. Men given the job of manually emptying the cesspools were allowed to go first, a humane gesture but one that rendered the shower an even more dubious source of hygiene.

AND SO THE PRISONER patients felt a glimmer of hope when told they were to be moved again, this time to Bilibid Prison back in central Manila. As with Pasay, the Japanese told the prisoners that Bilibid had a clean, well-supplied medical facility with beds, medicine, and plenty of food and water. But when they passed through the prison's gates at nightfall, their hearts sank once again. The penitentiary, built by Spanish occupiers a century earlier, had been deemed unfit for criminals and closed by the Filipinos. The Japanese reopened the jail to use as a way station from which captured prisoners would either be dispatched to prison camps around the Philippines or shipped to Japan.

Bilibid stood at the corner of Azcarraga Street and Quezon Boulevard, a familiar intersection to Barton. He had clipped by it often in those early weeks, tanned and khaki clad, on his way to one of the area's many shopping destinations or lively nightspots. Now, under the watchful eye of the Bilibid guards, he could only gaze beyond the prison gates and recall his early infatuation with the city.

Manila's narrow streets, mix of architecture, and overlays of culture from foreign dominions had mesmerized him. Seventeenth-century Spanishbaroque buildings stood next to native huts of bamboo, nipa palm leaves, or grass, and they, next to shuttered stucco buildings with balustrades. There had been fresh fruit stands everywhere, piled high with pineapples, sweet mangoes, and neat lines of amber-streaked papayas, so fresh the stems were still damp from the picking. Tart calamanci limes nestled beside his favorite: the small native bukos. Barton would buy all he could hold of the succulent baby coconuts with their soft, sweet insides, just like the vanilla pudding Nelly, his family's cook, had made for him as a child.

Women with crosses around their necks had walked in twos and threes balancing goods in woven baskets on their heads. Barton had darted between automobiles that crept among pedestrians and calesas, the ubiquitous Filipino horse-drawn carts. The locals, even the children, had always met his gaze, smiling and nodding as they passed.

The earth at the intersection of Azcarraga and Quezon was still brown as tamarind, but the mingling aromas of tropical foliage and mashed peppers simmering in vinegar were gone. Cars were burned and turned on their sides, and calesa carts were smashed alongside bloating animal carcasses. Air attacks had left the streets pitted and impassable, and during the nighttime blackouts, looters finished the destruction the Japanese had started. Sandbags barricaded shops and buildings, and glass from shattered windows glittered on the sidewalk.

The Yangco Market, once a bustling bazaar of native products, stood cratered and vacant across the street. Barton had shopped for Christmas presents for his mother in its small, colorful booths. He had never mailed the bright hats, slippers, and linens he'd bought, nor even his first letters home. Were the packages still perched proudly on his dresser at Manila's Army and Navy Club—so close to where he stood now? Were the letters to his parents in New Jersey and to Benny, Bill, and Eve, the enchanting girl he'd met at Pearl Harbor, still sitting atop them?

When the sorry band of prisoners approached Bilibid's forbidding iron gates, sympathetic Filipinos along the route had been downcast, some tearful. A few daring young boys flashed their signature V signs before the gates slammed and locked behind the last prisoner. The Japanese had failed to calculate the degree of loyalty the Filipinos felt for the Americans, who had set up health clinics and new schools and established a representative government. The United States had also promised the Philippines its complete independence by 1946.

By contrast, the Japanese viewed Filipinos as impure Malayan inferiors and treated them brutally. In the short months since their occupation, the Japanese military had bullied and slaughtered thousands of citizens, ignoring the lessons of the revered ancient Chinese samurai Sun Tsu. In his treatise *The Art of War*, Sun Tsu instructed samurai warriors to "treat . . . captives well and care for them . . . By these means [the samurai] make their governments invincible." Sun Tsu might have predicted the result of Japanese cruelty toward the Filipinos: a heightened allegiance toward the Americans and mistrust of Japan's propagandist assurance of a united, prosperous Asia. Thus far, the Greater East Asia Co-Prosperity Sphere the Japanese had touted equaled only barbaric subordination, bloodshed, and starvation.

When Barton wasn't daydreaming about his peacetime life, he would join his expanding group of friends, usually huddled in the cool shadow of the prison's twelve-foot-high perimeter wall. In the evenings, from their crumbling cells, they would sit together and listen to the bombing and battering of the besieged Bataan Peninsula. And they continued to strain their ears for evidence of approaching reinforcements. Just one week earlier, in a surge of optimism, they had gathered for Easter worship and prayed that Bataan's defenders would hold on until the reinforcements could reach them.

They were sure that they'd heard the distinct *wrrrhh* of an American plane versus the *buzzzz* of the Japanese Zero airplane engine the evening before. At such times they'd laugh, maybe slap one another's backs, and then listen some more. Their fervent prayer on Easter Sunday had been to a common nondenominational God that surely loved them and would show

His mercy. Defiant church bells stung the air in the streets beyond, seeming to confirm that their solemn entreaties would soon be answered.

So when the news of Bataan's surrender hit Bilibid four days later, it shook the prisoners as hard as the earthquake that hit Manila that same morning. Many despaired that they'd been betrayed twice: first by MacArthur and then by God.

WITHIN DAYS OF THAT bitter news, the prisoners were ordered to prepare for another move, this time to a place called Cabanatuan, sixty kilometers (thirty-seven miles) north of Manila. Their misanthropic guards once again shoved the prisoners in line for another march past queues of long-faced Manilans.

The guards were hot, tired, and full of loathing for their charges, a sentiment that had only intensified during the long siege of Bataan. The best Japanese soldiers were reserved to fight the war; those put in charge of prisoners were either disgruntled conscripts or minimally trained third-tier recruits who were all too ready to turn their wrath on the prisoners.

Under the Bushido code—the ancient samurai code of conduct taught to every Japanese boy from an early age—surrender was among the most dishonorable of acts. For a soldier to allow himself to be taken alive or, worse, to surrender, was unthinkable; either brought permanent shame to the individual, his family, and his country. In fact, Japan had declined to ratify the 1929 Geneva Convention because of its opposition to the clause condoning the notification of relatives upon a soldier's surrender. This would not only bring permanent shame upon the soldier, but disgrace to his family as well. Perhaps Ashihei Hino, the Japanese wartime reporter, best described his country's view on this subject in his account of the surrendered men on Bataan: "I feel like I am watching filthy water running from the sewage of a nation . . . which has lost its pride of race."

Thus, by their way of thinking, all prisoners of war deserved only disgrace and hardship. The prisoners were well aware of their captors' disposition as they set out for Cabanatuan. Despite sore temptation, they dared not scavenge discarded American rations scattered among the war debris littering the roadside.

Barton had quickly learned to avoid all but necessary eye contact with his captors. Looking down was the best way to fend off fear—and to hide it. On these brutal marches, designed to weaken, demean, and humiliate, he would lock his eyes on the footsteps in front of him and follow their pattern hypnotically. And like so many of the prisoners, he would fixate on memories of home: of Lilac Hedges, of family, of the Jersey Shore and hours of diving into Atlantic waves and happy picnicking afterward.

Conjuring these images of life when it was whole and full of possibilities renewed his strength. There were the fragrant lilacs, cicada orchestras, postcard images of rolling farmland, summer orchards weighted with ripening fruit, and roadside stands piled high with tomatoes and sweet corn. And there were the family images, too: of Benny, Bill, his little sister, Rosemary, and, of course, his parents. But he lingered most on his mother, though this also brought stabs of pain.

His mother had come to represent everything he had wanted to escape, and only now, in his first experience of deprivation, could he see how much his efforts to distance himself from her had hurt her. Yet these regrets also impelled Barton. He wanted desperately to make amends; for her to know that he loved and appreciated her. He also wanted to make her proud, which he was sure he had long failed to do. If he were lucky enough to see her again, he would run to her, not away from her, and show her the gratitude and affection she had so persistently been denied.

2

★ ★ ★

BENNY

IN LATE NOVEMBER 1941, barely two weeks after Barton sailed for Manila, Benny and the crew of the USS *Enterprise* received abrupt orders from their commanding officer. Admiral William "Bull" Halsey's curt directive to sortie from Pearl Harbor for an undisclosed location "as soon as possible" was unprecedented. Benny could not recall a single instance in the past eleven years when shore leave had been cut without notice.

Even more curious were the twelve F4F Wildcat fighter planes being towed to *Enterprise*'s F-9 berth. The propeller-driven aircraft were hoisted onto the flight deck, after which a dozen marine pilots boarded with hastily packed luggage and very recent orders of their own. Why were these planes being loaded in addition to *Enterprise*'s own 140 dive bombers, fighters, and torpedo planes?

There was good reason for apprehension. Negotiations between Japan's ambassadors and officials in Washington had dragged on fruitlessly for months and tensions were rising fast. Prime Minister Tojo had ticked off a

long list of demands—including that Japan be given a free hand in its occupation of China and Indochina and that the United States cut diplomatic
ties with Chiang Kai-shek, China's leader-in-exile. In addition, Japan had
demanded President Roosevelt reverse his recent order freezing Japanese
assets and restore the flow of American gasoline to its fuel-starved ports,
not to mention halt the buildup of American forces in the South Pacific. As
near as Benny could tell, little had been offered US negotiators in exchange.

Given the worsening standoff with Japan, Admiral Halsey's order unleashed a torrent of questions from the air and gunnery crews. But duty-
bound Benny was not one to second-guess Halsey or any other naval
superior. They needed to do as instructed and fast, he told them. Benny
had quite a few things of his own to do before departure. No telling how
long they would be at sea, and he had to get a letter off to his mother. He
knew she would be anxious about his visit with Barton before he pushed
off for Manila, and there was much to tell.

November 27, 1941

USS <u>Enterprise</u>

Dear Mother,

   Barton has come and gone—this is the first chance I've
had to write you about it and I don't know when I'll have a
chance to write again. I was on the dock to meet him as he
came in. He looked healthy, he was smiling, and happy to be
in that uniform!

   I had the ship's station wagon for the day and took him
sightseeing. Together with two friends of mine, we made a
party of it. First we took him to the Pali overlook, then
to the other side of the island for a cocktail party at

the home of Webley Edwards, the local radio announcer for
Hawaii Calls. The daughter of the family took Bart for a
swim at the Outrigger and Canoe Club at Waikiki beach and
he enjoyed himself hugely.

The Moanna [sic] Hotel is just next door and I took him
over there for a drink. I couldn't raise a bit of sympathy
from Bart about the loneliness in my life. He laughed and
said that crocodile tears were streaming down his face!

Later I called up a young lady friend, Eve, and we
went out to a local night spot, the South Seas, saw the Hula
shows and they danced and danced right up until it was
time for Bart's ship to leave. But when we took him back to
his ship we waited and waited and nothing happened. It
seemed that things had worsened in the Pacific and his
route had to be rearranged. I doubt now they called at
Shanghai or Hong Kong, which is too bad.

We finally left the dock around 3 a.m. after Eve had
collected about 20 flower leis that Barton and the boys
threw her from the ship. She liked Bart a lot, and went
down to the dock again the next day. She works at an office
downtown and saw that his ship was still there and got time
off to go see him again. Bart seems to have all the ladies
eating out of his palms. He had 3 of them running circles
around him here. All the way from 18 to 40.

Mother, I gave him the best advice I could. He isn't
in the best spot in the world right now, but he is young
and has his whole life before him--two years or so there
should be a great experience, providing he keeps a grip on
himself. Bill gave him the best advice of all--to do a good
job and guard his health and his money. If he does that he
will be o.k.

He should be there by now, and I really believe that he will be fairly safe. He'll be on shore duty, from the gist of his orders. That is far better and safer if anything breaks in the Pacific. The Japs won't take the Philippines easily, even if they send an invading force. Remember Mother, Manila is protected by the guns of Corregidor, plus the Army's Air Force, plus the Asiatic Fleet, plus a half million men in the Filipino army, plus our own forces. They will find the Filipino army trained by General MacArthur--a pretty crack outfit and a tough one.

And remember, meanwhile, while they are doing that, we aren't here in Pearl for nothing. Anyway, the next few weeks will tell the story. They may back down completely if we stand firm, in spite of the terrible loss of face they would sustain. The Japanese man in the street is sick of war. They've had severe restrictions now for years, and they don't like it. Of course the Big Boys may decide on national hari kari [sic] and take the big chance. There's always that angle with those people.

I told Bart what it would be like out there in paradise and not to throw pesos around just because there are two of them for a dollar. I advised him to get up with a couple of the boys and get a house in Cavite. Then they could hire a cook and a house boy so they wouldn't have to worry about food.

I agree with what you said about the rest being up to Bart. I warned him to guard his values and judge those around him carefully.

Your loving son,

Benny

P.S. I also told him to remember that it's only 8 or 9 days by
Pan Am Clipper to New York--and to write you often.

Benny had been the first of the three brothers to leave Lilac Hedges for
Annapolis. That was in 1926, and he was one of the lucky 1930 graduates
to receive an officer's commission. The Naval Academy was not immune to
the economic reversals of the Depression, and peacetime commissions for
rising ensigns were no longer automatic. He departed for Norfolk, Virginia,
that June for duty on the aircraft carrier USS *Lexington*.

When the schedule of orders was posted at graduation, Benny had been
disappointed to draw an aircraft carrier. In most navy circles, the battleship
was the peerless ruler of the seas. The then-prevailing view was that a carrier's best use was to support battleships by scouting, range finding, and
providing defensive air cover. Still, to Benny, a shipboard gunnery assignment was a dream come true.

The joke at Annapolis was that salt water, not blood, coursed through
his veins, and there was more than a little truth to that. Benny could predict a
change in weather long before it was announced on a barometer and seemed
to thrive on a mixed aroma of salt air, gun grease, and a naval officer's mainstay of strong, scalded coffee. He was, as the saying goes, a real sea dog.

After a following stint at the navy's ordnance testing lab in Washington,
DC, Benny was noted in his performance review as "cheerful, enthusiastic,
cooperative, and honest" and recommended for promotion. It was a happy
time for him and his new bride, Jeannette, whom he married in 1933. In
1934 they welcomed a baby girl, Jeanne Marie. But Benny's promotion
came with new orders that uprooted the young family and sent them across
the country, first to Bremerton in Washington State and then to the naval
port at San Diego. The moves with a small child took an increasing toll on
Jeannette, who had not wanted to leave the heady social swirl of Washington, DC in the first place. Benny's lengthening sea deployments strained
the marriage further.

In 1940 the entire Pacific Fleet, including his new ship, USS *Enterprise*, was transferred to the US naval base in Hawaii. The move was intended to curb Japan's expansionist zeal, but it only infuriated Japanese leaders. Mutual mistrust had only intensified since. Worse for Benny, Jeannette announced that she and Jeanne Marie, now in kindergarten, would not pull up stakes again; they were going to stay put in San Diego with her mother. It was the first overt sign that the marriage was in trouble. Reluctantly, in May 1940, Benny shipped off to Pearl Harbor alone.

From Pearl, *Enterprise*'s primary role was to patrol the vast seas between Hawaii and California. The two other carriers available to relieve her, *Saratoga* and *Lexington,* were older and frequently in drydock for repairs. *Enterprise* filled the gap time and again. Perhaps it was just as well that lonely Benny and *Enterprise* had been on nearly continuous deployment since moving to Hawaii. At sea, his fellow crew had become an increasingly important source of ready companionship.

Since Annapolis, Benny had learned a great deal about gunnery and fleet practices and his views had evolved considerably. By 1940, he was part of a growing contingent of officers that saw carriers as the navy's primary offensive weapon, even though only a handful of them were in operation. These powerful and self-sufficient floating airports with their multiple air squadrons had many times the offensive reach of battleships. That view, however, had yet to be adopted by top brass.

AS *ENTERPRISE* EXITED PEARL Harbor Channel on November 28, 1941, and hove into the open sea, Benny was at the rail in Sky Control, his command station, scanning the water's surface through his ever-present field glasses. Rising not quite six feet from the steel deck, his eyes were deeply creased for a man of thirty-three, and he was as stout as navy regulations would allow. But his visual acuity of 20/15 was better than perfect, and he had yet to miss an errant ripple on patrol. "His eyes burn brightly, scorching the dainty wings of fair moths that fly his way," quipped the 1930 Naval Academy yearbook, *Lucky Bag*, beneath his photograph.

Sky Control was a partially enclosed platform on the tripod mast. At 110 feet above the waterline it was the best vantage point on the ship. Benny had a commanding view of the southwest corner of Oahu as *Enterprise* cleared Barbers Point. Shortly thereafter, an escort group of three cruisers and nine destroyers joined the carrier. Once in formation, all bows pointed due west.

Compounding the mystery of *Enterprise's* present mission was the mimeographed order that was handed Benny next: to supply all aircraft with war-ready torpedoes and live ammunition. It also directed him to arm the ship's mounted guns and antiaircraft batteries with the same. Benny sent a message back to *Enterprise's* captain, George Murray. If they prepared the torpedoes for war shots, they wouldn't be able to participate in the scheduled battle exercises on their return to Pearl. Word came back promptly: "Prepare torpedoes for war shots."

Such preparation took scores of men hundreds of hours. Stored ammunition was loose, and a million rounds had to be belted, clipped, and installed on all the guns on the ship. Torpedo gangs had to attach TNT warheads to the carefully stored bombs. At the same time, the ship's mechanics worked around the clock to put the marine planes in top-notch condition; there were no servicing facilities wherever they were going.

When the flotilla was safely at sea, the mission was announced at last: transport the twelve fighter planes and their pilots two thousand miles to Wake Island. The strategic mid-Pacific American base, with no fresh water source and only one known mammal—the rat—needed immediate fortification. After the 2,800-strong *Enterprise* crew and pilots were notified, yet another startling order circulated the ship and, by signal, transmitted to all escort vessels. The announcement was signed by both Captain Murray and Admiral Halsey, *Enterprise's* flag officer:

CV6/A16-5(10-11t)

USS Enterprise

At Sea

November 28, 1941

BATTLE ORDER NUMBER ONE

1. The <u>Enterprise</u> is now operating under war conditions.

2. At any time, day or night, we must be ready for instant action.

3. Hostile submarines may be encountered.

4. The importance of every officer and man being especially alert and vigilant while on watch at his battle station must be fully realized by all hands.

5. The failure of one man to carry out his assigned task promptly, particularly the lookouts, those manning the batteries, and all those on watch on deck might result in great loss of life and even the loss of the ship.

6. The Captain is confident all hands will prove equal to any emergency that may develop.

7. It is part of the tradition of our Navy that, when put to the test, all hands keep cool, keep our heads, and <u>fight</u>.

8. Steady nerves and stout hearts are needed now.

G. D. Murray (signed)

Captain, US Navy,

Commanding

Approved, November 28, 1941

W. F. Halsey

Vice Admiral, US Navy

Commander Aircraft,

Battle Force

Enterprise at war? Scuttlebutt regarding the strongly worded memo shot from one end of the ship to the other. The crew shifted to an unfamiliar state of high alert, and more than one school of fish drew torpedo fire along the way. But the convoy's crinoline wakes were the only visible disturbance on the water's surface all the way to its destination.

On November 30 *Enterprise* crossed the International Date Line, and the calendar skipped to December 2. At daylight the next morning, the marine pilots boarded their planes, took off in a line, and lowered onto the largest of Wake's three tiny spits of coral, sand, and scrub.

On December 3, under blackout orders and radio silence, *Enterprise* and her escorts swung around and immediately began the trek back to Pearl. Having regained a day at the 180th meridian, they sailed through two December fifths. On the first of these, a young flyer named Ensign John H. Vogt returned from his patrol and reported seeing ships' masts through the haze at the outer perimeter of his search; the information was logged but not acted upon.

On the second December fifth, the convoy ran into a tremendous squall. High winds lashed and battered the convoy. Thirty-foot waves broke high over *Enterprise*'s bow as the carrier rose and fell in heaving seas. Benny lurched along slippery, crazily slanted walkways as he moved from gun emplacement to gun emplacement. He was not alone in wondering whether getting to Pearl on December 6 as scheduled was more important than getting there in one piece. Benny's concern was that pelting rain was blinding his already raw-nerved gunners, not to mention challenging their tenuous holds on the gun mounts.

Only when powerful trade winds collided with the mountainous seas and threatened to crack the bows of two destroyers did a reluctant Admiral Halsey order reduced speed. The convoy's scheduled arrival at Pearl Harbor was thus postponed to Sunday morning, December 7.

Benny and the crew were as relieved as they were disappointed. The slowdown eased their nerves, but after nine grueling days at sea, the delay also meant no Saturday-night dissipating at the Moana Hotel or Sunday on the links. Adjusting to the news, the men going off rotation gravitated to the gymnasium-like hangar deck to watch Gary Cooper in *Sergeant York*, a movie about a draftee-turned-World War I hero who saved hundreds of his comrades' lives while braving a hailstorm of enemy fire.

As the men settled into the film, *Enterprise* and her escorts slowed their eastward pace but remained on a near-convergence course with another convoy, *Kido Butai*, a mammoth six-carrier Japanese armada complete with 414 planes and 49 support vessels pounding southeast from its own late-November sortie, a remote anchorage in the Kurile Islands. The Japanese convoy was traveling under radio silence outside normal shipping lanes to avoid detection.

At dusk on December 6, scout planes again returned to the ship after their customary two-hundred-mile scan in all directions. Flyer D. W. Halsey (no relation to the admiral) jumped from his dive bomber, still zipped in his orange jumpsuit. He had an urgent report. Young Halsey felt sure he had observed the top of ships' masts on the horizon at the end of his northwest search. The admiral questioned sternly why he didn't investigate further. He quietly responded that he would not have had enough fuel to return to the ship. Because the pilot was relatively inexperienced, Captain Murray and Admiral Halsey decided to disregard the uncorroborated report.

In the predawn hours of December 7, Benny was on the "dog watch," which ran from 0400 to 0800. Damp cold and edgy nerves had him on full alert that morning. He paced back and forth in Sky Control, alternately raising his field glasses to scan the obsidian sea and swilling from a bottomless cup of coal-black coffee. At 0500 the day's first general quarters ("man your battle stations") sounded. Flight quarters ("pilots, man your aircraft") then blared from the loudspeakers.

It was customary to send one air squadron to Pearl Harbor ahead of the ship on the day of its arrival. This duty was sort of a rotating perk among the flight squadrons. Leaving *Enterprise* several hours early to arrange for the convoy's berthing allowed the pilots to greet anxious wives and girl-friends in two short hours instead of the five or six it took *Enterprise* to get there. On this particular morning, the honor went to Scouting Squadron Six, led by Commander Brigham Young.

As the pilots assembled, Benny sent an inquiry to the flag bridge as to whether the live bombs and antiaircraft ammunition were to be removed from Scouting Six's planes. After some delay, a runner brought word back from flag staff: remove the bombs but leave the ammunition. Benny nod-ded and transmitted the message. After Battle Order Number One, why should this surprise him?

Out on the Sky Bridge, he could see the pilots suiting up and prepar-ing for takeoff. Crewmen huddled around them, asking the flyers to notify loved ones of the ship's impending arrival. *Enterprise* had departed so sud-denly that many of them hadn't had the chance to explain that they might be gone longer than a routine weekend of maneuvers. Benny always felt a quiet pang overhearing the men chattering about wives and families waiting for them. Once again, nobody would be waiting for Benny.

Benny had already said his good-byes to Scouting Six pilots Vogt and Roger Miller, the men who had joined him for a day of revelry during Bar-ton's stopover. They made a fast plan to go to Waikiki the following week when they all had leave. At 0615 the flight deck was finally cleared, and Squadron Six's eighteen planes took off and set a due east course. They would do a 180-degree sector sweep ahead of the ship, then land at Ford Island, the islet in the center of Pearl Harbor, by morning colors.

TWO HUNDRED AND FIFTY miles north of Oahu, nearly the same distance that the *Enterprise* now stood west of her port, the Imperial Japa-nese fleet pressed southeast at flank speed. Its twenty-seven submarines were already well ahead of the fleet. At 0550 the Japanese Imperial Navy's six aircraft carriers and escorts had commenced the launch of 184 attack planes.

★   ★   ★

AFTER THE *ENTERPRISE* PLANES took off, Benny fiddled with
the radio dial until he found the squadron's flight frequency. This had become a habit in Sky Control on approach to Pearl, often just to relieve the
boredom. The bravado chitchat among the pilots, usually on the bawdy
side, was always a source of amusement.

About 0745, through the crackle and buzz of interference, Benny was
jolted by the pilots' voices rising with alarm over the radio transmitter. They
were shouting to one another.

"Hey, did you see that army plane shooting at me?"

"That's no army plane! That's a Japanese plane! Look at the red circles
on his wings!"

"That bastard! I'm going to shoot back!" The charged back-and-forth
continued as Squadron Six and the equally surprised Japanese pilots tan-
gled in view of Pearl Harbor.

Relieved of his watch, Benny raced past the duty bugler and the officer of the deck, then past the quartermaster and the helmsman. He was
heading for the secret radar console between the flag bridge and the ship's
bridge. Benny found Jack Baumeister, *Enterprise* radar officer, hidden behind a long black curtain. Heart at a gallop, Benny told Jack what he'd heard
on the pilot's frequency. "Can we get anything on radar?"

Perspiring, Jack leaned forward in his chair and peered at a cluster of
echoing blips of unknown origin making their way across the screen of the
ship's new radar machine. "It's strange," he said. "I've got a lot of bogies, but
I shouldn't be getting any. We're a hundred and forty-four miles away, so
they have to be flying really high for me to even get them on radar—I mean
at least twenty thousand feet."

"Have you reported this?" Benny asked, incredulous. Jack replied that
he had, but his tone betrayed a lack of confidence in the new radar tech-
nology. By then, however, numerous planes had sent messages back to

Enterprise confirming the worst. Benny and Jack stood together staring at the screen, the top half seeming to crawl with ants. Within seconds, the ship's sirens screamed. The radioman had received an official coded message: "Enemy air raid on Pearl Harbor X This no drill."

The quartermaster pulled the general quarters alarm, triggering its seventeen spine-chilling buzzes. The message blared repeatedly over the ship's loudspeakers as men scrambled to their battle stations. Back in Sky Control, Benny issued rapid but succinct instructions in preparation for a possible attack on *Enterprise* itself, first to the men on the large five-inch antiaircraft mounts and on down the line to the machine gunners amidships.

As Benny barked orders to his gunners, Halsey issued his own from the flag bridge. After sending up a combat air patrol (CAP) to search for enemy ships, the admiral motioned to the signalmen. In a finger snap, a new set of multicolored flags were yanked from their flag bag and hoisted up the yardarm. The message to the fleet: "Prepare for battle." With *Enterprise's* battle flags now flying from her forepeak, the signal went out to the ships in the convoy to do the same. Wordless, from the ship's highest perch, Benny watched the opening scenes of *Enterprise* at war.

OVER THE NEXT TWO hours, the enemy force, commanded by Japanese admiral Isoroku Yamamoto, leveled the American fleet at Pearl Harbor. *Enterprise's* Squadron Six, outnumbered ten to one, fought the swarming Zeros with everything it had. The pilots' voices through the crackling radio static rang in Benny's ears for days, especially that of Ensign Manuel Gonzales. "Please don't shoot! This is Six-Baker-Three, an American plane!" Next came Gonzales's urgent command to his rear gunner, "We are on fire—bail out!" The transmission went silent after that. They disappeared without a trace.

Brigham Young carried Admiral Halsey's staff officer, Lieutenant Commander Bromfield Nichols, in the rear of his plane. Nichols was carrying the classified report on *Enterprise's* delivery of the fighter planes to Wake. Through the wind and static, Benny heard Young say something about antiaircraft puffs over the harbor and army planes over the marines' aviation hub, Ewa Air Station.

Next, Nichols shouted that bits of their left wing were gone. The next thing Benny heard was a long series of invectives, and then nothing. He later learned that Young barely made his landing on Ford—after taking more fire from confused US gunners on the tarmac than the Japanese pilots in the air.

News of the rest of Squadron Six trickled in. Lieutenant Clarence Dickinson and Ensign Bud McCarthy had been lucky. Under attack by six Zeros, they shot down one but were no match for the rest. Both their planes were riddled, but the men bailed out at low altitude and survived to tread water off Battleship Row, witnessing firsthand the entire horrific show. Ensign Edward Deacon landed in the water short of the runway. Holding his wounded gunner, he grabbed his raft from the sinking plane and paddled ashore.

Squadron Six leader Earl Gallagher miraculously avoided the enemy planes by flying back out to sea, low above the water. He felt sure the enemy ships had retired to the northwest. He then landed on Ford Island amid more confused American gunfire. After refueling, Gallagher flew 175 miles in the direction of the retreating planes but found nothing but empty seas. When the worst of it was over, Benny asked around for news of Ensigns Vogt and Miller.

Vogt's Dauntless dive bomber was last seen by marines at Ewa Station in a dogfight with three Zeros, firing his fixed and free guns with everything he had. Then he got on the tail of one of them and poured tracers into it, but it pulled up so sharply that Vogt collided with it. He was able to bail out but his parachute failed to deploy, and he died after slamming into a tree. Roger Miller managed to take out a Zero also, but he, too, was killed. Benny's two good friends had been struck down within minutes of each other in the first hour of the war.

STILL A RELATIVELY SAFE distance from Pearl, *Enterprise* searched for the retreating Japanese fleet for the next twenty-four hours. The Pacific

Ocean had become a vast hiding place for an invisible foe, however, and the attackers were nowhere to be found.

The search was abandoned late on Monday afternoon, December 8. At sunset, *Enterprise* and her convoy nosed up the channel and into Pearl Harbor. It was a silent, ghoulish glide through thousands of feet of smoldering wreckage and floating bodies. Soot-smudged soldiers manning antiaircraft guns lined the docks. "Hey, you better get out, or they'll get you too!" yelled one shell-shocked sailor. Another cried, "Where the hell were *you*?"

A dumbstruck Benny surveyed the devastation from the ship's superstructure. Grim-faced sailors lined the ship's rails, and thousands of faces fastened on the horror from every gun mount, hatch, and portal. *Nevada* was overturned and aground, *Utah* blown to pieces, its remains slouched in harbor mud. The capsized *Oklahoma* had rolled 150 degrees, her tripod mast jammed deep into the sludge.

Only the bottom of *Oklahoma*'s hull was visible. As the *Enterprise* crew gawked helplessly, word traveled that hundreds of *Oklahoma*'s sailors were trapped alive inside. Men huddled on and around her hull, frantically working pneumatic drills to free them before their oxygen expired.

The spit-and-polish harbor *Enterprise* had departed nine days earlier was aflame and clogged with charred ship remains and floating death. A pall of black smoke fed by the still-burning *Arizona* hung heavy and low over the entire anchorage. For *Arizona*, it was too late for heroics. Four Japanese bombs found their mark on the ship, and 1,700 men perished, among them 23 sets of brothers. By Benny's count, at least twenty ships had been sunk or damaged. He wondered with dread how many of the dead he knew.

Enterprise put in at a new berth, F-2, just astern of the stricken battleships. *Utah* sat capsized and burning at her usual slot, F-9; she had docked there only after *Enterprise*'s sudden departure for Wake Island. The torpedo that felled *Utah* was no doubt intended for the larger spoils of flattop *Enterprise*. Thanks to the diligent surveillance of the spy Takeo Yoshikawa, a Japanese ensign disguised at one point as a Filipino dishwasher in the harbor's navy mess, the enemy had been well apprised of the harbor layout. Yoshikawa's last communiqué to Japan in late November had noted *Enterprise*'s abrupt departure, but it was received too late for Admiral Yamamoto to alter his attack plan.

Once the lines were secured, the *Enterprise* crew promptly shifted gears to reprovision the carrier for immediate redeployment to a hostile sea. By the light of the burning *Arizona*, Benny set about his next exhausting task: rearming the ship. The work had to be done faster and to a greater capacity than ever before. And while the antiaircraft magazines were packed to the brim, millions of gallons of fuel oil gushed into the ship's tanks, and storerooms were crammed with a myriad of supplies.

Hundreds of thousands of pounds of potatoes, flour, eggs, chicken, wrenches, gun grease, bacon, cooking oil, soap, paper, pens, bandages, toothpaste, aspirin, and shoes were hauled aboard and stowed. Coffee stores alone for 2,700 measured in the tons. Instructions were shouted up and down long lines of sweating sailors pitching in from the docks. During rare pauses for rest, the *Enterprise* crew could hear the agonizing tapping on *Oklahoma*'s overturned hull by the oxygen-deprived men trapped inside. By the time *Enterprise* loosed her lines, the voiceless *tink, tink, tink* had stopped—and 429 sailors had presumably suffocated to death.

Benny's good friend Webley Edwards, KGMB's popular *Hawaii Calls* radio announcer, came down to the docks to see him off. The last time they had seen each other was at Webley's house—laughing and talking over rum punches with Barton and Ensigns Miller and Vogt. The flickering *Arizona* lit their faces.

"It's up to you carrier boys now," Webley said, clasping Benny's hand in a farewell handshake. "You're all we've got left."

At 0400 on December 9, barely a dozen grueling and traumatic hours since arriving, *Enterprise* and her escorts pushed back through the wreckage and headed northwest. With the harbor under blackout orders, their departure was illuminated only by oily water, still aflame. Her orders were to clear local seas of enemy submarines and repel subsequent attacks.

Swinging west to east and back again, they scrutinized Oahu's every seaborne approach, searching for a killer fleet that not a single pair of American eyes had seen. The lookouts reported so many sightings of Japanese submarines that dozens of depth charges were dropped and hundreds of gallons of precious fuel were expended in pursuit. An exasperated Admiral Halsey finally signaled to his task force: "If all the torpedo wakes reported are factual, Japanese submarines will soon have to report home to reload, and we have nothing to fear. We are wasting too many depth charges on neutral fish. Take action accordingly."

After breakfast on December 11, Benny picked up the ship's newspaper on his way back to Sky Control. He glanced down at the headline and stopped dead in his tracks to reread the headline splayed across the top of the typed mimeographed sheet: "Cavite Navy Yard Smashed." Casualties were estimated in the hundreds, with more feared.

Whether it was the instant remorse over the confident assurances he had just sent his mother or fear for Barton's life, Benny felt his knees go weak. There was no denying any longer that Barton was in the bull's-eye of a dangerous war zone. Benny's next call would be to Bill in Washington to see whether Barton had survived the attack and, if so, where he was now. If anyone could find out, it would be Bill.

3

★ ★ ★

HELEN

AT LILAC HEDGES ON Sunday night, December 7, Helen and Arthur Cross settled gloomily by the fire after turning off the Victrola. They had been fastened to the newscasts for hours while their dinner sat cold and untouched. They had been trying to reach Bill in Washington since hearing the news, assuming that he had more information than had been broadcast, or could get it.

But all of Washington was reeling, too. Even Bill could not supplement their meager information stores by bedtime, though he promised to do everything in his power to find out. Before retiring to a sleepless night, Helen unscrewed her fountain pen and took a long draught of blue-black ink from a porcelain inkwell. She opened her black leather diary with "1941" stamped in green on the cover and leafed to the seventh page of the last month.

Blackest of all Sundays! At 2 today, we got word that Japan foully attacked Hawaii while her 'ambassadors' talked peace in Washington.

Poor laddie Bart at Manila, getting his baptism by fire, he who never
had a thought of hate for any man. Poor Benny on the Enterprise in
Pearl Harbor! God be at their side.

After listening to President Roosevelt's declaration of war and address
to Congress the next day, she wrote:

Let the Philippines not become another Dunkirk! The Japs according
to radio are swarming like locusts. Have we got proper air protection?
And Benny, on those boundless waters, looking for death from above and
below! What have mothers done to deserve such grief? I stare numbly
at my Christmas cards and packages, longing to stow away the gaudy
reminders.

To her British-born husband, Helen revealed a stalwart and pragmatic
side, but to her diary, she indulged fiery opinions, fierce indignation, and
withering insights. Her entries the preceding several months had amounted
to a dread-filled countdown to the hour of Barton's departure for the Philippines: the cholera shots, the farewells to friends and neighbors, and the final
family dinner at the Russian Tea Room before the mournful trek to Grand
Central Station to meet Barton's transcontinental train.

On his last evening at home, she wrote, "I must steel myself for the hour
when dread imaginings give place to reality and he is gone. Every moment
of his life has blessed me and I am truly grateful—and ashamed of my weak-
ness."

Her emotions were not just those of an anxious mother relinquishing
a grown child to a dangerous world—painful enough, any mother knows.
Barton was much more than a son to Helen Cross. He was the very symbol
of her own reincarnation in a promising second marriage. As if to cement
that success, she had insisted on naming him after her new husband: Arthur

Barton Cross—Jr. With this, Helen had permanently cast off the forsaken image of failed wife and mother. Her apparent preference for this youngest of her three sons may have read as favoritism, but it was, more accurately, a mantle of gratitude for the miraculous second chance his arrival signified.

HELEN ESTELLE CHAMBERLAIN WAS born in New York City in 1883 of recently emigrated parents. Respectively, her father and mother were of English and Irish descent. Soon after Helen's birth, the young family moved to the historic and progressive township of Framingham, Massachusetts. By all accounts, Helen was focused and determined from an early age. She was an industrious child who excelled in school and spent after-school hours developing a mastery with the needle and thread. This was likely due to the County Cork needlecraft talents conferred by her mother, née Annie Lynch.

According to family lore, Helen's father, William Lincoln Chamberlain, was one in a continuum of prosperous enough English merchants. Though he supported the family well, Helen and Annie formed an alliance familiar among Irish American women in the late nineteenth century and one that supplemented their household incomes: fine embroidery and skilled needlework. For Helen and Annie, there was never a shortage of orders for their handiwork, particularly around Christmas.

Whether or not the independence gained from that experience was the reason, Helen joined the slim 3 percent of American women at the turn of the century who pursued a college degree. Triumphantly, at age seventeen, she made the brief but seminal journey from Framingham to nearby Wellesley College in September 1900.

Helen double majored in German and Latin, perhaps believing that mastery of Goethe, Virgil, and Horace gave her a certain gravitas that widened the distance from a relatively unremarkable childhood. Her superior showing in Wellesley's elocution classes completed Helen's transformation from ambitious student to a refined and elegant—if strong-minded—young woman.

The first decade of the new century was a time of expanding opportunity for American women, and Helen approached her 1904 graduation with optimism and self-assurance. Soon after her commencement, she was thrilled with the offer to teach Latin at a high school in a small New Jersey borough. But the social dictates of the time also stressed that young women should marry, and in the borough of Rockaway, Helen Estelle Chamberlain fell in love and did just that.

In the young and attractive Dr. Raymond Mott, Helen saw a promising future. Raymond in turn was delighted to have drawn such a prize. The town dentist, Dr. Mott descended from a long line of Motts, dating back to their arrival on Long Island from Saffron Walden, Essex, England, in the early 1700s. Rockaway Township, named after a historic Indian tribe that roamed its hills and fished its streams long before the American Revolution, was a close-knit community with a strong social fabric, and the surrounding Jersey countryside was an idyllic tapestry of stone mills, fields, streams, and woods threaded with old Indian paths.

Born into this stable and secure world were two Mott sons, Elias Bertram and William Chamberlain—Benny and Bill—in 1908 and 1911, respectively. The family lived in a white frame house with dark-green shutters a short distance from Mott Hollow, a once-thriving hive of mills and other business concerns settled by Dr. Mott's Quaker ancestors more than a century earlier. The young boys ran free with friends whose families had been neighbors for generations. Rockaway's general store, barbershop, soda fountain, and five-and-dime were all run by merchants who knew Benny and Bill by name. They also enjoyed a close circle of grandparents, aunts, uncles, and cousins.

Their grandfather, Elias Briant Mott, was Rockaway's grand patron. His large personality won him local adoration, and his civic and community activities were legion. Elias held the august position of Morris County clerk, was a patriarch of the Independent Order of Odd Fellows, and served as a standing member of the Improved Order of Red Men. The

Red Men were said to have descended from the Sons of Liberty, who, famously disguised as Mohawk Indians, boarded three East India Company ships and tossed ninety-two thousand pounds of English tea into Boston Harbor. Being grandsons of Elias Mott was the closest thing to royalty that little Rockaway had.

Raymond, the youngest of Elias Mott's four children, was overshadowed by his eldest brother, Bert. The most successful of the siblings and heir apparent to their father's revered community role, Bert became a bright and gregarious lawyer and founded many of the town mainstays, including First National Bank of Rockaway and the Rockaway Building and Loan Association. He succeeded his father as clerk of the conservative Morris County and rose to state Republican Party chairman. Under Bert's tutelage, the county GOP maintained consistent majorities of twenty thousand votes over Democrat opposition, a statistic of which he was very fond.

Raymond, a quiet man by comparison, chose dentistry as a solid if less prominent profession than his brother's. From a young age, he was deeply affected by his father's preference for Bert, and his early insecurities metastasized into overwhelming melancholia when he became an adult. Raymond's family life and marriage to Helen came to suffer as a result. Perhaps for fear of falling short of his wife's expectations in the same way he felt he had his father's, he sought refuge in the quiet world of his dental office and possibly relief from anxiety in his supply of the calmative ether.

While Raymond saw to his dental patients, the diminutive Helen rose in stature at the local American Association of University Women chapter as well as at Wellesley's local alumnae chapter. She became friends with the well known and well respected, including fellow Wellesley graduate Madame Chiang Kai-shek, the future first lady of the Republic of China. Helen also aspired to the intellectual and social world of nearby New York City and relished her Wellesley Club teas and lectures in the city. When Benny and Bill came along, she proved a caring, if emotionally contained, mother.

Then something went terribly wrong, though accounts vary. Did Dr. Mott's melancholia tear at the fabric of the marriage? Did the former Quaker village of Rockaway become too limiting for his ambitious and intellectually curious wife? Whatever the truest answer, Dr. and Mrs. Mott's marriage ceased to flourish in that environment. At first, young Benny and Bill were only vaguely aware of the growing distance between their parents, but the boys grew anxious as their mother spent more and more time away from them. Rumors spread that the marriage was on the brink.

In an era when divorce was rare, Helen and Raymond parted ways in 1915. Helen returned to teaching and relied on family to care for her young boys, now seven and four, when she was at work. Society of the day looked unkindly on divorced mothers, and Helen wanted nothing more than to be released from that stigma and a second chance at a respectable and re spected life.

In 1916 she met a prosperous British textile merchant, Arthur Barton Cross. Arthur was handsome, well dressed, and worldly. She was captivated from their first meeting while on an outing to New York City. He had attended the Citadel in Charleston, South Carolina, and then returned to England for university in the renowned textile city of Leeds. Within five years of his graduation, he had achieved high professional regard in the burgeoning international textile and cloth-making industry.

Arthur had offices in both New York and the textile-rich town of Rock Hill, South Carolina. With a casual, high-born manner, he smoked Chesterfields and drove a Model 30 Cadillac. He was interested in observing the birds of America and in purchasing good art, and had the time and money to indulge in both. Within six months, Helen and Arthur became engaged.

At Arthur's insistence, they traveled to England to wed, leaving Benny and Bill behind in the care of relatives. After the nuptials, they took an extended honeymoon trip throughout the British Isles. When they returned to New Jersey, the newlyweds launched their new lives with enthusiasm.

They collected Benny and Bill and moved to an old farm estate in the afflu-
ent borough of Eatontown in Monmouth County.

The main house was a large, gabled Victorian with scalloped cedar shin-
gles and green-striped awnings that stretched over a broad span of south-
facing windows. Its ample, manicured grounds met an acres-wide nursery
of English boxwoods in the rear, beyond which was an apple orchard and
a broad expanse of farmland on the western border. But the estate's most
prized feature was a full surround of mature, brilliantly purple lilac bushes
that passersby would famously stop and admire every spring. The property
was named Lilac Hedges.

Despite her newfound happiness, Helen had been shaken by the failure
of her first marriage and occasionally fretted that she couldn't live up to
Arthur's idealized image of her. She confided to her diary:

> Ah me! I can only give Arthur what life gave me . . . what my good
> blood called for and which life nearly squeezed out of me. Is there not
> virtue in struggle, in attainment through one's own effort, in the simple
> joys of love and work well done, even if spent by the effort?

Arthur was a decent enough stepfather, easing Helen's concerns over
the marital transition's effect on Benny and Bill. But the new family arrangement had not eased the boys' anxiety. Though they had been quite young,
their parents' divorce made them freshly aware of hidden messages in adult
behavior that before had eluded them. Benny and Bill also became highly
sensitive to their mother's priorities, even before they knew what those really were. Her behavior toward them had always been more matter-of-fact
than affectionate. Occasionally, however, her habitual coolness was interrupted by spells of genuine warmth and interest in them, and the two responded hungrily to such moods. They worked fervently to maintain her
approval and win what affection might be granted under these new circumstances.

Most afflicted by the sudden change in family life was Bill. In neither parent, it seemed, could he find reliable emotional sustenance. His mother's remarriage compounded by irregular contact with his father ultimately pushed him toward his schoolwork, at which he excelled. The kindness and positive reinforcement of his teachers and, later, his professors and professional superiors seemed to compensate for the early parental shortfalls. The consequence of Bill's early childhood was a hyper-self-reliance fueled by a determination to excel.

Though Dr. Mott never remarried, he overcame his difficulties with the loving help of the extended Mott family and local community. But his ongoing emotional frailty made being around him increasingly awkward for his young sons. Their grandparents Elias and Lauretta Mott stepped in and filled this gap admirably.

They performed all the requisite parental duties, from bathing and feeding to nightly reading, and, with the help of their great-aunt, Mathilda, taught them the family art of making bread with scalded milk. Lauretta nursed Bill back to health during an early battle with typhoid fever when neither parent could minister to the bedridden boy. But after Helen and Arthur returned from England, Bill and Benny made the permanent move to Lilac Hedges.

One year after Helen and Arthur married, two brothers became three. In April 1918, with the lilacs in full bloom, Arthur Barton Cross Jr. was born. He came into the world the same joyful year that saw the end of the Great War, which President Woodrow Wilson declared would be the "war to end all wars."

Barton was born a month premature, and Benny and Bill were protective from the start. That Barton was their half brother was no more than a biographical detail to the older boys. In fact, the ensuing years were happy ones for Helen and Arthur and Benny, Bill, and Barton.

They spent long summer days at the Jersey Shore, where the boys played endlessly in the waves. Their painted woven beach basket was always filled with the family's summertime favorites: cold shrimp and potato salad, sandwiches, shortbread cookies, and a jug of freshly squeezed lemonade. After hours of play in the cold water, the boys would rejoin Helen and Arthur to picnic on the beach, she always under a broad-brimmed, brightly colored hat, and never without a book in hand.

When they returned home from these outings, siblings William and Nelly, their southern black live-in housekeepers, would have the chores done and dinner under way, the house full of aromas drifting from the large, well-stocked kitchen. The antique dining table was set nightly for five. When their new baby sister, Rosemary, arrived, a mahogany-and-cane high chair was added in the corner.

Arthur presided over these meals, tapping the butler's button under his foot from time to time should they lack for anything. He was always the initiator of well-chosen conversation, in keeping with his orderly British upbringing. Helen's place at the long, polished table was across from Arthur. Barton sat by himself to his mother's right, freeing his right hand to toy with his food or to slip minty chops, scraps of tenderloin, or fresh cherry pie to his cocker spaniels. Benny and Bill always sat together, across from the favorite young son and to their mother's left.

The older brothers were delighted with their new siblings—first Barton, and then fiery and quick-witted Rosemary, nicknamed Muff for reasons lost to history. They did not seem to care or notice that Barton and Rosemary had nicer clothes, more toys, and the majority of their mother's and stepfather's attention. The older brothers attended public schools and worked paper routes to earn their spending money, while Barton and Rosemary were privately educated and flush with pocket money from their parents, who seemed to not want them to take on odd jobs.

AS BARTON GREW, THE older boys welcomed him into their lives with open enthusiasm. They taught him how to fish, catch lizards, race across the millpond, and both impress and spy on girls. They also vigorously defended the undersized Barton against countless would-be bullies. One eleven-year-old neighbor in particular taunted him mercilessly, calling Barton a runt and—slamming him in his Achilles' heel—repeatedly jeering "Mama's boy!"

Bill famously picked the young fellow up by his hair one afternoon, ignoring his screams for mercy. The alternately crying and whimpering miscreant begged to be let go. Even Barton was beginning to feel sorry for him. When Bill finally released the boy on condition he keep away from Barton and Lilac Hedges or else, he ran as fast as his eleven-year-old legs would carry him, not once looking back.

When Barton was finally big enough, Benny and Bill introduced him to touch football. They gave him tips and took him to high school games. The school football team had long been the star of the surrounding boroughs. Every boy between eight and eighteen dreamed of someday being its quarterback.

But Barton never developed an appetite for the primal aggressions of gridiron warfare. It was baseball that became his favorite activity with Benny and Bill. The three brothers spent hours each night after dinner on the broad south lawn of Lilac Hedges, playing their improvised game with one pitcher, one hitter, and one outfielder. They made bases out of anything they could get their hands on, including the dried hide of an unfortunate squirrel. Barton was neither fast nor much of a hitter, but he loved the game just the same. Unusually tall for their adolescent ages, Benny and Bill towered over him. Their height endowed them with that much more star quality to Barton, ever undersized for his age.

They taught him what they knew without a trace of older-brother bravado. They only smiled when he took up the bat with his left hand, and frequently slowed the action in the outfield to let Barton score. Barton grew accustomed to this preferential treatment over the years, which later made it difficult for him to survive, not to mention realize his full potential, outside a system not specifically calibrated to optimize his chances.

Nonetheless, their mother was as pleased by the brothers' bond as they were themselves. On summer nights, she and Arthur sat on the wide, covered porch watching them play until circling bats began their nosedives toward the airborne ball and the long shadows of twilight reached the fields beyond. Helen would call to Barton to come in for a bath and bed while the two older brothers routinely stayed behind, gathering up the tools of their play. Then they walked together in the gathering darkness toward the house.

Benny and Bill would do as she expected, and that was good enough for them, it seemed. Their twin imperatives were to cultivate their shared role as Barton's elders, ensuring at least sparing maternal affection, and to prepare for a life in which they would almost certainly be expected to take care of themselves.

4

★ ★ ★

BILL

AT THE OFFICE OF Naval Intelligence (ONI) in Washington, DC, Bill
Mott had worked forty one straight days since Pearl Harbor was bombed
and war declared. By mid-January 1942, the Navy Department was running on a twenty-four-hour schedule and still struggling to keep pace. With
two brothers in the Pacific—Barton listed as missing in action and Benny
facing mortal danger by the hour—Bill needed no reminder that superior
intelligence was the Navy Department's top priority. But shortages of naval
officers schooled in codes and ciphers were acute, even as blame for the
mishandling of pre–Pearl Harbor intelligence was cast and recast in the
daily newspapers.

Bill retrieved the *Washington Times-Herald* from his icy Chevy Chase
walk each morning to read of the Roberts Commission, a formal government panel assembled to "report the facts" leading to the disaster. To the
navy, its mission seemed more a search for scapegoats rather than facts and
answers. Like many divisions within ONI, the one in Bill's charge—Secret

Dispatches, Letters, and Documents Branch—had been besieged with inquiries and subpoenas, even as it sought to run a world war around the clock.

Washington's naval leaders felt the hot glare of a global spotlight and an enraged citizenry. The American public viewed the Pacific War as the navy's war and the unspeakable losses at Pearl Harbor theirs to explain. These woes were compounded by daily reports pouring into the Navy Department of American tankers being sunk much closer to home—by German U-boats off the Atlantic beaches of New York, New Jersey, Delaware, and other East Coast states. Germany, Japan's ally, had declared war on the United States four days after Pearl Harbor.

The Germans' race to sink more US ships aiding Britain than the latter could buy, build, or borrow had continued unabated since. More than thirty were lost in January 1942 alone, eight on a single night within sight of New York Harbor. Burned bodies and thousands of ship remnants were washing up on coastal beaches all along the Eastern Seaboard. It appeared that the US Navy couldn't even protect American shipping within swimming distance of its own shores.

Washington's ordered society and stolid military establishment had been slapped awake on December 7, 1941. By mid-January, a world had turned. The nation's capital, long accustomed to its southern-leaning traditions and unhurried pace, was now in a chaotic struggle to ramp up and run a war that suddenly spanned the globe. Hastily minted reserve officers descended from Pullman cars at Union Station only to form long queues and crowd the city's rickety trolleys and small pool of taxis.

They headed for all manner of temporary lodging in boardinghouses, barracks, hotels, and apartment buildings, most of which were already overbooked with long waiting lists. Nearly seventy thousand Washington initiates—from fresh inductees, to eager purveyors of war goods, to stenographers and government workers of all ranks—swelled the city's population to overcapacity in no time. In less than six weeks, the district government had issued more than 1,500 new building permits and still couldn't keep pace with the soaring demand—the housing bottleneck just one small piece of the shocking transition to a previously unimaginable second world war.

Upgrading the security at Washington's military departments and the White House was another major undertaking. Machine guns were mounted on the bridge leading to the Lincoln Memorial, and guards with tin hats were posted outside the State and War Departments. The White House had installed bulletproof glass in the three south windows of the Oval Office, and a bomb barrier was poured along the west wall. General Electric was commissioned to design special outdoor lighting to dimly illuminate the grounds without casting light on the house itself. An air raid shelter was built under the newly constructed East Wing.

The lights at Naval Intelligence burned nightly as the bitter struggle for control of the world's oceans intensified. All eyes were on the men who could read the codes and divine new threats before a widely dispersed enemy could strike again. Recruiting and detailing of naval intelligence officers had reached a frenzy by January 1942. Desperate to crack the Japanese naval codes and keep abreast of the Germans' changing ones, senior officers routinely pulled rank to detail personnel from one office to another according to which intelligence functions were deemed most critical.

Around this same time, President Roosevelt decided to set up an intelligence center of his own in the West Wing of the White House. He had come up with the idea after Winston Churchill's White House visit in late December. To command Britain's war with Germany, the prime minister maintained an underground headquarters in London full of maps; when traveling, he carried with him a matching set on which staff continuously updated enemy movements. During his December 1941 visit to the White House, he had set up the vivid portable display in the room across the hall from his quarters, the Queens' bedroom, on the second floor.

"Franklin, you must have a map room of your own," Churchill effused, and even temporarily loaned him the aide traveling with him at the time, one Sublieutenant Cox, to get the project under way. Roosevelt needed no convincing; he immediately ordered his naval aide to "Fix up a room for me like Churchill's." A ladies' coatroom on the ground floor, located between the Diplomatic Reception Room and the president's physician's office, was thus hastily converted into the new chart room.

Cox was also charged with training Lieutenant Robert Montgomery, an American naval reserve officer and well-known actor who was also familiar with Churchill's London map room, having recently worked for the US naval attaché in England. Montgomery built on Cox's preliminary work setting up the new White House Map Room, but within weeks, he requested a reassignment to join the hunt for German U-boats in the Atlantic. A replacement was needed in short order, preferably someone who would not also be tempted to depart for the war front.

The search for Lieutenant Montgomery's successor was intense, and speculation was thick in the staff-strapped Navy Department on who might ascend to the position. There was no application process for Roosevelt's military aides; the president's men did their own scouting. Their scrutiny of potential naval aides was particularly focused. As a onetime assistant secretary of the navy, Roosevelt had a strong preference for his naval representatives over other military aides.

Officially, naval aides served as the formal liaison between the White House and anything relating to the US Navy, but under FDR, the position entailed much more. They were the president's intelligence officers, chargés d'affaires for heads of state visiting the White House, unofficial executors of special requests from Mrs. Roosevelt, and now, overseers of the Map Room. Intellect, personality, and discretion were essential qualities, as well as one's ability to work long and unpredictable hours.

Captain Joel McCrea, Roosevelt's senior naval aide, told the president, "I have my eye on a chap named Mott—an Academy graduate and naval reserve lieutenant. I want to bring him over here to take over from Montgomery as executive of this operation . . . I like the cut of Mott's jib. He's intelligent, quick witted, and a take-charge doer . . . Since I spend so much of my time at the Navy Department, I need my Map Room deputy to be a 'take-charge guy.'" McCrea further stipulated that the Map Room was to be a primarily "naval operation," although all theaters of war would be covered. And he wanted its executive to remain in the position for the war's duration. Mott's nearsightedness, he surmised, would permanently disqualify him for sea duty.

BILL'S 1929 NAVAL ACADEMY appointment came three years after Benny's. Unlike Benny, however, who was happy enough to do well, Bill had stood at the top of his high school class and undertook every academic task with near-fanatical intensity. Beneath his senior yearbook picture was the quote "Some are born great, some achieve greatness, and some have greatness thrust upon them." Under it, his English teacher, Mrs. Carpenter, had written, "To Bill, the best English student I have ever had."

The prolonged economic depression following the stock market crash his plebe year had a near-catastrophic effect on Arthur's business. As he struggled to recover, Bill's Annapolis appointment was not only a goal attained, but also an economic necessity. The fact that Uncle Sam covered the cost of a midshipman's education was a luxury-turned-saving-grace.

Budgetary cutbacks forced on the navy by the Depression, however, had an even worse effect on Bill's graduating class than it had on Benny's three years earlier. Only half of the 1933 graduates received officer commissions; the rest were honorably discharged and offered a place in the naval reserves. Any shortcoming among classmates competing for commissions was grounds for the dreaded cut. In the spring of 1933, as Bill's June graduation approached, he was met with an obstacle that prevented him from taking the same coveted course as Benny.

Each midshipman had to undergo a rigorous physical examination prior to receiving any postgraduation orders, and among the most dreaded of the compulsory tests was the vision exam. Perfect eyesight was an absolute prerequisite for a naval officer, particularly for sea duty. Failure to observe the slightest threat—a light, a periscope through the mist, a critical guiding star—could jeopardize the ship, not to mention the lives of thousands. The eye test was therefore especially exacting.

Replacing the familiar reading charts that hung in eye doctors' offices everywhere (because they could be memorized) was the Snellen tester, which was manipulated by the examiner to make letters of various sizes slide into view horizontally and pop up vertically in constantly changing order. The eyes were dilated beforehand, then refracted with a homatropine solution that was applied every ten minutes, several times in a row. A retinoscope then threw light on the pupil at a distance of one meter to determine if the eye was myopic or near- or far-sighted, and if so, by how much. These refractions were conducted on each midshipman by four naval eye specialists.

"Son," the Academy physician said to Bill after his exam, "you're a fine midshipman. But you can't go active with those eyes, eyeglasses or not."

Bill was stunned. When he entered the Academy, his vision had been 20/15 in both eyes. The shock that his less than perfect vision was enough to bar him from the navy career he'd been planning as far back as he could remember rocked him to the core. He was crushed, not accustomed to the sort of setback he couldn't overcome with tenacity and hard work. After receiving sunglasses to protect his dilated eyes from sunlight, he pulled his cap down low over his watering eyes and began formulating the unimaginable: an alternate life course.

If the career of a naval officer was not to be his, Bill concluded, he would not join the Reserves, at least not right away. He loathed the idea of civilian life, but with few other choices in view, he moved directly from Annapolis to Washington, DC, and began searching for a job. His first stop was the northwest gate of the White House on Pennsylvania Avenue.

In hand was an article Bill had obtained from the stacks at the *Washington Times-Herald* summarizing the commencement speech that President

Roosevelt had just delivered at his Annapolis graduation. Bill politely asked the gate guard if he could speak with the president. When the surprised guard queried further, Bill explained patiently that the chief executive had offered to help any of the noncommissioned Academy graduates—and pointed to a passage in the accompanying news article: "Now, I can't promise you anything," Roosevelt said, "but if any of you boys who are not commissioned need help, well, you know you have a friend in Washington."

Bill waited for some time as the message was carried inside the White House and debated. Finally, a man came out and introduced himself as Steve Early, FDR's press secretary. Trying to conceal his irritation, Early smiled and, with a southern drawl, said, "Well, it's nice that you came by, but I'm sure you know the president's comment was, well, you know, rhetorical."

Bill said, "Well, I took him at his word, and I need a job."

Early sighed, exasperated. "Okay, I'll tell you what," he said. "Give me your telephone number, and I'll look into it."

The next morning at about seven thirty, Bill received a call at his boardinghouse. He was to report to the Washington Navy Yard as an ordnance inspector, charged with examining lead castings eight hours a day. The work was stunningly boring, but he endured it long enough to gain acceptance to George Washington Law School (which he attended at night) and get a job as a patent examiner for the US Patent Office.

Bill worked at the Patent Office by day to pay for law school and living expenses. In the evenings were classes and many a solitary dinner at Ford's or Child's, local counter-and-stool eateries where he could study his law books and, for forty cents, fill up on specials such as pot roast, mashed potatoes, string beans, and coffee. Despite late-night classes, studying, and the tedium of patent work, Bill excelled academically and moved up in professional rank. By the time he was admitted to the DC bar, he was a senior patent examiner in the General Counsel's Office and confident that a lucrative career in patent law lay ahead.

Despite the promise of fame and fortune the US Patent Office offered to eager young inventors, it was a classic federal bureaucracy, slow and leaden. Bill battled daily stacks of applications and rote procedures but greatly enjoyed the dogged energy of the entrepreneurs who streamed in and out of his office. As the son of a dentist, he had more than a passing knowledge of that profession and unwittingly became the resident expert on patent applications for fluoride removal from drinking water. Fluoride was thought to be the cause of brown spots on children's teeth. Dental scientists discovered subsequently that fluoride actually protected tooth enamel from decay and might even have tooth-hardening properties. Two years later, Bill oversaw the patent process for *adding* it to municipal water and toothpaste.

This wasn't the military career that Bill once dreamed of, but it was a secure and respectable profession during grim economic times. Meanwhile, his affinity for the navy never extinguished, he sought every opportunity to stay involved with his Annapolis classmates and colleagues. He was an officer in the US Naval Academy Alumni Association, a position that gave him considerable control over local distribution of army-navy football game tickets, a source of stature regardless of rank. He visited Annapolis often for alumni meetings, and befriended Academy football coach Rip Miller. Bill always brought Rip fresh intelligence on promising high school football players with the academic potential to enter the Academy.

In 1938, he organized the first of what would become an annual army-navy-game rally at Washington's Ambassador Hotel, smartly securing the attendance of the secretary of the navy, the secretary of commerce, the postmaster general, the chairman of the Maritime Commission, the chief of naval operations, the Marine Corps commandant, and the coaching staffs from West Point and Annapolis. Bill also arranged for starlet Linda Darnell, one of Hollywood's loveliest, to lead off the event with the help of an NBC radio commentator. Cocktails were generously served. A popular and patriotic event, the rally was broadcast throughout the country.

Such good-natured and high-spirited gestures earned Bill respect and fellowship among Washington's political and navy elite. Further, his 1938 marriage to witty and astute Rosemary "Romie" Baker, a Madeira School and Sarah Lawrence College graduate, was considered a union of one rising star to another. The couple became regulars at the right parties and weekly tennis matches at the exclusive Chevy Chase Club.

One cool afternoon in September 1939, Admiral Walter Anderson, chief of Naval Intelligence, introduced himself to Bill Mott in the Chevy Chase Club men's locker room. The admiral had noticed the young man's Naval Academy ring. Both half clad, they struck up a conversation. The only other person in the locker room was the club's bootblack, busy spit polishing Admiral Anderson's shoes. After chatting at length about tennis, the court conditions, and a brief game of navy who's who, Admiral Anderson's demeanor grew serious. At once the world's democracies seemed under siege and daily war headlines were on everyone's mind.

Nazi Germany had just invaded Poland, prompting declarations of war against the Germans by Polish allies Britain and France. And Japan's slaughter of Chinese civilians and unceasing incursions across Southeast Asia had prompted US cancellation of its commercial treaty with that country, removing all obstacles to an outright trade embargo against the import-dependent Japanese.

"So when did you graduate the Academy, son?" Anderson asked, pulling on a white athletic shirt marked with the club's red-and-black crest.

"Class of thirty-three, sir, but I wasn't commissioned because I'm near-sighted. Now I'm a patent lawyer. Not my first choice, of course, but it's a good job."

Admiral Anderson listened quietly, then continued. "Are you in the Reserves? There's going to be a war, you know, and I could use you down on Constitution Avenue. If I get the paperwork drawn up, would you accept a commission in Naval Intelligence? I happen to run the place."

Surprised but not displeased, Bill hesitated.

"Well, thank you, sir, but no, I'm actually not in the Reserves right now.

With all due respect, I hear they treat reserve officers like shit down at the department."

The bootblack raised one eyebrow without looking up.

Amused by Mott's candor, Admiral Anderson replied with a chuckle, "You let me worry about that, Mott. You may be sure that if you fit the bill for what I have in mind, nobody's going to treat you like shit, as you would say. Can you be at my office at 0800 Monday morning?"

"Yes, sir, I can," Bill replied, smiling.

A flurry of letters followed, waiving Bill Mott's vision disability, and in 1940 he was back in the navy, as a lieutenant. By restarting his military career as a Naval Intelligence officer, Bill became an expert at the incipient enemies' military codes, as well as deciphering the department's byzantine protocols of power, rank, and advancement. He was placed in charge of the office that received, circulated, and stored top secret correspondence at the Office of Naval Intelligence.

The Secret Dispatches, Letters, and Documents Branch ("Office A-3-c") had custody of the most highly classified telegrams and intercepts (diplomatic and military) coming into ONI. With the recent and top secret breaking of the complex Japanese cipher system (code-named Purple) used to transmit that country's diplomatic cables (decryptions were code-named Magic), Bill came to understand the looming war threat better than most.

He was frequently called on to summarize the essence and import of these communications for both the director of naval intelligence (DNI) and the chief of naval operations (CNO). The intercepts were selectively shared on an "eyes only" basis and were never to be copied. They were hand carried to a handful of designated recipients who read them on the spot and handed them back. After circulating in this manner, they were returned to A-3-c, where they were filed and placed under lock and key.

Bill also became familiar with Ultra, the code name for British decryptions of German military signal intelligence but which eventually expanded to include those of the Japanese and Italian military as well. These decryptions were challenging to paraphrase, but he developed a reputation for synthesizing them without sacrificing accuracy.

By early 1942, Bill's unusual combination of talents were increasingly sought after. When ONI's Admiral Frederick Horne declined Captain McCrea's request for Mott to report to the White House, he offered alternative officers—all discreet and versed in the communications and cartography (the science of creating maps). But McCrea turned them down. The White House was superior to Horne and all the other navy admirals combined, and McCrea, not accustomed to negotiating for personnel, simply ordered Bill Mott to 1600 Pennsylvania Avenue. With this, he became the full-time overseer of the new White House Map Room.

DESPITE THE TORMENT BILL felt over Barton and his failure to locate him, his demeanor gave little away on his first day at the White House. Captain McCrea introduced his new recruit to the president, his family, and the close-knit White House staff.

Bill was gregarious and smiling as he was ushered around the West Wing's rarified environs, shaking hands, exchanging pleasantries, and generally endearing himself. Roosevelt clearly enjoyed the banter with his new aide, particularly when conversation digressed to navy football. FDR also took a keen interest in Bill's family, empathizing as a parent might over Barton's disappearance in the Philippines and the constant perils Benny faced. It marked the beginning of a friendship that would last until the end of the president's life.

In March 1942 Bill wrote Benny from the White House:

> My new job is quite interesting, and even with my
> Republican background I can't help but like and admire
> the man. He certainly is interested in the Navy, as well

as being very human personally. I have talked with him
many times about you and Barton and he asks me after every
Pacific engagement if you are alright . . .

I'm glad to see your luck is holding out and that the
good work carries on. Believe me I follow your movements
with an anxious eye. I am always immensely relieved each
time you come through.

The Map Room was twenty-seven and a half by twenty-two and a half feet, but it had a close feel to it, with its low-slung ceiling, blacked-out single window, and unusual furniture arrangement. Desks and file cabinets formed an island in the center of the room and the walls were overlaid with fiberboard on which large-scale charts, covering all theaters of the war, were hung. The room's design and the height of the maps allowed Roosevelt to navigate around in his wheelchair to study them at close range—and occasionally confirm the remote location of a postage stamp from his collection—without having to stand.

Battle areas were covered with clear plastic and continuously updated with grease pencils to reflect the ever-changing locations of Axis and Allied forces. The ocean areas were sprinkled with different-colored pushpins to identify ships by country—blue for American vessels, red for British, black for German, and so forth. An impressed War Secretary Henry Stimson confided to his diary, "Every task force, every convoy, virtually every ship is traced and followed in its course . . . as well as the position of the enemy ships and enemy submarines, so far as they can be located." Pins of various shapes denoted types of military vessels: round heads for destroyers, square heads for heavy cruisers, etc. . . . Different pins indicated the location of the Allies' Big Three: a cigar for Winston Churchill, a cigarette holder for FDR, and a pipe for the Soviet Union's leader, Joseph Stalin.

The president visited the room twice daily, usually on his way to his office in the morning and again in the afternoon after visiting the doctor's office across the hall where he had his polio-withered legs massaged or his congested sinuses packed. Roosevelt's closest aide, Harry Hopkins, and CNO Admiral Ernest King were also regular visitors, as was the army chief of staff, General George C. Marshall, and War Secretary Stimson.

Under Bill's tutelage, the Map Room—which was also the sole repository of Roosevelt's diplomatic correspondence—quickly assumed an aura of permanence. He took what had been started under Cox and Montgomery and refined systems for receiving, distilling, and securing top secret information. Within weeks of Bill's takeover, a decimal filing system for classified documents was established and a codification manual was created to ensure that critical documents could be retrieved in short order.

New practices simplifying the charting and recharting of Japanese, German, and Italian military forces and their estimated aircraft distribution were also put in place, as well as an improved system for monitoring merchant ship and submarine activity. He also improved upon the system for charting and recharting orders of battle and supply line threads that, literally, stretched around the globe.

Locked leather pouches containing classified cables, military memoranda, and other Top Secret and Most Secret documents were delivered around the clock to the heavily guarded room. The deliveries were logged, studied, and summarized, and then relevant updates were applied to respective war theater wall charts. Subject files were created so that the president could draw on them easily to formulate policy and draft correspondence. Bill also set up a system for logging, distilling, and distributing situation reports from all theaters of war, as well as daily intelligence summaries gleaned from translated Ultra and Magic enemy intercepts.

While the Map Room started as a center for naval war information, it expanded quickly to cover all theaters of war. Bill had a staff of six: three army and three navy watch officers, all members of the Reserves. He required that all watch officers memorize the secret center's critical priorities and protocols. For example, whatever important news might be breaking, all communications between Roosevelt and Winston Churchill, followed by his communications with Generalissimo Chiang Kai-shek and Joseph Stalin, took absolute precedence. Either Bill or Captain McCrea walked intelligence summaries and these priority cables straight to the Oval Office or, depending on the hour and urgency, to Roosevelt's private quarters.

Reliable and discreet staff were critical, and Bill held his watch officers to the same standards he expected of himself. Ensign George Elsey, a Princeton-educated naval reserve officer whom Bill had hired back at Naval Intelligence, was his first recruit. When Elsey and Bill's subsequent hires first entered the Map Room, Bill would close the door and point to a "three monkeys" cartoon taped to the back. Under the first monkey, whose eyes were wide open, was printed "sees everything." Below, in pencil, was written "something." Under the second monkey, holding a hand behind one ear, was printed "hears everything"—the penciled note below: "a little." The third monkey, hand over his mouth, "tells nothing." Below, in pencil: "less."

Bill would then disclose that the penciled annotations were the work of Secretary of War Stimson, as dictated to him one evening in the Map Room by FDR himself. This made the point that Bill's imperative of extreme discretion was dictated straight from the top. He would then simplify his expectations: "I explain a task or clarify a complex matter to you once, and from that point forward, I expect you to act promptly and precisely with respect to it." Their boss was a stern taskmaster, but both the army and navy watch officers felt a strong loyalty toward him. Confidentiality, accuracy, and speedy access were the three imperatives of Bill Mott's operation, and they were all enhanced by that loyalty and seamless teamwork. By the spring of 1942, the White House Map Room had become the de facto epicenter of Allied war planning.

Both the president and his closest advisor, Harry Hopkins, were impressed, as well as with Bill's deft handling of non–Map Room matters, including quick and charming responsiveness to requests from Eleanor

Roosevelt. His temporary detail from Naval Intelligence to the White House was soon made permanent, and a promotion to lieutenant commander came with it.

Throughout the exacting early months in his new job, Bill found time each day to pen inquiries about Barton. His search had been a roller coaster from the start. Though "Casualty and Missing-in-Action" manifests were infrequent and error-ridden, he reviewed every single one; Barton was not listed on any of them. He wrote Captain Joel Newsom, commanding officer of Barton's ship, now docked at Port Darwin, Australia. Replies to his urgent missives yielded a few answers, but each generated new questions in turn. He learned that Barton had been wounded during the bombing at Cavite. He had survived and was hospitalized at Sternberg. But then what?

Bill had felt a surge of confidence when he learned that MacArthur had commissioned a hospital ship to ferry Sternberg's wounded to Port Darwin. The ship had departed within hours of the fall of Manila. There was no manifest to examine, but Bill contacted Australian naval authorities and requested that Barton be tracked down and instructed to call him. White House operators were placed on full alert: "Put Barton's call through no matter what time, day or night." The head operator, Louise "Hacky" Hackmeister, had been on duty that day. She swiveled away from the switchboard's gnarled panel of wires and insistent beeping to face him. She was calm and sympathetic despite her tether to the humming board. "Believe me, son," Hacky said, "I'll call you at once if anything comes through."

But weeks stretched into months with no call from Australia.

Helen peppered Bill week after week with fresh rounds of questions to which there were no immediate answers. His mother had scant idea how much effort he was expending to learn Barton's fate or how troubling what little information he had secured was. But the family continued to hold out hope for Barton's survival, in no small part because Bill projected confidence—real or forced—that Barton had surely pulled through. He would make every effort to perform on that assurance. The unrelenting pressure he was putting on himself was not just because he loved his brother and was worried about his mother. It was because, despite the purest of intentions in helping Barton attain his commission, Bill felt fully responsible for thrusting him in harm's way.

5

★ ★ ★

CABANATUAN, SPRING 1942

AFTER MARCHING FOR HOURS in the midday sun, the navy patients and other Cabanatuan-bound prisoners arrived at the Manila train depot. A north-facing freight engine hitched to a dozen boxcars awaited them. The men were ordered to disperse along the platform and climb aboard. After medics took over the deceased patient, Barton stepped onto the black, heat-buckled floor of the second boxcar. It quickly became impossible to see any activity on the platform as he was forced to the rear of the car by continuously boarding prisoners. Barton's uneasiness grew in the new surroundings: a dark, ten-by-six-foot, furnace-hot steel crypt. Worse, Charles had boarded a different car, either by mistake or by force.

What happened next was unimaginable. Yelling from the direction of the engine, a Japanese soldier signaled to the guards standing at each boxcar door. Impervious to protests from the prisoners, the guard at the second boxcar shouldered the creaking metal door closed. The men heard the exterior latch slammed down and hit twice, as though barely able to contain its cargo.

Pinned between the car's back wall and a wall of sweating flesh so close to his face that he struggled to breathe, Barton felt a wave of panic. Even before the train lurched forward, men began to gasp for air. Little could be heard above the moaning, the helpless splattering of defecation from the dysentery-ridden, and knees thudding to the floor by those losing consciousness. Those that remained conscious endured something potentially worse, an hours-long terror that they would die before the journey's end. Barton struggled to contain his own rising claustrophobia, possibly remembering he had survived it once before.

In 1930, when he was twelve years old, his parents took him on a very special outing into New York City to take in the view from the top of the brand-new Chrysler Building. At 1,050 feet, it was the tallest building in the world and its gleaming steel spire seemed to reach the heavens. The opening-day tickets were to its viewing gallery on the top floor. One by one, the guests filed into the building's thirty-two gearless electric elevators, among its many modern inventions. Their elevator car was dimly lit, with polished wood panels, and there was an operator wearing a uniform and cap with shiny gold buttons. But with so many people eager to get to the gallery, the car quickly overfilled.

When the operator cranked the brass doors shut, Barton felt a fear he had never experienced before and began perspiring heavily. The second the doors opened, he burst past the exiting guests into the viewing gallery. When his bewildered mother finally found him, he dismissed her concerns and moved toward one of the enormous triangular windows to take in the view. It was never formally diagnosed, but Barton's established fear of tight, enclosed spaces was for him at least as powerful as any triggered by armed Japanese.

THE FREIGHT TRAIN'S RUSTED black cars came to a merciful halt in the late afternoon at Cabanatuan City, the north central terminus of the Manila railroad. While unconscious prisoners were dragged out of the boxcars, Barton and the others staggered onto the train platform, gulping fresh air. As more and more dazed men stumbled into the blinding sunlight, small groups of Filipinos and their children began materializing from side streets and alleyways near the tracks.

Nervously shuffling bare or sandaled feet, they gawked silently at the pitiful scene of the prisoners exiting the boxcars and bodies being laid out on the platform. While Barton scanned this mixed sea of faces in search of Charles, Filipino boys began darting toward the men and thrusting pieces of sugarcane into their hands. Encouraged by the boys' success, others approached the prisoners with bananas, panocha (a Filipino sweet made with peanuts), and cane candy. Some offered cassava cakes or balls of rice wrapped in banana leaves, while still others set down cups of water as close to the prisoners as they dared.

Suddenly aware, the head Japanese guard shouted an angry command. His comrades immediately turned on the crowd, pushing and striking at will. They withdrew, but defiantly hurled their remaining goods over the picket of guards to the prisoners. Men all around Barton reached up desperately, like spinsters for a bride's bouquet. In this sudden display of hands and arms, there was a familiar one, long and freckled.

The combination of the edibles and relief at finding one another revived both Charles and Barton, whose crisis-born friendship seemed to strengthen by the day. In fact Charles seemed to be improving, perhaps because of it; he was unusually resilient after the train ordeal. And while captivity seemed to bring out the worst in him, it also had given him a reason to live. "Not gonna let a bunch of goddamn Japs decide whether I live or die," he declared, and not for the last time.

No food or water had been issued the prisoners since morning, and little then, but none was offered by their captors after they exited the boxcars. Instead, the guards ordered the men to reassemble in four-abreast columns. Minutes later, the prisoners set out again, first dragging through the heart of Cabanatuan City and then turning east onto a rutted dirt road.

It was near the end of the dry season in the Philippines, the hot and windless stretch of months that precede the drenching monsoons. While acacia, papaya, and banana trees lushed the distant landscape, the shade-less road was inches deep in dust. The powdery soot exacerbated the men's thirst, settling onto their swollen tongues, between their teeth, and in the rims and corners of their eyes. Several prisoners staggered out of the columns from heat prostration and were loaded onto trucks trailing the marchers. Others passed out completely and were tossed like cordwood onto the truck beds.

While these horrors demoralized many of the prisoners, it had the re-verse effect on others, including Barton. It tapped in him a wellspring of desire to live. In fact, this difference marked an early divide in the burgeon-ing prisoner population. Mistreatment and deprivation destroyed the wills of some, eventually killing them. But it strengthened the resolve of others. Strong religious faith and a positive personality were predictors, but the galvanizing power of anger can also be credited. Whatever their motivat-ing muse, Barton and these others seemed to intuit that making the simple mental choice to live could make all the difference in their survival.

At dusk, the marchers came to a halt in front of a squarish barbed wire stockade. The entrance faced the road on one side; the other three abutted open land. The prison camp's interior was flat, barren, and chalk dry. Bam-boo barracks with roofs of thatched nipa palm leaves were its only adorn-ments other than the manned, forty-foot-high machine gun emplacements marking each corner of the compound.

Ordered to stand at attention, the exhausted prisoners waited forty-five minutes for their "welcome" instructions from the camp commandant. Their legs trembled, and they swayed almost drunkenly in the searing heat. Finally, a dwarfish man in an immaculate uniform emerged from his make-shift headquarters. Lieutenant Commander Masao Mori had a coiffed, bristling moustache and was wearing knee-high boots polished to a high shine. He puffed out his chest, folded his arms, and gave his new charges a long, contemptuous look. He then addressed the prisoners through an interpreter.

The Cavite-based ensigns were in collective dismay. Like Takeo Yoshikawa in Pearl Harbor, "Lieutenant Commander" Mori's prewar occupation—running a bicycle shop in Cavite City—had been an apparent cover for a higher calling: assessing the layout of Cavite Navy Yard for its incipient attackers.

It was a reminder of the unflattering saying the Filipinos had for the thousands of Japanese domiciled in the islands, disliked for their arrogance and airs of superiority over them. In Tagalog, their native tongue, the phrase was *"Pasukab kung tumingin, parang Hapon,"* meaning, "He eyes you in a treacherous manner, like a Jap."

The Cabanatuan commandant's manner had changed since his tip-seeking bicycle repair days. Mori's speech was terse and harsh. Punishment for violation of any of the camp rules was death. Prisoners would be put in groups of ten. If there was an escape by one in the group, the remaining nine would be executed. He then reversed direction with a flourish and returned to his headquarters.

At Mori's exit, the ravenous and desperately thirsty men were each given a ball of rice and a canteen cup of water, after which they were assigned to barracks according to rank and branch of service. Work orders would be issued in the morning after *tenko*. Barton and Charles were familiar with that drill and knew exactly how they would handle it.

The interior of their barrack, where they were quartered with other naval officers, consisted of two long, wooden planks divided by a dirt aisle. Each platform was split into five sleeping bays. Prisoner discouragement over their new home was palpable, but on that first night at Cabanatuan they could only collapse on the hard wooden bays. Some drifted to sleep mulling escape, others contemplating how they would survive, and others, their souls already crushed beyond repair, hoping only for death's merciful release.

★　　★　　★

SOON AFTER BARTON'S GROUP arrived at Cabanatuan came
the defeated Corregidor defenders, and soon after that the defenders of
Bataan—all prisoners now. The state of the Bataan prisoners shocked the
Cabanatuan residents, even in the context of their drastically altered living standards. They horrified all who heard their tale of a brutal hundred-
kilometer (sixty-two mile) march from the Bataan Peninsula to their
first prison hold, a place called Camp O'Donnell, where thousands, they
learned, had died already.

One Bataan survivor told of not only impossible thirst, starvation,
and beatings, but of Japanese guards driving American trucks over fallen
prisoners and then sticking out rifle bayonets to slit the throats of lines of
marching men. Others that fell out of the marching columns were shot by
rear-guard "buzzard squads." But the horrors of Cabanatuan were plenti-
ful, too.

Without sanitation, clean water, and adequate food, an average of
thirty men a day died during Barton's first months there, not counting ex-
ecutions. The most common causes were malaria, beriberi, diphtheria, and
dysentery—and despair, too, though despair was not formally listed as a
cause of death. The Japanese kept their distance from the prisoner hordes,
wearing masks when near them and throwing food into their barbed wire
enclosures.

With the majority of prisoners weakened or sick, their dependence on
one another became primal. It was in this context that Barton began to see a
role for himself. He started small by organizing groups on work details while
they chopped wood or buried their dead. His idea—and that of a growing
number of prisoners—was to pool their resources and restore the weak-
est among them to at least a functional state. This would be accomplished
by giving the most infirm larger rations and, if they could get their hands
on them, medicines such as quinine. Such supplements could be obtained

through Cabanatuan's emerging black market, where medicines and food could be purchased from Japanese guards who had procured them to sell to their captives at a fat profit or as barter for gold watches or rings. That such a market existed at all, however, infused a measure of hope among the prisoners, a precious commodity at Cabanatuan. Even the strongest among them knew they could become the next needy patient.

Such brotherly acts forged powerful bonds among the men and spawned a determination to pull one another through. Barton understood, either consciously or unconsciously, that he had been mostly a recipient in his life, and that this one-way generosity had diminished him. That he had the physical and emotional capacity at Cabanatuan to help others survive was more satisfying than all the times in his life he'd been singled out for special treatment. He couldn't help but reflect whether his family might recognize him less and less as his imprisonment lengthened, and not just because he was dirty, unshaven, and underweight.

6

★ ★ ★

WHITE HOUSE MAP
ROOM, APRIL 1942

WITH WAR EXPLODING ON every ocean and continent, Bill Mott worked late again on April 17. At seven o'clock, the Map Room was in a rare lull. The radiator under the blacked-out window hissed and clanked as Bill examined the pins and grease pencil markings on the Pacific-plotting map. At thirty years old, Bill stood nearly six feet and was fighting trim. He had the bearing of a military man: high cheekbones, a thicket of jet-black hair combed straight back, gilt collar leaves reflecting his recent promotion, uniform crisp, and shoes shining like mirrors. But anxiety roiled under that polished exterior.

Crossing parabolas of tacks plotting Allied and Axis movements across a seventy-million-square-mile Pacific war front were measured in degrees and centimeters. To the middle left was Cavite, where Barton had been wounded during the Japanese air attacks in December.

A few centimeters to its right was the Bataan Peninsula, where the largest-ever defeat of American forces had occurred the previous week.

A thumbnail beyond it was Corregidor, which, Bill knew, would also be forced to capitulate. Somewhere between those three hot spots, Barton had disappeared without a trace.

Long before it was public, Bill knew of the decision not to reinforce the flagging garrisons in the Philippines. The die had been cast in December 1941 during Winston Churchill's emotional Christmas visit to the White House. The prime minister made the lengthy trip shortly after the US declaration of war on Japan to ensure Roosevelt's commitment to a "Europe First" strategy. Churchill understood the rage the American public felt toward the Japanese and wanted to prevent emotional diversion of American resources from Britain's defense against the Nazis to the Pacific.

Available Allied resources to wage global war were stretched to the limit and had to be prioritized. Churchill's Yuletide mission and persuasive charms ensured that helping Britain defeat Nazi Germany would take precedence. War Secretary Stimson's reluctant entry regarding the Philippines, which he confided to his diary during Churchill's visit—"There are times when men have to die"—was the cruel verdict.

Within the context of other threatened Pacific bases, the consensus that the Philippines could not be won back quickly or easily—and that Allied troops there would be abandoned—had been reached thanks to cold military math. By that same calculation, Australia, still in Allied hands, had to be held. Otherwise supply-and-communication lines would be severed and Allied access to the entire Southwest Pacific lost. Australia was also the only Allied base left in the region for staging countermoves against Japan.

It was an open secret that Roosevelt had little affection for Douglas MacArthur—and was wary of the Republican general's presidential aspirations. But he agreed well before the fall of Bataan that MacArthur should be evacuated to Australia both to protect it from Japanese seizure and to prepare counteroffensives against Japan. The decision took a number of factors into account. There were no other generals in the region to put in charge, and Roosevelt could not afford the political fallout of General MacArthur falling into enemy hands. Home front public opinion played a role in the president's decision.

MacArthur and his public relations team had released more than a hundred press communiqués from besieged Corregidor, which were picked up by every newspaper in the country. They touted the general's bravery, genius, and leadership in the face of a scurrilous enemy. Reeling from serial reversals on the world stage, the American public gobbled up the flowing heroic narrative; babies were named after MacArthur and streets renamed after him.

So there would be no outcry or even a congressional inquiry into why all the general's planes in the Philippines were destroyed on the ground, wingtip to wingtip, despite repeated pre-attack directives ordering him to launch them. Nor would there be an investigation into his inexplicable nonresponse to the War Department's advance war warnings. Bill had been at the War Department that entire night, waiting tensely with others far senior to him for MacArthur to acknowledge receipt of the warnings and to confirm that defensive air measures had been taken.

The first cablegram, sent seven minutes after the bombs began dropping on Pearl Harbor, warned specifically that Manila and greater Luzon were Japan's next likely targets. MacArthur neither replied nor commenced air operations, with tragic results. With American airpower destroyed, Cavite Navy Yard was the obvious next target—easy pickings without air protection. Bill was not the only naval officer to question MacArthur's reckless military judgment in the Philippines.

He then ordered over seventy-five thousand American and Filipino soldiers to the Bataan Peninsula in compliance with a pre-war defense contingency plan. Yet inexplicably, all but minimal stocks of food, ammunition, and medicine were left behind. These errors appeared grossly shortsighted to navy brass, who were further incensed that MacArthur *blamed* the navy for defeat in the Philippines by not heeding his demand to send ships to rescue the very men he put in harm's way.

The two-inch circle on the Pacific plotting map marked the widening Japanese-controlled perimeter around everything north of Australia, making it increasingly difficult to get reliable information on those men left behind. Thus far the Japanese, not a signatory of the 1929 Geneva Convention, had refused to discuss adherence to its provisions on prisoners of war. Requests for updated casualty lists were also proving futile. Unconfirmed reports indicated that quiet exchanges of noncombatants, mostly Filipinos, had taken place, but not military men.

Barton's whereabouts was not Bill's only concern in the Map Room that evening. A quick calculation of speed, distance, and a glance at the clock meant that the top secret convoy stealing across the Pacific to bomb Tokyo had reached its rendezvous point. With *Enterprise* leading the covert task force, no doubt Benny was on high alert up in Sky Control at the moment. Backed by steely determination and burning revenge, the covert plan had been approved unanimously by top brass, despite the severely handicapped state of the US Navy.

Shortly after Pearl Harbor was bombed, President Roosevelt asked his military planners to find a way to strike Tokyo. America desperately needed a win to stem sinking public and military morale. FDR understood the importance of bolstering outgunned soldiers on every front, not to mention rationed citizens who were also being asked to build a massive war arsenal.

The December 7 losses had been staggering: 2,400 killed, another 1,200 wounded, 18 warships and 188 aircraft destroyed, and an additional 159 damaged. And bad news had piled up ever since. Guam, Hong Kong, Singapore, Burma, Sumatra, and the East Indies had all fallen to the Japanese in the following four months. And now the Philippines were lost; Americans were in a vengeful, morose free fall.

In February 1942, partly in response to the national mood, Roosevelt had ordered the sequestration of more than a hundred thousand Nisei—US residents of Japanese ancestry—at internment camps across the United States (including Pearl Harbor spy Takeo Yoshikawa, to an Arizona camp, though his misdeeds had not yet been discovered). Even this action failed to shake Americans out of their malaise, but Roosevelt knew what would: bombing Tokyo. Such a bold and aggressive initiative, he believed, would unify the country, restore confidence, and offer Japan a taste of US resolve. The logistics, however, were formidable.

An aircraft carrier would have to get within two hundred to three hundred miles of mainland Japan for its small, carrier-based fighters (F4F Wildcats) to strike Tokyo and have enough fuel to return to the ship. But it was far too risky to send the few remaining ships in the Pacific Fleet that close to Japan. Only the army's burly B-25 bomber had the size and range necessary for such a mission. But B-25s had never taken off from an aircraft carrier, and it was physically impossible for them to land on one. So the president ordered the army and navy to work together on a solution to that problem, and fast.

Bill had known about this mission for months and had been long preoccupied with its high risk and poor odds—the worst so far for Benny. In fact, Bill knew to a footnote the scope and perils of every *Enterprise* mission well in advance of Benny. Though they wrote each other often, wartime censorship prevented Bill from sharing such classified details, including any mention of this daring operation. Understanding the dangers Benny faced yet unable to warn him was an acute source of anxiety for Bill.

The state of the floating navy, moreover, was deplorable. To lose the slim surviving strength of the Pacific Fleet would be to virtually relinquish US naval presence in the entire region. The recent dispatch from Admiral Chester Nimitz, CINCPAC (Commander in Chief Pacific Fleet), that Bill had distributed, eyes only, offered no comfort:

TOP SECRET

Pacific Fleet markedly inferior in all types to enemy. Cannot conduct aggressive action in Pacific except raids of hit
and run character which are unlikely to reduce pressure on
Southwest Pacific. Logistical problems far surpass peacetime
conception and always precarious due to fueling at sea and
weather . . . Unless this fleet is strengthened, it is in unprecedented danger and its effectiveness . . . is limited.

Nimitz

According to the punctilious Map Room clocks, it was 0700, Saturday, April 18, 1942, on the other side of the international date line. They should have executed by now, if indeed *Enterprise*, *Hornet*, and their escorts had made it to the launch point where Colonel Jimmy Doolittle and his B-25 squadron were to take off. All there was to do now was wait. The bank of clocks on the far wall ticked away the seconds in every time zone, and the teletype taunted from the corner, its incessant repetition as ominous as it was monotonous: *click, reset; click, reset; click, reset.*

Bill had learned to display grace under pressure at a young age, thanks to tumultuous family circumstances, but that day tested him. The Pacific map's vast watery expanse off mainland Japan's coast offered no consola-tion. Were he to press his whole hand over the convoy's route, it would touch no land relief at all—only enemy-infested waters; an enemy that was superior in size, strength, and sea power. Another worry roiled also. If the Tokyo bombing mission was successful, would the resulting Japanese rage further endanger Barton, who, under the best of circumstances, had been taken prisoner?

His mother's letter, delivered to the White House that same afternoon, throbbed in Bill's ears. "My mind," she wrote, "swings like a pendulum, Bar-ton, Benny, Benny, Barton . . ."

Bill stepped over to a typewriter, scrolled in a blank sheet of paper, and began typing.

The White House
Washington

To: Lt. Comdr. X. B. Taylor
Bureau of Navigation

If the Regulations permit, I should like to be notified first in the event of the death of either of my brothers, Lt. Elias Bertram Mott, II, at present serving on the USS Enterprise, and Ensign A. B. Cross Jr., missing after the bombing at Cavite in Manila. I feel that I could more easily break the news to our mother, Mrs. A. B. Cross, than could a stranger should either such unhappy events come to pass.

Lt. Cdr. W. C. Mott

7

★ ★ ★

"THIS FORCE IS BOUND FOR TOKYO"

JUST HOURS BEFORE SEVENTY-FIVE thousand troops on Bataan surrendered to the Japanese, the USS *Enterprise* and her escorts once again nosed out of the ships' channel at Pearl Harbor in single file. After clearing the channel, the task force's heavy cruisers and destroyers fanned out into protective positions. Admiral Halsey then issued the order to head northwest, and *Enterprise* signalmen relayed the directive to the rest of the convoy.

Three long days and nights passed, with the crews in the task force still unaware of their destination. They pressed inexorably north and west into cooler and cooler latitudes. The goose-bumped crew finally changed out of their tropical uniforms into long-unused cold-weather gear.

On Sunday, April 12, Benny Mott was once again on the watch in Sky Control, discerning what he could through the filmy morning mist. Down on the flag bridge, thirty-five feet below, Admiral Halsey was locked in his familiar pugilistic stance, his cap down low over his face, obscuring a set jaw, beetle brows, and unruly silver hair. Benny didn't like not knowing their destination or mission but just then it didn't matter. He believed to his core this man would get them there and back, recalling the fear, admiration, and camaraderie Halsey inspired during his midshipman years.

BACK THEN, CAPTAIN HALSEY had been commanding officer of the Academy's Annapolis station ship, the USS *Reina Mercedes*, a former cruiser captured during the Spanish-American War. Among its functions was to imprison transgressing midshipmen. Benny was glad he'd never met Halsey under those circumstances; their interactions had only been at pleasant social gatherings the Halseys hosted for upperclassmen, whom the couple treated with emphatic warmth. During these more relaxed affairs, Benny and Captain Halsey often discussed navy football and another common passion: the underappreciated virtues of their shared home state of New Jersey.

Halsey had relished these chest-beating interludes about the state: "The home of Alexander Hamilton, Thomas Edison, and Albert Einstein!" he would crow in mock exasperation, drawing wide grins from Benny every time. At Annapolis, Benny and Bill were both known for their proud defense of the Garden State—against routine mockery. They even embraced their nickname, "the Jersey Brothers," despite its implicit derision. Was it Halsey who started that? Benny couldn't remember, but it stuck.

The feisty *Reina Mercedes* captain enjoyed his own Jersey-native spiel— he was the product of generations from the august town of Elizabeth, one-time state capital, founded in the seventeenth century by English settlers. He groused that it was now known less for its critical submarine industry or as the birthplace of the electric car than for being the base of the notorious "Jersey family," the oldest US Mafia syndicate in La Cosa Nostra (Sicilian) and the only one indigenous to New Jersey. The persistent media spotlight on the Mob irritated the state's proud and long-established natives, including Captain Halsey and Midshipman Benny Mott.

Benny would chime in with his own New Jersey yarns. "Well, sir, we love a spirited defense of our much-maligned state. You see, the Motts arrived with the Quakers back in the seventeen hundreds, but they didn't just sit around pritheeing this and pritheeing that!" Halsey always appreciated Benny's family high notes, including the Motts' ancestral link to members of the iconic fraternal order that boarded the tea-laden vessels *Dartmouth*, *Eleanor*, and *Beaver* in Boston Harbor in 1773. The rest of the story is textbook history, but rebel-hearted Halsey would laugh and clap Benny on the back every time. Between the two of them, New Jersey's reputation was restored every time.

The whole *Enterprise* crew felt Benny's combination of awe and affection for Bull Halsey. Before every mission, Halsey reveled in his anti-Japanese epithets and scowling, serial invectives, like a football coach before the big game. The men loved his bellicose quips, including "Hit hard, hit fast, hit often," and his "perfect willingness" to divide the Pacific Ocean with Japan: "We'll take the top half, and they can take the bottom." And they reliably whistled and clapped when he staked claim to Emperor Hirohito's white horse when it was all over. Halsey would trot it right through Tokyo, he declared, and the Japanese language would only be spoken in hell when he was done with them.

Never mind that Halsey was a late admit and graduated near the bottom of his 1904 Academy class. Nobody cared. The man they knew was a trained pilot, schooled in intelligence, and knew aircraft carriers like the back of his hand. "He can calculate to a cat's whisker the risk of an operation" was the oft repeated quote among *Enterprise*'s 2,700-strong crew.

That faith was needed more than ever right then. While they didn't know their destination or the purpose of this mission, they did know that the odds were stacked against them. Two months earlier, a triumphant *Enterprise* had returned to Pearl after its first enemy offensives in the Gilbert and Marshall Islands. They had damaged or sunk a dozen or more Japanese vessels and downed more than forty planes. When *Enterprise* entered the channel, slid through the torpedo nets, and returned to port, every sailor in Pearl Harbor had lined the rails, cheering and shouting. Ships blew sirens and horns, and men of every rank whistled and hooted. Admiral Halsey was grinning from ear to ear on the flag bridge, taking it all in.

In those early raids, *Enterprise* had been outnumbered but not outwitted, giving its sailors—and the country—a needed shot of good news. Still, it had come at a price. Though *Enterprise* had brought home the war's first victory, the Gilberts and the Marshalls had been a trial by fire for its untested crew.

While retiring from the engagement, *Enterprise* came under surprise attack by enemy bombers. Benny's machine gunner on the port catwalk, George Smith, was killed, becoming the carrier's first gunnery casualty of the war. An enemy plane had dropped out of formation and aimed straight for *Enterprise*'s deck. Its right wing hit the ship, killing Smith before skidding into the sea. Fuel from the plane's ruptured tanks drenched half the carrier, all the way up to the superstructure. This first-known airborne suicide attack had stunned Benny and his men. None of them had even considered the possibility of an enemy plane flying directly into their ship.

George Smith's funeral gave the *Enterprise* crew their first taste of burial at sea. They'd stood at attention on the fantail while an honor platoon came to parade rest before them. The men bowed their heads and prayed as gun salutes and the trumpeting of taps competed to be heard above the rushing, high-seas wind. The body bag—weighted with lead shells so that it would sink quickly—was placed beneath an American flag on a stand, angled feet-first toward the thrashing waters below. The draped figure was then released into the sea and disappeared beneath the ship's steady wake. Until then, this ritual had only been practiced, like so many other war exercises and drills, off sunny, peacetime Oahu.

ON THIS MISERABLY COLD April morning two months later, Benny turned his attention to the horizon. Tightening his plump fingers around the cylinders of his field glasses, he steadied his focus. With the weather stormy and foul and the rise and fall of the deck spanning 150 feet, he was not initially certain of what he'd just seen. Once assured that it was not the waters' pitch and hurl tricking his eyes, he motioned to Enterprise's Captain Murray and pointed to an approaching vessel. Murray was out the door at once.

By the time Murray reached the wing of the flag bridge, a wraith-like outline of seven more ships—two cruisers, an oil tanker, and four destroyers—appeared through the mist; a dull series of gunmetal-gray silhouettes against graphite seas and cinder skies. Within minutes, an entire convoy was in view.

The lead vessel was an aircraft carrier, the spanking-new USS Hornet, and it was carrying a mother lode of unusual cargo. Atop her aft flight deck in two parallel rows sat sixteen dark-green Army Air Forces medium-range bombers. Were those B-25s? They were twice the size of an aircraft carrier's elevators, which were used to raise and lower aircraft between the flight and hangar decks. "What in theeee hell?" Benny said aloud.

He wasn't the only one gawking. Speculation swept Enterprise, and within minutes, there were multiple theories about the force's mission: The bombers were being delivered to reinforce a base in the Aleutian Island chain that stretched westward from Alaska to Russia, just as Enterprise had done with the bombers to Wake Island in what seemed an eternity ago. Others speculated they were destined for a Russian airfield on the Kamchatka Peninsula. "Only God and Halsey know for sure," mused Benny.

But speculation ended minutes later when they heard the admiral clear his throat over the ship's loudspeaker. The men were quiet, expectant.

"This force is bound for Tokyo!" Halsey bellowed.

Wild cheers erupted from every one of the ship's steel compartments. Benny shivered with excitement and disbelief. Down on the flag bridge, Admiral Halsey reacted to the elated chorus with a broad, satisfied smile.

"This force is bound for Tokyo" was flashed in code to all the other ships. The *Hornet* and *Enterprise* convoys then maneuvered into a single force, named Task Force 16. It was composed of the two carriers, four cruisers, eight destroyers, two tankers, and two submarines. All bows of the largest assembly of American warships since Pearl Harbor pointed west at a determined twenty-three knots.

Benny felt a surge of pride being part of the USS *Enterprise*. Despite the chronic fatigue and persistent anxiety over his troubled marriage and the well-being of his baby girl, his powerful bond to his shipmates was as inextricable as that of any family. Benny would do anything for this crew, and the feeling was mutual.

While docked at Pearl, he had overseen the installation of state-of-the-art Oerlikon 20-millimeter antiaircraft guns throughout the ship, a vital upgrade ordered by Halsey after February's tactical air strikes in the Gilbert and Marshall Islands. The old water-cooled cannons were removed, and potent new guns with unprecedented range and precision were positioned on catwalks and walkways on every level. Word traveled quickly regarding the powerful new artillery, and he'd gotten several heartfelt kudos and shoulder claps since their departure. *Enterprise* and her crew was his entire world now, and these gestures of confidence had come to mean everything.

All too often, Benny lay awake during the brief intervals he was supposed to be resting on his hard, narrow sleeping rack. Before their departure, Jeannette had not only informed him that she wouldn't ever be visiting at Pearl but also that her lawyer would be in touch. He was still reeling from it. A thousand times, he had sworn to himself that no child of his would ever endure what he had endured as a child. Now the full weight of her leaving him and taking their little girl was upon him, and he was powerless to alter her plans—especially from out here in the middle of the Pacific Ocean.

He careened from despondence over his own troubles to wrenching anxiety over what had become of Barton. Was he alive, or had he been bayoneted and cast aside, never to be found? Had he been taken prisoner? This night, even steaming toward Tokyo, was no different for Benny. He needed the rest—desperately—but he had received no mail from home in weeks and was endlessly anxious for news. He watched for letters like a perched falcon, especially for those carrying a White House or Lilac Hedges return address—anything.

After tossing, turning, and staring at the blank metal ceiling for what seemed like hours, he switched on the tiny light over his bunk and pulled out a piece of onionskin letterhead proudly embossed with a sketch of his ship. He needed to shake off the miserable scenarios gathering strength in the dark.

USS Enterprise

At Sea

April 12, 1942

Dearest Mother,

    I don't know when I shall have another letter from you but I hope it will be soon. I enjoyed reading the diary entry that you sent about your trip to the shore. Guess I've read it through three times and each time it is like going home for awhile. It is so much you and conjures memories of our early days, of Sea Bright, Ocean Grove, Red Bank, the grand Atlantic and its wonderful swimming. If I could only have a little bit of that now I'd be rested and ready for anything. I guess that is not to be my lot for a while though.

    Bill has written me all about his new job. One of grave responsibility and trust. I hope he believes now that he can serve much more usefully there than at sea. Also, I've had a couple of letters from Dad. His letters were interesting and he seems quite proud of both Bill and me.

Mother, I want to do something nice for you. I can afford it and I want to. The money is rolling in now and frankly I have no opportunity to spend it. So while I am saving (I am anxious to know if you received the bond I sent for safekeeping by the way) I feel there will be plenty of time left to buy and pay for war bonds.

I want you to take the enclosed check and get yourself something nice. The time may soon come when you will no longer be able to obtain many things, if indeed it is not already here. You deserve it Mother, and don't worry, we'll still be buying bonds.

I had in mind a nice coat for next winter, and I mean a really nice one--please go do this while the getting is good!

Know that I love you Mother, and know that I will press on until I reach Barton. It keeps me going even on the worst of days.

Please write and be brave.

Your loving son,

Benny

p.s. I am enclosing some pictures of me with several war correspondents. Am not sure if they can be sent but if they are not at least one can try. Anyway, they will be in many newspapers so perhaps you can see them there.

Benny was mindful that it was April 12, Barton's birthday, and it was sure to be a bad day for her, particularly with the fresh crop of bad news coming out of the Philippines. After rereading the letter, he placed it and his signed-over allotment check in an envelope. He reached up and switched off the light; perhaps sleep would be his reward before the midwatch.

TASK FORCE 16 CONTINUED its strong westerly course, covering three hundred to four hundred miles each day. With *Hornet's* flight deck unusable thanks to the tightly parked B-25s, *Enterprise* search planes scouted two hundred miles out on both flanks while her fighter pilots patrolled protectively above. April 17 dawned raw and cold and the seas were rough. Still a thousand miles east of Tokyo, the carriers and cruisers fueled one last time before they left the tankers and destroyers behind for the final dash to the launch point. Throughout the afternoon and night, they rolled and pounded through the heavy seas. The screening ships were barely visible through a steady drizzle and low, pumice-colored skies.

At 0315 on the morning of April 18, for the first time in six weeks, the insistent electrical clambering of the general quarters alarm ripped through the ship. Benny was standing the midwatch. He scanned the horizon through his binoculars—back and forth, over and over, without pausing as he awaited the next set of signals. Nothing.

Then *Enterprise* jerked so sharply to starboard it nearly knocked Benny over. Seconds later, Captain Carey Randall, the marine commanding officer aboard, burst through Sky Control's door. Jack Baumeister's radar had picked up two surface contacts ten miles ahead, he reported; the task force was turning to avoid detection from the suspected Japanese patrol vessels. Together they waited, studying the horizon for forty-five minutes. Finally, the task force turned back, resuming its westerly course. They were still seven hundred miles from Tokyo; hundreds of miles from launch point.

At 0500, an *Enterprise* scout bomber flew low over the deck. The pilot reached out and dropped an orange beanbag with a scribbled message attached. He had sighted another patrol vessel, fifty miles ahead. Worse, he was sure he'd been spotted. Even with that news, gutsy Halsey pushed on for thirty more minutes, gaining another eleven miles that the fuel-strapped B-25s wouldn't have to fly to gain safety after their raid.

Suddenly, through the fog and rain, Benny made out two ships' masts and a low black hull, about a hundred feet long, off the port bow. He immediately reported it via *Enterprise*'s sound-operated telephone. "We have a setup on enemy vessel. Request permission to fire five-inchers [guns]." He waited an interminable three minutes for a reply. But Admiral Halsey said no and instead dispatched the cruiser *Nashville* to sink it. The Japanese vessel fought back with its single gun until its rounds finally fell short, and the ship started sinking fast. Heart pounding, Benny picked up another patrol vessel in his field glasses. *Enterprise*'s fighter planes began to strafe it, but soon it too was sunk by the *Nashville*.

Halsey wasted no time with his next order. There was no longer any doubt that they had been reported to the Japanese military by at least one of these civilian-manned "picket boats" surveilling the distant waters arcing around the home islands. At 0800, 650 miles from Tokyo and 150 miles short of the objective point, Halsey sent a signal to *Hornet* telling Lieutenant Colonel Jimmy Doolittle to launch his planes:

```
To Col. Doolittle And His Gallant Command


        Good Luck And God Bless You--



                                        Halsey
```

Benny watched *Hornet* turn into the wind and speed up for the launch. Between the forward velocity of the carrier and the winds churned up by the stormy weather, the pilots had the benefit of a forty-six-knot (approximately fifty-five-mile-per-hour) headwind. The plane directors on *Hornet*'s deck also tried to time the launches so that the heavy bombers could take off on the up-pitch of the bow.

Hornet's bow lifted and plunged violently as Jimmy Doolittle's plane was the first to race across the carrier deck, catching the bow as it rose on a wave crest. The crew from the *Enterprise* cheered wildly into the howling wind. There was a split-second pause before the second plane was released from the flight deck's trip wire. Benny watched, relieved one second and horrified the next, as the plane took off on the down-pitch of the bow. He closed his eyes as it slanted toward the sea and hung precariously low over the water for hundreds of yards, straining to become airborne before finally gaining altitude.

When Benny reopened his eyes, the plane was still struggling to pull up; it was no more than a foot or two above the water. For more than half a mile, it hung so close to the heaving sea that it seemed certain the plane would crash. Benny and Captain Randall stood together in the tower chanting over and over, "Pull up, goddamn it! Pull up! Pull up!"

And the next fourteen planes—"in a nicely judged bit of timing," Benny would later regale his audience in the officers' wardroom—"observed first-hand the advantages of taking off on the bow's *up* pitch."

Despite the difficulty gaining altitude, all sixteen planes finally lifted skyward and disappeared single file into low, fast-moving clouds. They headed due west in the direction of mainland Japan even as *Hornet's* and *Enterprise's* scout bombers reported fifteen more patrol vessels, several of which they sank. With no time to waste, Task Force 16 immediately reversed course and boiled their wakes to a high froth in a breakneck twenty-five-knot race for safety.

Benny and a gaggle of other officers gathered in the wardroom annex to relieve excited anxiety and speculate on the raid's success. Estimating that Colonel Doolittle was nearing his target about that time, they tuned the dial to Radio Tokyo, which happened to be broadcasting an English-language propaganda program.

A little after 1400 hours—noon Tokyo time—the announcer, in stilted, heavily accented English, laughingly read a Reuters News Agency report—strictly embargoed but inexplicably released—that Tokyo had been bombed. The broadcaster went on at length about how this was a ridiculous joke played on the Japanese people: no foreign bomb or shell had ever landed on Imperial soil. As he looked around him on that lovely spring day in Tokyo, he said he saw nothing but calm, serenity, and cherry blossoms.

Suddenly sirens sounded in the background, and his voice gave way to frantic Japanese—then he abruptly went off the air. Benny turned and smiled at Captain Randall and slapped his knee; it was the best he'd felt in months.

8

★ ★ ★

BARTON, 1930–1941

GROWING UP, BARTON HAD not approached academics or any of life's other responsibilities the way his older brothers had. Nor had he adopted their relentless imperative for self-improvement. Instead, friends and social activities had been at the center of Barton's early life. A happy-go-lucky boy with a seemingly endless reserve of goodwill, he took an unusually genuine interest in others. Peers and adults alike were drawn to his warmth, puckish wit, mischievous sense of humor, and amusing collection of arcane facts, sports-related and otherwise.

Yet Barton always seemed to fall short of his father's expectations; in academics, sports, even in his height. Helen did what she could to bring her husband's lofty goals for Barton to fruition. She alternately prodded and upbraided him about his lessons, particularly math and science, two basic assets of any Annapolis candidate, which they were determined he would be. He actually did well in literature and poetry studies and had a perfect ear for music, but these strengths were not encouraged. Barton handled the strain by appearing not to care, and his mother's expectations by appearing not to try.

Things got worse after Benny and Bill departed for the Naval Academy. Only eleven when the second of the brothers left home, Barton soon found life at Lilac Hedges quiet, lonely, and uncomfortable. While he adored his young sister, Rosemary, she couldn't replace the loss of his brothers. What had once been the epicenter of fun and boisterous camaraderie suddenly felt all wrong, and his parents' angst over his studies only exacerbated his unhappiness. To Barton, all their gestures equaled reproof, and he became increasingly restive and brash. Disciplinary issues both at home and school spiked.

The town movie theater offered refuge, all the better if the occasional girl was involved. The fairer sex was apparently beginning to find Barton Cross quite attractive and witty. He also developed a taste for good tobacco at a young age, and for the occasional beer. When Helen reproached him for these transgressions, he replied that it was her own liking for Benson & Hedges that sparked his interest in the first place, and she could hardly criticize him for a little beer considering his parents' not infrequent scotches with a dash of soda. This left her stammering for the appropriate response to the little scamp, which never seemed to occur to her in time to do any good.

Beset by business crises, Arthur was rarely available to help. The textile business, already wobbling from labor strikes, was on its knees after the stock market collapse. Mills and plants were shuttering, and ships carrying cloth sat idle at coastal docks. It was growing ever clearer that Helen could not cope with Barton's burgeoning adolescence by herself. She hoped that at least one of the older boys might return home before the launch of their careers, but it was not to be.

And so it went until one evening in 1932 when an exasperated Arthur had finally had enough. Barton was fourteen years old, and "Little Lord Fauntleroy," as he sputtered to his wife, needed a paradigm shift. Arthur turned to his longtime friend David Page Harris, headmaster of Christ School for Boys in Arden, North Carolina. With its motto "The school that makes manly boys," Christ School seemed the perfect antidote to Barton's persistent lassitude.

No one was more surprised than Helen by how well her coddled son took to his new environs that fall. She both feared and hoped he might return to Lilac Hedges after a disastrous first week or two. Yet daily chapel, classes, and chores—making beds, waiting tables, cutting wood, and feeding chickens—all, as it happened, delighted Barton. Even digging up tree stumps, so arduous its assignment was reserved for repeat rule breakers, gave Barton a sense of satisfaction. His droll humor and high-spirited bonhomie won him fast friends, and his quick-wittedness snagged him a spot on the *Warrior*, the school newspaper.

After expecting the worst, Barton not only adapted to life at Christ School but also thrived on its structure and the constant companionship of fellow boarders. He performed surprisingly well in academics, too, even in the once-dreaded subjects of math and science.

Barton was also intrigued by the morning services in St. Joseph's Chapel, the spiritual center of Christ School life. At home, the Episcopal Church equaled monotone sermons followed by droning bids for contributions and coffee hours that bored him to despair. At Christ School, the daily sounding of the chapel carillon, known as the Angelus bells, called students to worship but also to hear homilies on such topics as "Failure is a chance at a new start, not a measure of self-worth" or "When we work together, we cannot fail." The effect on Barton of these daily sermonettes—simple but profound guideposts—was like spring rain to a dormant garden. Almost subconsciously, he began applying their lessons.

But perhaps best of all, the school's top sport was baseball. Unlike other secondary schools where football reigned supreme, baseball had been Christ School's athletic mainstay since its founding in 1901. Barton had never been on a real baseball team before. Likely due more to his

knowledge of the game and his unmatched command of professional baseball statistics, he was given a spot on the school's second team. He would
always remember the day he became a "Greenie," even the weather—a
cool spring afternoon—when he returned to his log cabin and laid out the
uniform—crisp and white, bearing Christ School's green insignia—on the
simple woolen blanket that stretched across his bunk.

The chores at Christ School did as much to educate Barton as the homilies and classes, but so also did the presence of a different society of boys
than he had known near Lilac Hedges. While some were of the same background as he, a number of others were on scholarship. Some had no mothers, some no fathers, and still others were orphaned entirely.

Such circumstances seemed unimaginable to Barton. These particular boys often worked the hardest to succeed—and succeed they did, academically, athletically, and socially. He pulled himself up on this developing
wisdom, and it gave rise to self-confidence, a previously unfamiliar feeling.
By graduation, Barton had a reputation as one of the smartest, if nearly the
smallest, in his class. And while his inner prankster put him at the top of the
penalty work list (and claim to the most excavated tree stumps), he finished
Christ School with the second-highest GPA in the class of 1934.

Arthur was delighted when Barton gained acceptance to his alma
mater, the Citadel, the Military College of South Carolina. The few coveted
congressional appointments to the Naval Academy were taken that year
and the Citadel had been Barton's next choice. He was also quite young for
a high school graduate, having finished Christ School at age sixteen; a year
of maturity in a military environment ahead of the Academy was a prudent
move, his parents concluded. Helen was determined that her boy would
try again for the Naval Academy the following year, but he was Charleston-
bound for now and determined to make the best of it.

THE CITADEL'S STERN WHITE stucco buildings topped with
medieval-style turrets accurately reflected its rigor. And while Barton may

have thought his legacy status might shield him from the legendary hazing that cursed the life of a plebe cadet, or "knob," he was not so lucky. Barely an hour after passing through the Citadel's Lesesne Gateway that steamy August morning, he found himself at the start of Hell Week.

Fresh off a year of being on the receiving end of such treatment, the second classmen were spiteful; it had been done to them, and by God they would now have their turn inflicting the torture: ear-splitting shouting of orders and questions; slapping; food deprivation; marching knobs down to the low-country swamp to stand at attention, waist-high in muck, while swarms of mosquitoes feasted on them.

The first few days of this working-over broke more than a dozen of them; they simply packed up and went home. But Barton showed surprising pluck. Determined to survive the mistreatment (possibly motivated by the imagined disappointment on his father's face had he not), he urged on his new colleagues as well. With a spirit of defiance, humor, and an ever-present helping hand, he exhorted them to stick it out. "We're not going to let them beat us at this game!" he would say over and over.

Barton did everything he could think of to coax his miserable fellow knobs. He also vowed to himself and others that he would never engage in these black arts toward future initiates—if he got that far. "We'll show these bastards how officers are supposed to behave when we get the chance," he'd say. But Barton also learned at the Citadel how to avoid drawing unwanted attention.

Lesson One was to conceal that his father was a Citadel alumnus. Legacies, presumed to be overentitled braggarts, were traditionally given double the treatment. Lesson Two was to absolutely do what he was told, however absurd, however many times, whatever time of day. The fact that he was a legacy gave him additional fortitude in this, so anxious was he to not disappoint his father. By heeding these lessons, Barton survived knob year, if not happily.

Barton became popular in his company, less for drill proficiency than for wicked mimicry of his superiors, well-told jokes, and hilarious attempts at the distinctive Charleston drawl with New Jersey inflections. Dormitory pranks were another source of amusement. Painting slumbering colleagues' fingernails with pink enamel was a knob-barracks favorite, since polish remover was a scarce commodity on the Military College of South Carolina's campus.

Nonetheless, as the year progressed, the option of leaving Charleston for what Barton imagined to be the gentler Annapolis became a paramount goal. One year at the Citadel, he concluded, was plenty.

And so, at long last, Barton Cross was accepted into the Naval Academy's class of 1940. Delighted, Benny and Bill were full of counsel and stories. After all the halcyon tales from their own Annapolis days, Barton expected nothing less than a pleasant high-seas adventure. He was ordered to report to "latitude 38°58'53" N, longitude 76°29'08" W" (Annapolis) the first week of June. Barely returned from Charleston, he bade his parents farewell again, this time at the main entrance to the Naval Academy. With a mix of pride and anxiety, Helen and Arthur watched as Barton fell in line with another class of plebes to begin a fresh series of unremitting humiliations.

AFTER PASSING THROUGH THE Academy gate, Barton was directed by uniformed guards to the administration building. Turning right past a nest of mounted naval guns from the Spanish-American War, he walked up the steps of administration and took his place in a line of other would-be naval officers waiting to be processed by the chief clerk. Following receipt of a date-and-time-stamped instruction sheet, the inductees marched awkwardly across the Yard to that most hallowed of buildings, Bancroft Hall. There they were herded and hustled—from physical exam to haircut to supply store—right up to that momentous hour: their swearing in as midshipmen of the United States Navy.

The apprehensive assembly faced the great marble stairway leading to Memorial Hall and the Academy's most treasured relic: a dark-blue flag bearing the phrase "Don't Give Up the Ship." The revered banner, quoting the dying words of Captain James Lawrence, had been hoisted by a defiant then-Master Commandant Oliver Hazard Perry as the US Navy battled the British at Lake Erie during the War of 1812.

When the moment came, Barton raised a slightly trembling right hand and pledged: "I, Arthur Barton Cross Junior, of the state of New Jersey, aged eighteen years, having been appointed a midshipman of the United States Navy, do solemnly affirm that I will support and defend the Constitution of the United States against all enemies, foreign and domestic; that I will bear true allegiance to the same; that I take this obligation freely, without any mental reservations or purpose of evasion; and I will well and faithfully discharge the duties of the office on which I am about to enter: so help me God."

Following the ceremony, the orders came fast and furious. It did not dawn on Barton until it was too late that he would have to endure another year of plebe purgatory before things had any chance of improving for him.

As with the Citadel, it was the second classmen, or "youngsters," who were charged with conferring a range of cruelties on the entering class: Only walk down the center of corridors. Turn square corners and walk head up, shoulders squared, chest out. Fingers along the seams of your trousers. There was a new language to learn as well. Bancroft Hall walls were "bulk-heads," floors were "decks," stairs were "ladders." Plebes were told when and where to form lines and how to march to and from them (double time, meaning at a run), where to sit for meals, and how to eat them. Endless in-structions covered every minute of the day, from reveille to taps.

The midday meal became its own source of dread. Barton was ordered to eat many plebe-year lunches *under* the dining hall table, thanks to his fail-ure to correctly answer a firestorm of questions on an array of arcane naval facts spat out by one especially unkind youngster. These included the birth and death dates of any number of navy greats and the width and length of the deck planking on a particular class of ship. The hazing worsened over time as others in the class above him sensed Barton's vulnerabilities. Unlike at the Citadel, he had a hard time staying below his Annapolis tormentors' radar.

Barton's sole extracurricular activity at Annapolis was the Academy Chapel Choir, where his rich and well-trained tenor voice was enthusiastically welcomed in a choir replete with baritones. In fact, his solo pieces gained some acclaim—a rarity for him at Annapolis.

As his difficult plebe year wore on, Barton began to develop a visceral dislike for the Naval Academy—for all things naval, in fact. Demerits were given for everything; by Christmas, he had more than forty, and the time and effort it took to work them off only yielded more deprivation and hard work. Daily room inspection required that floors (decks) be washed and waxed; blinds be dust free, at "half-mast," and opened; shower walls be clean, dry, and unspotted; and light fixtures be white-glove spotless both inside and out—among two dozen other requirements. Even on days when Barton managed to pass inspection, he frequently failed a second unannounced "spot" check, which could occur at any time during the day. He compiled dozens of demerits for violations of this particular banality alone.

Barton's distress was compounded by letters from friends who had gone off to "normal" colleges, an experience he increasingly desired. The creep of self-doubt was unstoppable. He had never been much interested in fighting or hurting other men. Why, then, had he landed in these places where learning to excel at that very thing was a core requirement? It simply wasn't his nature, any more than football's block and tackle. If his experiences at the Citadel and now Annapolis were any clue, the military life was not a promising line of work for him.

Sensing trouble, Helen traveled to Washington for a month to monitor Barton's progress. She insisted it was only to hear him perform with the Academy choir in Sunday chapel—among the rare times parents were allowed on campus. It wasn't long before she learned of Barton's hazing. Bill's wife, Romie, had told her of one particularly upsetting incident shared by a visiting midshipman at a Washington cocktail party. Bill would likely have taken Romie to task for leaking the tale to his mother, knowing full well how such matters tended to play out. After promising her daughter-in-law that her source would remain anonymous, Helen promptly wrote Barton inquiring if the rumor was true.

Surprised, he emphatically denied the incident had occurred and implored his mother to drop the subject. Her pursuit of the matter could only hurt him, he insisted. But unable to subdue her anxiety, Helen penned a letter to the Naval Academy's superintendent, David Foote Sellars:

My dear Admiral Sellars,

Against the advice of everyone, I should like to talk with you about my son, Arthur Barton Cross, now a midshipman in his plebe year. He is the third of my sons to enter Annapolis. . . .

To most civilians, you are simply the austere trainer of men, but I am presuming you also possess that trait of sympathy given the youthfulness of plebes. My son went into his recent examinations ill in body and I fear subnormal in spirit and mind. No boy was ever braver than he—he knows about hazing and expects it—he learned that at The Citadel, I can assure you.

Barton has not written or spoken a word of this to me or to his father, but a classmate of his mentioned the cruelties he is undergoing to his older brother in Washington. Through devious means unknown to either the older brother or the lad himself, news has reached me.

This "youngster" [3rd classman] has peculiar tendencies—almost sadistic one might think. To beat a boy until blood appears, to force him to hold heavy objects of furniture on his bare head while balanced on billiard balls—all to the breaking point. He was forced to crouch and

do knee bends, and this youngster told him he will see to it he cannot
study and will fail his examinations.

    To continue torturing devices for two-hour periods—is this
necessary to make officers? This youngster's name suggests Germanic
extractions, I believe.

    Both older sons, my husband, everyone, says, nothing can be done,
and I would only hurt Barton by publicizing it. In fact, my husband
says that even if he fails his examinations, he must never know that we
know.

    Naturally I would not go to my Senator who appointed Barton
to report it, but surely there is some remedy for this. Will the Service
lose this splendid young man because of petty, vicious, contemptuous
persecution? I know you do not condone this.

                            Yours sincerely,
                            Helen C. Cross

Barton would never tell his parents what really happened that terrible night—or on so many others nearly as bad. No good came of ratting out fellow mids, despite nominal rules against hazing. His suffering was all thanks to the intractable grudge of one Midshipman "R.," who had no family wealth or navy legacy to tout and resented those who did. His determination to settle the score with those more fortunate than himself was insatiable.

Returning from the showers to continue studying, Barton had been summoned by R. to his room once again—this time the evening before his Steam Enginery exam. But the hours-long torture that night left him physically and emotionally shattered. He stood on two billiard balls and, per orders, lifted and balanced R.'s desk while R. playfully jabbed him in the ribs with the business end of a wet broom, demanding answers to a string of obscure nautical questions. At some point, the towel dropped from Barton's waist and the torture continued while, wet and naked before a growing throng of revelers, he struggled to stay balanced. When it was over, his ribs were bruised and he was bleeding from the repeated jabbing.

In the end, Barton didn't cry; he didn't "break." But he could not return to his studies after R., in mock disgust, finally released him. Miserable, humiliated, pained, and exhausted, Barton collapsed on his hard, narrow bed and slept until morning bells. He awoke to a pounding head, every inch of his body aching. Completely unprepared, he dressed to face the dreaded Steam exam.

It was unclear whether Helen's comment regarding "my Senator" was a veiled threat, but Admiral Sellars responded to her letter promptly, assuring "drastic and summary" action. The admiral wasted no time broaching the topic with a much-surprised Midshipman Cross. Barton stood at attention in Admiral Sellars's office until he was gently told to stand at ease. Then, with a stunning degree of specificity, he inquired of Barton whether the incident had taken place. Barton never altered his facial expression; he just listened to the admiral describe his own nightmare in remarkable detail.

When allowed to speak, he said, "I'm sorry, sir. I've had it rough here and there, but no, sir. It never happened." He repeatedly denied the incident, refusing to rat out his tormentor. The commandant impressed upon Barton the importance of his obligation to tell the truth, but Barton responded evenly that he'd "been asked a few stern questions from time to time," but not physically abused. He was sure this was a case of mistaken identity, sir.

Admiral Sellars wrote Helen again, asking for the name(s) of the accused. He wanted to get to the bottom of it for his own reasons and was becoming insistent. At this, she balked, realizing that if Barton refused to cooperate, she stood alone. She wisely deduced that if she took the matter any further, she would bring her entire family down on her head. Midshipman R.'s identity would not be hers to reveal, she decided reluctantly.

To Admiral Sellars, she replied:

My dear Admiral Sellars,

I should hate you to think me a silly, hysterical mother. My only aim is that Barton should have had freedom of mind to pass that steam examination . . . We have never been able to get corroboration from him except, "I am having it rough but I can take it." You see I must not hurt his pride and of course shall not mention our correspondence on the subject, EVER, to anyone.

In my eyes the Naval Academy can do no wrong, and I already have two fine sons to prove this. Therefore I have complete confidence in your wise handling for the situation. It has distressed me deeply—I think interfering mothers are most disagreeable.

In Sincere Appreciation,
Helen C. Cross

Barton could not figure out how Admiral Sellars had learned of the incident, but he held firm that he would not be a tattler. Helen retreated back to New Jersey, realizing that many a Naval Academy mother before her had tried and failed to gain exceptions for their sons. Perhaps Admiral Sellars had her in mind with his often-repeated response to the question of why barbed wire was strung atop the school's perimeter. It was not, he would reply, to keep midshipmen in, but meddling mothers out.

IN PREVIOUS ENVIRONMENTS, BARTON had survived on varying degrees of cleverness. He had done well in group dynamics, too, from which he had drawn personal strength. But he was finding it more and more difficult to get by on these assets at Annapolis. The atmosphere, in his view, was emphatically not collegiate.

Rather, it was designed to train and mold men to a specific shape and culture. While Bill and Benny had toughed it out—and became misty-eyed over Academy traditions and monuments—Barton was intimidated and irritated by them. Every building, every road, and every structure was named after one or another of the navy greats. Reverence for past naval icons was ubiquitous. Nowhere on the grounds were monuments to the likes of Barton Cross, overwhelmed and undersized.

The summer after his first year was spent on the midshipman cruise, a weeks-long training in practical seamanship. To Barton, the cruise mostly meant cold saltwater showers, bad food, and grueling chores. With trousers rolled, he scrubbed teak decks with sandstone by day and served endless midnight watches shivering on deck or in the suffocating boiler room. He studied marine engineering, turbines, boilers, and the ship's auxiliary machinery. He hated every minute of it and rejected the notion that some sort of hallowed bond would develop through a round-the-clock regime of punishing duties aboard a ship.

Nonetheless, Barton returned to Annapolis for a second year of personal and academic crucifixion, with the new perils of naval tactics, gunnery training, and increasingly rigorous mathematics. He made it through the fall semester, landing near the bottom of his class. But things got tougher in the spring. Barton failed the final mathematics examination; and though he was allowed a reexamination, for which he studied hard, he failed it, too—by seven-hundredths of a point.

If hazing was a factor in his fatal academic stumble, he never let on. No exceptions were made at the Naval Academy for those who failed a course, despite Barton's good standing in other subjects (particularly English literature and history) and his legendary voice in the Academy choir. He was compelled to withdraw, in shameful comparison with his two brothers. Helen and Arthur were crushed.

Helen poured her heart out afterward in a five-page letter to the Academy's new superintendent, Admiral Wilson Brown. Her tone had decidedly changed from her last letter to Admiral Sellars:

My dear Admiral Brown,

I realize that you are a very busy man and there is nothing to compel you to answer civilian criticism.

I do agree with your intimation that mathematics did not come easily to my son, Ex-Midshipman Barton Cross. However, he has a brother who fell to 1.9 percent on one occasion in the same subject at Annapolis. He got through by a fair reexamination or perhaps by virtue of his luck, drawing a particularly good instructor when he needed one. When he left the USS Lexington's engineering department, his Captain remarked, "I hope Annapolis will send us a few more like you!" Someone saw through his fractional mark and gave him a chance to develop speed and facility.

Unless of outstanding brilliance, getting through the Naval Academy is largely a matter of luck. Grant and Pershing [at West Point], and many Admirals at Annapolis, including William Halsey, were near or at the bottom of their classes, and the country is grateful for this element of luck, this avoidance of the fatal fraction!

Your methods appear unpedagogic. You permit enrollment of 740 or more Plebes, knowing that half of them have to be failed, rather than build up 370 good candidates with proper instruction. Some of those you fail go on to distinction in the very subjects you fail them in. One boy I know led his class in Mathematics at Brown University, another at Cornell. Are we to conclude that the great universities of this country are inferior or that your product is superior? Neither is true but the universities do have civilian instructors who can teach, not bewildered young lieutenants.

*In Barton, I believe you had a lad of considerable latent
ability, who stood number 12 in a Citadel class of 400, and whom
[Citadel's] General Summerall spoke of as "fine officer material with
exceptional ancestry and fine family naval tradition behind him." The
reexamination that he took failed 21 of the 28 who took it! Was this fair
or just an ouster to necessarily reduce your numbers? Barton's loyalty
and love of the Service, and good marks in other subjects counted for
naught against 7/100 of one point in one subject? Yet you have boys there
right now skimming in several subjects, and many more who intend to
quit the Service as soon as allowable and a free education obtained—I
know because I've heard them talk on many occasions.*

*For this, crushing humiliation has been brought on his two brothers
in the Service who wanted so to see him with them and who know
his abilities, a feeling of abasement, and a loss to the Service of one
worth keeping. Your Academic Board must be made conscious of the
unfairness of that reexamination.*

Yours Sincerely,
Helen C. Cross

Before filing away the letter—alphabetically under the letter U for
"Unpedagogic Methods"—Admiral Brown penned a note to his subordinate, ordinarily charged with responding to these sorts of letter: "We won't
answer this one," he wrote, "but the point of view is interesting."

A DEFEATED BARTON CROSS returned to Lilac Hedges, feeling
all the worse that his own wounded pride and humiliation extended to his
family. Unable to endure forced conversations with his shell-shocked parents, he made plans to go into New York. He said he might just quit school
altogether, damn it, and get a job in the city. At a rare loss for words, Helen
and Arthur raised no objection.

Barton felt awkward in the first civilian clothing he'd worn in some time, and it may have added to his discomfort with incipient manhood. In fact, he was still a struggling postadolescent. A bullet of a young man, Barton was now presumably full height at five feet nine inches. His face radiated a boyish pink hue and his cheekbones were high and prominent. Cropped brown hair went this way and that, as resistant to conventional taming methods as he himself had been growing up. A high, broad forehead gave him a likeness to his brothers, though his eyes were a playful green instead of blue.

He trudged out the front door, down the painted porch steps, and headed toward the train station. His parents were working in the vegetable garden that day, desperate to appear normal and busy. But the angst on their faces revealed that the alkaline balance for growing perfect tomatoes was the furthest thing from their minds.

But Barton had a plan. Once in Manhattan, he made his way to Radio City Music Hall and proceeded to fill out an application for a spot in their chorus, a fantasy he had quietly entertained for some time. The *Radio City Christmas Spectacular* had become an annual family highlight after the hall's opening in 1932—his mother especially loved it. Until now, Barton's young life had been defined by the expectations of others and by their criteria for success. Perhaps this offered a unique opportunity to please both his parents and himself.

Barton had shown considerable musical talent throughout his life, despite his parents' efforts to interest him in more "acceptable" pursuits. Maybe now they would see fit to let him chase his own dreams. That night, he followed up with a letter to Admiral Brown, requesting a reference. The Barton Cross letter file in the Academy superintendent's office would grow thicker still:

Dear Admiral Brown:

I have taken the liberty of referring a prospective employer to you, as a character witness, in order to help me

obtain a position in New York . . . Having had much choral
experience prior to Annapolis and also in the Academy
Chapel Choir, there is perhaps an opportunity for me at the
Radio City Music Hall.

Naturally I showed my prospective employer my Academy
resignation, feeling that he would not be concerned over
the fact that I fell just short of the required grade in
mathematics. As a reason for my resignation, I told him
that I was perhaps unsuited for a naval career. If this
particular is referred to, I trust that you will realize
that this was not my heartfelt sentiment, only an answer to
an interviewer's question. In view of the circumstances, I
feel you will do all in your power to help me get started in
civilian life.

Respectfully Yours,

A. B. Cross Jr.

The letter displayed a combination of determination to pursue a career
that matched his abilities and absence of guile in approaching the Naval
Academy commandant to recommend him for a singing career. It was both
courageous and refreshingly naïve. Before Admiral Brown received any
follow-up inquiries from Radio City Music Hall, however, Barton's parents
regained control of the situation.

A chagrined Arthur made a telephone call to the University of North
Carolina's president, Frank Porter Graham. It took only this gentlemanly
phone conversation to ensure Barton's acceptance and transfer to Chapel
Hill. Helen and Arthur were weary from the struggle and hoped that North
Carolina's southern graces would be a better fit. In any case, they were de-
termined to short-circuit any further talk of a singing career.

Barton did indeed take to the easier manner of Chapel Hill and flourished there. Ironically he declared a math-heavy major in business and commerce and did well. Helen savored that this richly proved her point about the Academy's "unpedagogic methods" versus other fine universities. Still, Barton's departure from Annapolis had stung and left her feeling rejected herself.

Bill wrote to Barton at Chapel Hill regularly with newsy discourses on his newlywed life, including the proud arrival of Adam Sutherland Mott, his firstborn child. He also ventured the occasional navy update—to the degree he thought it would be tolerated, if not appreciated. He ended each letter with the same refrain, which he knew would be unpopular but was increasingly urgent: despite his Annapolis experience, Barton must enter Chapel Hill's Naval ROTC program; war news threatened, and he wanted Barton poised for reentry into the military as an officer should the country go to war.

Benny wrote to Barton too, sharing lengthy news about his own navy man's life on the West Coast. But from Barton's pleasant perch at Chapel Hill—where he happened to be having the time of his life—Bill's domestic bliss and Washington career trajectory and Benny's colliding worlds of marriage and life at sea sounded more like weighty, joyless commitments.

So instead of NROTC, Barton joined a fraternity, Chi Phi, the oldest and most pedigreed order on campus. His pledging ceremony was far more gracious and refined than any experience during his Citadel or Naval Academy tenure. The Chi Phi creed—"So then let modesty and dignity go hand in hand with loyalty"—was much more to his liking. He was a Tar Heel now, and had taken well to Chapel Hill's southern charms. And, as ever, he had also attracted a broad and fun-loving group of friends. His father's respected business presence in the South spared him the dreaded Yankee label in a town where, even seventy-five years after the Civil War, northerners were not welcomed.

GRADUATING CHAPEL HILL IN June 1940, Barton prepared for a career in the mercantile world. By then, however, Britain, France, Poland,

and other European Allies were at war with Nazi Germany and its new ally, Fascist Italy, and his and every other young American male's future was clouded by it. Since derision of the army was a favorite pastime of his family's, that option was out of the question—but he didn't have the appetite for more torturous rejection by seeking a naval officer's commission. The matter was thus deferred again.

Instead, Barton chose to participate in the war effort on his own terms: as an iron and steel procurement officer at the British Purchasing Exchange, located just off Wall Street. His academic background had actually prepared him well for the position, and he quickly mastered the accounts amassing American scrap iron for Britain's fight against the Nazis.

Respected and well liked at BPE, Barton worked hard. Being in the city energized him and restored his sense of *potential*. He and his father took the train into Manhattan together each morning, and, after parting ways near Arthur's offices, he proceeded downtown by subway. Barton frequently exited several stops ahead of Broad Street station, preferring to walk the rest of the way.

Jaunty and distinguished looking, he clipped along the bustling streets of New York threading among pedestrians, streetcars, and fresh fruit and flower stands setting up in the morning cool. His argyle socks were tucked neatly into polished cordovan shoes, and an open overcoat and scarf flapped in the breeze. Barton could usually be seen rounding the corner of Broad at 8:55 a.m. Ever genial, he greeted acquaintances and nodded to the Exchange doorman at 15 Broad before disappearing into the lobby. By 5:45 in the evening, he was headed back up to Midtown, usually to parties or clubs populated by New York's young cosmopolitan set.

Barton was the gin-and-tonic fellow with a pack of Luckies in his breast pocket and always seemed to have a pretty girl at his elbow. He was treated to more than a few overnight stays in the city when it was too late to return home by train. Different girls were invited to Lilac Hedges on weekend retreats as well. His mother scrutinized each and every one—but, both to her disappointment and relief, Barton never became steady with any of them.

Despite his earnest role at the Purchasing Exchange, heightening war news was making Barton ill at ease. News stories of battlefront horrors intensified daily. The miraculous rescue of some 200,000 British troops cornered by the Germans at Dunkirk, France, had a grip on the Cross household for days. Moreover, many of Arthur's English friends were being bombed out of their homes by the Luftwaffe's relentless London blitz.

Then one morning in September 1940, as the family sipped their coffee and waited for breakfast to be served, Arthur returned to the dining room with the damp morning paper. Barton's hair was in disarray, and his eyes betrayed another late night out. He barely noticed his father's reticence after reading the front page.

Arthur handed the paper to Helen, telegraphing his concern with a certain look. She scanned the headline and article, and then heaved a deep sigh. The news was that Roosevelt had signed the military draft bill into law, calling up the first nine hundred thousand men. It had been expected, but the reality of *mandatory* was something different, particularly when combined with the other news of the day—that Japan had joined Germany and Italy to sign the Tripartite Pact, which formed the Axis powers. Breakfast that morning ended with plenty of leavings for the dog. Barton was now a prime candidate for the draft.

Two months later, this family of avid Republicans was further disappointed by Roosevelt's besting of the GOP's Wendell Willkie to win a third presidential term. The Crosses despised Roosevelt's pervasive approach to boosting the economy, the so-called New Deal, which they viewed as aggressively antibusiness and fraught with ever-expanding government subsidies. Anglophile Arthur pointed out to whomever would listen that the real reason for the economic uptick since the Depression was not Roosevelt's

New Deal, but spiking textile and other war-materiel orders from his native Britain.

On the night of November 5, 1940, Helen wrote in her diary:

Election Day! Roosevelt, the glamour voiced lad, made the grade— elected by 24 million against 20 million for Wilkie. The Electoral College of course shows proportional representation—there one sees the fine hand of the bosses in the big cities. Let's hope that those 20 million protesting votes will curb him to some degree. We did not sit up for returns, feeling the results in our bones.

Barton began to feel sidelined as 1940 stretched into 1941. He returned home each night to Rosemary studying for her Waves exam [Women Accepted for Volunteer Emergency Service] and his mother's Bundles for Britain sewing circle. The women were gathered in the drawing room around the Victrola, listening to Edward R. Murrow's nightly broadcasts from London—ablaze from German bombing raids. "This . . . is London," Murrow would begin, as the spellbound women knitted away at scarves bound for Royal Air Force fighters battling the Luftwaffe.

Unable to escape the significance of events unfolding an ocean away, Barton began to yearn for a chance to reenter the navy. For a while, he had convinced himself that the British Purchasing Exchange *was* helping with the war effort, but with the mandatory draft, he knew he would be called up eventually. In the spring of 1941, Barton decided to swallow his pride and see if Bill could help.

Meanwhile, Bill had been formulating an idea of his own, one that matched the navy's needs with Barton's business degree and training. When the call came through from Lilac Hedges, he jumped at the chance to take responsibility for Barton's naval future—and an opportunity for maternal recognition for his mother's oft-overlooked middle son.

And so Barton's prestigious appointment to the Supply Corps, the navy's business managers, was Bill's doing. "I had planned to have you ordered down here as one of my assistants," Bill wrote Barton, "but I hesitate to do anything that would deprive you of a commission in the Supply Corps; it is the best opportunity offered any applicant these days. You have the right background, and the advantage of learning things that will be of great value to you in the business world, should you later leave the Navy."

Supply Corps commissions in 1941 were a hot commodity, but Bill knew how to maneuver along the navy's inside track to ensure that one of those coveted commissions went to Barton. After that, Bill pushed for his brother's acceptance into the Harvard Supply Corps training program, recently incorporated into its business school. At Harvard, Barton would master the rigors of the Supply Corps with FDR's son, young John Roosevelt. Bill followed his brother's progress with barely concealed pride and enthusiasm.

The new ensign's orders arrived quickly after his return from Boston that September. Congress had finally loosened its purse strings for an all-out fortification of an increasingly vulnerable American base in the Pacific: the Philippines.

It was a good opportunity, Bill assured Barton—although their mother was of a distinctly different mind. The evening his orders to the Philippines arrived, Barton joined Helen and Arthur for a glass of sherry on the porch. He tried to comfort his anxious parents and reminded them that this was the course they had long wanted for him. There was a clutch at Helen's heart when Barton raised his glass in mock celebration and toasted, "Here's hoping the Japs don't get me, Mother. I'd hate to give all this up!"

9

★ ★ ★

THE PERILS OF ESCAPE—
AND A LITTLE BASEBALL

THE POSSIBILITY OF ESCAPE crossed every prisoner's mind, but during the summer of 1942, Barton abandoned the fantasy for good. Men who had tried and failed were brought back to camp and beaten, mutilated, and tortured in public view. Nothing focused the mind on the perils of escape more than the particular return of three prisoners—two army colonels and a navy lieutenant—who were each summarily stripped naked, marched across the camp to the entrance, tied up, and flogged to insensibility.

They were then kicked to their feet, led out the front gate with their hands tied behind them, and strung up to hang from cross-pieces of wood several feet above their heads. A two-by-four was placed beside them, and when any Filipinos passed by on the road, they were summoned by the Japanese guards to pick up the timber and smash each of the hanging prisoners in the face. Then the guards would follow up and lay on their whips.

The beatings, whippings, and subsequent screams could be heard everywhere in the camp. Even in the middle of the night, the cracking whip sounded in the darkness. At the end of the third day, the other prisoners watched through the barbed wire as the three men, miraculously still alive, were loaded into a covered truck and driven away. Soon, two shots were heard from the direction of the retreating truck. The prisoners later learned that the third man had been beheaded.

Barton was as traumatized, enraged, and disgusted by this savagery as the rest of the prisoners. But it wasn't just this incident that permanently put the temptation of escape out of his mind. It was the grim story of ten men selected for execution in reprisal for another man's attempted escape from a bridge repair detail outside Cabanatuan. While the stunned men in his outfit looked on, the captured escapee was forced to join the nine other men in his ten-person shooting squad to dig a large hole, line up at its edge, and be shot at close range one by one. One of the unfortunate victims, Staunton Ross Betts, called out to his older brother Edwin, whom he called "Jack," standing among the horrified captive audience. "Take it easy, Jack," Ross said. "I'll be all right. And take care of Mother."

This Japanese deterrent to attempted escape—which came to be called, variously, "the ten-and-one-rule," "the blood-brother system," or, simply, "shooting squads"—had the desired effect, especially since none of the POWs knew who his fellow squad members were. This prevented them from conspiring to escape together. It would be one thing to escape and die trying, but quite another to bring down that kind of horror on others, Barton decided. He resolved then to survive by other means.

THOUGH MEASURABLY WEAKENED, BARTON had so far avoided contracting the serious tropical diseases that raged at Cabanatuan. Oddly, the larger and heavier men tended to fall ill and die more quickly than did those of smaller build like Barton. In fact, he was among the healthier prisoners, allowing him to continue in his quest to boost the morale of a growing group of friends, some teetering on the edge of despair. It wasn't uncommon for those whose mental, physical, and emotional health had become so bruised and degraded to simply decide to die.

Providing succor to these depleted and fragile men in this newly confined world became Barton's calling. Hopelessness was as fatal as any disease at Cabanatuan, and having visited its dark provinces a time or two himself in life, he knew when someone was on the brink. He might notice one friend drooping into apathy, offering little or no conversation, retreating into solitude. Another, frail as balsa wood, might be found lying in the scratchy cogon grass, eyes staring blankly ahead.

So Barton would return to the barrack and shake out his shoe on a dirty board, yielding maybe only a handful of rice, still in husks. With gusto, he and his friends would beat open the husks using the side of their canteens. Barton always drew laughs and groans with his constant refrain, "Cold Rheingold, anybody?" He'd then swill some tepid water, pretending it was a beer, and wipe his mouth with a dramatic swipe of his forearm. "Ah, that was *good*!"

The discovery that adversity has its upsides was one of the powerful lessons Barton had learned at Christ School. It is unknown how many frozen pine stumps and their notoriously long root systems he was forced to dig out with a pickax and shovel in the Smoky Mountain winters, but given that he held his class's record for total accumulated demerits, it was more than a few. Stump duty was the stiffest of punishments and difficult work, but completing those excavations in the quiet winter woods always offered Barton a measure of satisfaction. Cabanatuan's world of deprivation offered a certain sanctuary, too—and opportunities for fulfillment that had mostly eluded him in his former life.

At Annapolis, he had been drawn to the humanities, particularly the study of William Wordsworth. His favorite of Wordsworth's poems was "Lines Written a Few Miles Above Tintern Abbey." Concerning the poet's reflection on his younger self, it addressed the burden of self-doubt and how it sparked him to perform selfless acts:

> *In hours of weariness, sensations sweet,*
> *Felt in the blood, and felt along the heart,*
> *And passing even into my purer mind*
> *With tranquil restoration:—feelings too*
> *Of unremembered pleasure; such, perhaps,*
> *As may have had no trivial influence*
> *On that best portion of a good man's life;*
> *His little, nameless, unremembered acts*
> *Of kindness and of love.*

Not until Cabanatuan did Barton come to personify the principles of this well-loved verse. He organized card games and informal prayer, commanded ready audiences for his jokes and wickedly good stories, and contributed his tenor voice and eclectic musical repertoire to a group of singers who strolled the camp, crooning everything from Christian hymns to Broadway show tunes. As he had at the Citadel and Annapolis, he was also a willing participant in brainstorming nicknames for their various tormentors—in this case, the prison guards: Big Stoop, Little Speedo, Clark Gable, Air Raid, Laughing Boy, Donald Duck, Many Many, Beetle Brain, Fish Eyes, Web Foot, Hammer Head, Hog Jaw, and Slime. A latent thespian too, Barton always provoked precious, restorative laughter with his inimitable renditions of various camp guards' struts.

But he also recognized—astutely—that not all Japanese guards were cut from the same nasty cloth, and he developed something of a rapport with one of them. Lieutenant Oiagi, the camp's quartermaster and a Christian, was a quiet sort who had played on Japan's Davis Cup tennis team in the United States in the 1930s. He treated the American prisoners with fairness and relative restraint, particularly in contrast to his Cabanatuan colleagues. Barton's friendly banter with Oiagi had other benefits. When his friend and barrack mate Ensign Jack Ferguson was suffering from malaria, Oiagi found some quinine.

Jack was grateful beyond measure when Barton proudly produced and administered the quinine. As they sat together, talk of their respective homes and families ensued, as was so often the case at Cabanatuan. Ferguson, who was from Pennsylvania, talked mostly about his mother: how smart she was, how pretty, what a hell of a time he and his brother had given her when they were kids. Such topics formed the core of thousands of hours of conversation among the prisoners: peeling back layers of memory through countless recollections of home and childhood. Each man came to know the others' personal history totem—their towns, families, sweethearts, neighbors, favorite foods, best friends, and homes—inside and out.

Barton learned all about Charles Armour's upbringing in Little Rock—an American subculture as different from that of New Jersey as could be imagined within the borders of a single country. Like Barton, Charles was his father's namesake and the firstborn son of a second marriage. Charles, too, had chafed under outsized parental expectations; he felt in particular that he had never quite measured up in his father's eyes.

Before Mr. Armour died, he had been a soda-pop bottler representing the popular NuGrape brand. To help advertise the business, Charles's father had a car built in the shape of a NuGrape bottle: it was painted purple, and its exposed radiator was designed to resemble a bottle cap. Riding around town in that distinctive automobile afforded Charles a solid adolescent identity and made him feel like he *was* somebody—a schoolboy celebrity, to be sure. But all that vaporized with the 1929 stock market crash. Charles told the ensigns the story one evening as they crouched behind the barracks sharing a contraband cigarette.

Folks weren't spending money on soda pop when they could barely put dinner on the table, Charles said. When things in the Armour household seemed like they couldn't get any worse, he continued, his father had a heart attack while driving. The car slammed into a telephone pole after he slumped over the steering wheel. It wasn't long after his father's death that Charles joined the navy. "You know, get the hell outta the Wonder State. See the world. We see how that worked out."

Barton learned from Charles that being four inches taller might not buy happiness after all. Charles learned from Barton that lots of money and a fancy education were no guarantee of it, either. But of their respective homes, they were unequivocal in their proud recollections. They took turns drawing sketches of their houses in the dirt: Charles, of the unique Craftsman bungalow his family built at 501 Holly Street in Little Rock; and Barton, of his beloved Lilac Hedges.

The Armours had built 501 Holly with special attention to detail throughout. It had an L-shaped porch, the longer segment facing west toward beautiful sunsets, and the shorter part wrapping around to the south side. Charles explained that his parents designed the house so it could catch a breeze from every direction, a key attribute in a town where the thermometer could top 100 degrees on an August afternoon. Its wide eaves protected it, both from torrential summer downpours and the relentless sun that beat down from the south and west. French doors throughout the first floor not only gave the interior added grace, but also allowed for air circulation from one side of the house to the other.

In turn, Barton proudly described Lilac Hedges's white clapboard facade and classic Victorian gables, its green-striped awnings and painted porches, his mother's lovingly tended flower and vegetable gardens, the sprawl of English boxwoods, and, of course, the bursting surround of lilacs. He thought about the place all the time, he told Charles, and sometimes in his sleep he could hear the creak of the porch steps and whine of the old screen door opening and closing.

In their current state of wretchedness, some of the men found it easier to black out such emotional keepsakes than to conjure them up. For Barton, this might have included the sumptuous al fresco meals on the south lawn (and William's lemon cake); the rustle of his mother's favorite chiffon skirts in the breeze; the rich, earthy, cherry aroma of his father's pipe tobacco, and the lilacs, always the lilacs, glistening in the spring sun like a cache of amethysts. Their fragrance was so distinct and memorable, he might have broken down if he'd thought of it for too long.

Still, the occasional urge to share how their lives had once been, dignified and whole, was irresistible. The prisoners surely knew more about one another's lives than friends or even spouses or girlfriends might have learned back home. This was as true of Charles and Barton as it was of any other two men who'd been together since the start of this hellish odyssey.

WHEN IT CAME TO interacting with his captors, Barton's relatively small stature conferred a surprising natural advantage: he didn't tower over the diminutive Japanese guards as many other prisoners did—which often infuriated them and alone brought reprisals. Barton further disarmed them with another tactic he'd learned in his adolescence: projecting a distinctly nonthreatening manner. His ambassadorial role in persuading the prison guards to allow a game of baseball was one of its rewards. Baseball was not only the great American pastime, but a game much loved by the Japanese as well.

The prisoners carved bats out of native wood, and a softball was produced by the Japanese. A diamond was laid out on the camp's former inspection grounds, and two teams of players were drafted: one of army prisoners and the other navy. In the first game, the navy squad defeated the army team 3–1. The would-be blue-and-gold cheering section was as happy as the players.

Another game was scheduled, this time against a local team of Filipinos. Though the Americans lost 6–3, Barton hit his first-ever home run. A small Filipino band played "Onward Christian Soldiers" as he rounded third base and made it safely, incredibly, home, just seconds before the catcher tagged him. When Barton Cross crossed home plate he was as electrified as he was exhausted, hungry, and dirty. He laughed out loud and nearly burst into tears. The absurdity that this was actually one of the happiest moments of his life struck him full force.

The games lifted the spirits of all the players—even one they played against the Japanese guards themselves, which they elected wisely to lose. But playing ball burned precious additional calories not made up for at dinner afterward: a serving of rice and the occasional addition of a watery soup called *lugao*, with a few floating bits of yamlike *camote*. The games on top of their work details left the prisoner-players more famished than ever, and they realized with some sadness that the added energy playing ball required had to be factored into the cruel calorie math that determined survival. With a diet of fewer than 1,000 calories per day, they were all losing weight. Eventually, baseball at Cabanatuan was suspended for lack of participants.

10

★ ★ ★

A BROTHER'S BURDEN:
THE SEARCH

THE DEMANDS OF BILL'S White House job grew exponentially during the first half of 1942, as did those at home, with Romie and toddler Adam increasingly wanting of his time, attention, and company. Bill did the best he could to balance the dueling claims for his primacy, not to mention those imposed by his mother, whose almost daily letters and telephone calls about Barton regularly refreshed his sense of urgency and feelings of guilt.

But replies to Bill's persistent calls and letters about his missing brother arrived at their own unhurried pace. One came from an army nurse in Australia who had been evacuated from Sternberg Hospital just before Manila fell. Bill had recognized the old family friend's name on the evacuee list. His letter expressed relief that she was safe, and then asked about Barton. Had she seen him after the Japanese attack on Cavite? Did she know his whereabouts?

She replied that in fact she *had* seen Barton: he was a patient at

Sternberg! He had been wounded in the foot and leg, she confirmed, but was expected to recover. Bill was euphoric at this—then dismayed as she proceeded to explain that only *army* wounded and their nurses were evacuated to Australia before Manila fell. She didn't know what had happened to either the navy patients or the naval medical staff.

By bits and pieces, Bill gradually assembled a fairly reliable composite of what had befallen Barton and where he was most likely being held. It was not intelligence he wanted to share over the phone or in a letter, so in early spring, he secured his first day of leave since war had been declared and booked a train for New Jersey. Helen's and Arthur's calls had grown more frequent and importunate, and he hoped this gesture would calm them. But his good intentions were preempted by an article in the *Red Bank Register*, their hometown paper.

ENSIGN A. B. CROSS THOUGHT PRISONER
WOUNDED AT CAVITE WHICH JAPS HAVE NOW

Ensign A. Barton Cross Jr., son of Mr. and Mrs. A. Barton Cross, is believed to have been captured from a hospital near Cavite Naval Base after the fall of Manila. While there is strict censorship regarding such notices as far as the general public is concerned, it was revealed that during the attack and just before Cavite was abandoned, Ensign Cross was engaged on the dock in duties surrounding the submarine tender of which he was executive supply officer. As the fires raged on the wharves from enemy air action the 22 year [sic] old officer, a former classmate at Harvard of John Roosevelt, was supervising the embarkation of men and supplies when he was struck by a shell splinter.

> Attempts are being made to trace Ensign Cross
> through the International Red Cross in Geneva Swit-
> zerland, but to date all efforts have been unavail-
> ing . . . General MacArthur and his Forces still hold
> Bataan and Corregidor, the island forts that guard
> the entrance to the harbor.

A telephone message from Arthur was on Bill's desk when he arrived at the White House that morning. After two weeks, with several phone calls and promises of follow-up in between, a letter from Bill arrived at Lilac Hedges:

                    The White House
                    Washington

                    April 2, 1942

Dear Arthur,

    I am sorry about the blow from the Register regarding
Barton. They must have pieced together reports (never
assuredly accurate, by the way) from the Red Cross. I was,
in fact, planning a trip to see you about this when you
[first] called. I regret how matters unfolded.
    Yesterday a casualty list came through and on it were
the names of five officers left behind in Manila after
the evacuation to Bataan and Corregidor. Among them were
three in the Medical Corps and one in the Supply Corps.
All of them were known to Admiral McIntyre, the Surgeon
General, who is often here at the White House seeing after
the President. Barton was not listed. Also, Barton's name
was not on the long list of dead that came in today from the

International Red Cross--further confirmation that he is
indeed alive.

I had the occasion to show these lists to the president
and Admiral King and we discussed the possibility of
sending our own doctors over there to tend to the wounded
from Cavite, as well as a great many other related subjects.
I hope to speak with you about this before the end of the
week.

Everyone seems confident that it will only be a matter
of weeks now before we get confirmed information (unlike
that in The Register) that he is alive and in the hands of
the Japanese, if not more.

                                        Love,
                                        Bill

But Bill's words brought scant comfort:

                                        Lilac Hedges
                                        Oceanport, New Jersey

                                        April 5, 1942

Dear Bill,

Thank you for your apparent efforts, but we continue
to feel terribly depressed by the press accounts we
read daily. Not just about Barton, but the Philippines
generally. Clearly it is becoming another Dunkirk. At
worst the situation may be the complete isolation of the

Philippines and the Japs bomb the hell out of them from
every direction.

Why are green men sent to the firing line? What of the
wounded? Is this just another instance of Naval stupidity?
We pray hourly for Barton and Benny's safety.

Love, Mother

Enclosed in the envelope was an additional note from Arthur:

Dear Bill,

What I cannot understand is that there is no
organization big enough to advise the world whether
Japanese prisoners are being treated as human beings.

Another puzzlement is that, up to the present, the Navy
Prisoner of War Bureau has never issued a statement. On the
other hand, the Army bureau is listing personnel weekly. I
cannot help but think they are functioning more efficiently.

It does point out to the layman very forcibly that the
Army's Colonel Bresee is really on the job. I know of an
instance where the Colonel wrote and told a mother how
to address letters to her son, in care of the Japanese Red
Cross, New York City.

We become incensed with the Navy when we hear these
things.

Trusting that this finds both you and your family well,

With Kindest Regards,
Arthur

                                        The White House

                                        Washington

                                        April 9, 1942

My Dear Arthur,

    You do the Navy an injustice when you assume the Army
Prisoner of War outfit is functioning more efficiently than
the Navy one. I have been in regular touch with Colonel
Bresee since I very first heard of the attack on Manila, and
he has had a chit on file in his office for months, reminding
him to call me with any news of Barton's whereabouts.

    You see, the reports on all branches come through the
International Red Cross in Geneva and funnel through
Colonel Bresee. The Prisoner of War Board is a joint board,
having both Army and Navy officers as members. Captain
Jackson, whom I know quite well, is a Navy member and he
also has a chit to call me the minute any news of Barton
comes in.

    What you say about the Army listing personnel weekly is
true, but it just so happens that the Japanese have chosen
to tick off their Army prisoners to Geneva before they get
around to the Navy ones. There is nothing the Navy can do
about this because we don't control the Japanese--yet. Once
more, please be assured that I am leaving no stone unturned
to get the latest intelligence on Barton from any and all
sources.

                                        With Best Regards,

                                        Bill

P.S. Colonel Bresee was very happy to hear that you think so highly of him.

Letters and toll calls continued apace between the White House and Lilac Hedges, but Bill's assurances failed to assuage Helen. She was soon to make matters even more difficult for her middle son. Angry and out of patience, she launched her own official inquiry into Barton's status. Pleas from Helen Cross's prolific pen began pouring into war-wracked Washington: to Red Cross officials, to Bill's former boss at Naval Intelligence (already struggling to locate thousands of missing and captured), and to United States senators, including New Jersey Republican senator William Barbour:

> Lilac Hedges
> Oceanport, New Jersey
>
> My Dear Senator Barbour,
>
> It never occurred to me that I should ever ask your good offices in a personal way—however the enclosed clipping from the Red Bank Register will explain the grief which has descended on this family.
>
> For three months we were not notified that our son Barton Cross was not with his ship—weekly letters have gone out as though to a ghost. Think also of our awful three months anxiety over him on a ship—a submarine tender loaded with explosives and unprotected—following its progress supposedly from Cavite to Darwin, to the Dutch East Indies—watching for sinkings, bombings. Now we read only "missing" opposite his name after being wounded at Cavite Dec. 10th—where or how he is now, I do not know.
>
> Are our naval officers allowed to disappear like this?
>
> Can you please find out for me if he is a prisoner of the Japanese as well as the following:

1. *How does he live, since no paychecks have been sent out to him since his arrival in the Philippines?*

2. *Will they clothe and feed him properly?*

3. *Could or will he be exchanged as a prisoner of war, so he could go to Corregidor with MacArthur or to the safety of Australia?*

Believe me, I am proud of my son, doing his duty on those blazing docks until struck down and removed to Sternberg Hospital. At 23 years of age, he met Hell unflinchingly. I have another son, an officer on that gallant airplane carrier which was at the Marshall Islands. So I know how to bear anxiety and grief.

I just want to know so that I may sleep again, if Barton is alive, if the Japs will feed him, if America cares about those prisoners at Cavite and Manila or is taking steps to find out about them.

Hopefully, and with appreciation of any reply you may send.

Sincerely,
Helen C. Cross

When his mother's letter to Senator Barbour and others crossed his desk (first routed from Capitol Hill to the Navy Department, then to Bill for reply), Bill was more irritated than embarrassed—but plenty of both. He immediately placed a call to Lilac Hedges, demanding his mother explain her apparent end run around him. Did she really think this would generate better information than he had given her? Did she really think this was appropriate, making inquiry to a United States senator about one missing man with a war spanning the globe going on?

After listening patiently to his rant, Helen explained sweetly ("My dear boy," she began) that she and Senator Barbour were old friends. Why would a little letter to an old friend upset him so?

Bill exhorted his mother to halt her letter-writing campaign, explaining what he would have thought obvious: that such unwanted attention could hurt him professionally, and would certainly not improve her store of information regarding Barton. Bill would have to reply to Senator Barbour, he said through clenched teeth, and with a workday that already spanned sixteen hours, such extracurricular tasks were not appreciated.

> The White House
> Washington

My Dear Senator Barbour:

The Navy's Bureau of Navigation has forwarded me your letter of inquiry for reply. Ensign A. B. Cross is my half-brother, Mrs. Cross being our mother. You may be sure therefore that my interest in his case is more than an official one. I have gone to great lengths to gather any and all information on his case. The unfortunate facts are that Barton was wounded in the bombing attack on Cavite and we've had no further confirmation of his whereabouts. Our fear is that he is now a prisoner of war.

Mother seems to feel there was some dereliction on the part of the Navy in not having notified her that Barton was missing from his ship; however I believe you will understand that it was, and is, impossible for the Navy to keep in constant radio touch with the Asiatic Fleet, especially regarding individual cases. When on or about the 15th of February I finally received the roster of officers from the boy's ship and found that he was missing, the Navy Department immediately took steps to try and find out what happened to him.

The Commandant of the 16th Naval District [the

Philippines] conducted an investigation which confirmed
that Barton had been wounded at Cavite and was treated
in a hospital in Manila. The reasons he probably did not
forward this information before he was quizzed by the
Navy Department were,

1) That he may have assumed Barton went out on some other
    ship after the Otus departed, or,
2) He had a war to fight and had not the time yet to take
    up the case.

Our mother has asked you a great many questions as to
how Barton is living, how the Japanese are treating him,
possibilities of exchange etc . . . None of these questions
have answers at present.

The Prisoner of War Division, working in conjunction
with the International Red Cross, is doing everything it
can to find out about conditions among our prisoners of war.
The Japanese have forwarded them very little information,
but all of which I have forwarded to our mother. You may
rest assured that I shall make such information as I may be
able to gather available to her.

As you know Mrs. Cross has another son in the Navy
besides Barton and myself, and I have also written him
about this matter since he is on duty in the Pacific and
may be able to turn up additional information. I have also
written to the Commanding Officer of Barton's ship.

Respectfully Yours,

William C. Mott, Lieut. Cdr.

Weeks passed before Joel Newsom, captain of the USS *Otus*, replied to Bill's inquiry. Finally, in mid-May, Captain Newsom sent his findings after consulting the ship's log of December 10, 1941, to supplement his recall of events that difficult day:

```
                              Submarines
                              United States Asiatic Fleet
                              USS Otus (AS20)


My dear Lieutenant Mott:


  I have purposely delayed replying to your letter of
March 17 until the latest information from Manila was
received. Now that Corregidor has fallen, further delay is
useless. As you say, our departure from Manila on December
10 was somewhat hurried.
```

Newsom proceeded to explain that Admiral Hart had ordered *Otus*—one of the Asiatic Fleet's few critical submarine tenders—to sortie immediately after damaging bombs glanced her starboard side during the Japanese air attack. In the confusion and haste, Newsom couldn't account for why Barton had turned up missing.

```
  Persons who left Manila after we did but before it fell,
stated definitely that Barton was in a Manila hospital with
shrapnel wounds. I cannot confirm whether he reported to
the Submarine Tender Canopus, nor has anyone I can locate
seen him since he was in the hospital. It is known, however,
that the hospital was not bombed. There is a possibility
that upon recovering and finding all naval vessels had
```

evacuated Manila, he escaped to join the guerrillas
in the mountain country, as some did. You are the best
judge of that possibility. I sympathize with you in your
uncertainty . . .

   I regret I cannot give you more encouraging news of
your brother. He was a grand shipmate and an excellent
officer. There is no doubt in my mind he is a prisoner
of war. From meager reports received, the Japanese are
treating their officer prisoners of war better than we
might expect from that nation, but reliable information is
scarce, at best.

Next came the news that *Canopus* had been sunk during the siege of
Bataan. After weeks of hoping that Barton had made his way to it, now the
family spent the next several weeks praying that he hadn't, even as they
braced for the ship's manifest and casualty report. When the lists finally arrived in June, Barton was not on either one.

Throughout the spring and summer of 1942, Bill reviewed every scrap
of intelligence from the Philippines—which had narrowed to a trickle since
the termination of all radio traffic at the fall of Corregidor. Even so, while
Barton was still listed as missing, Bill felt sure that Captain Newsom's intelligence was spot on: that Barton was wounded at Cavite, treated at Sternberg, and taken prisoner after Manila fell.

But where was he now? There was a measure of hope in one of Captain
Newsom's references, that perhaps Barton had "escaped to join the [Fili-
pino] guerrillas in the mountain country, as some [Americans] did."

This burgeoning guerrilla resistance movement had been confirmed by
other sources, but Bill was frustrated by the few and erratic details available
on these widely dispersed bands of unsurrendered American and Filipino
military. All that was known so far was that guerrilla groups were organizing
in isolated centers throughout the islands. They were made up of American

officers who had fled to remote hill and jungle communities and banded with armed, resistance-minded Filipinos who knew the terrain. This much was known because some had set up clandestine shortwave radios and were attempting to relay to the world what was happening in the Philippines. These crude broadcasts were first thought to be Japanese feints but had since been authenticated; they were being picked up in Australia as well as at receiving stations as far away as San Francisco. Their repeated requests were for arms, food, and other supplies that would help them resist the Japanese.

The Red Cross, along with the navy and army intelligence operations, built on their meager reserves of information, but limited interaction with the Japanese through Swiss delegations had yielded little more than enemy demands regarding their own prisoners in the Pacific. There were other bits of information coming in that were so disturbing Bill would not share them with Arthur, much less his mother. They were learned via intercepted Japanese communications and other classified documents dispatched to the Map Room. The first, a quote by a Kempeitai official regarding Allied prisoners, had appeared in the *Japan Times*: "They cannot be treated as ordinary prisoners of war. Their defeat is their punishment. To show them mercy is to prolong the war . . . An eye for an eye, a tooth for a tooth. Hesitation is uncalled for and the wrongdoers must be wiped out."

Another dispatch was so disturbing that Bill sought multiple translations to confirm that it had not been an error. In a memo to Captain McCrea, Bill elaborated:

The following excerpt was taken from a Japanese diary captured on New Guinea: "Because of food shortages, some companies have been eating human flesh (Australian soldiers). The taste is said to be good." (Note: Because of the incredible implications of this statement, it was concurred in by three individual translations.)

Another entry several days later contained the following crude haiku:

```
When we ran short of rations,
We devoured our own kind to
Stave off Starvation.
```

After writing the memo, Bill put on his cap and walked out of the Map Room in the direction of the Rose Garden. On that early-summer afternoon, a group of military nurses evacuated from the Philippines had been invited to the Executive Mansion. The nurses, bedecked in their crisp whites, were now stationed at Walter Reed Hospital in Washington. When Mrs. Roosevelt heard of their arrival in the nation's capital, she invited them to the White House to officially recognize their good works. Bill was more than happy to escort the nurses to see the First Lady, with whom he had a warm relationship.

After an initial exchange of pleasantries, Bill ventured an inquiry about Barton to the gathered nurses. "Oh yes!" exclaimed one, Mary Lohr. "He's your brother? Oh my, yes, I knew him!"

She explained that she was working at Sternberg Hospital in December when the navy wounded were brought over from Cavite. Barton was wounded in the lower leg and foot, she said; she nursed him from the time he arrived until she was ordered to Corregidor on Christmas Day. He'd told her exactly what happened to him.

Bill was speechless as his new angel of mercy continued her tale.

"He said he heard shrapnel clicking on the road behind him. He'd been running, carrying something, when he got hit. Then he said, 'The good news is, now I'm here with you!' He was always cracking jokes, trying to buck us up," she added.

Bill's questions poured out.

"Yes, he was still there on Christmas, when our group of nurses left for Corregidor. In fact, on Christmas Eve he asked me to send a telegram to his parents, in New Jersey, I think, but from Manila's Army and Navy Club, not the hospital. He didn't want them to know he was in the hospital."

That was the last time she saw him, she said.

Mary couldn't say why only the army wounded were ordered out on the *Mactan*; by then, she was on Corregidor. "There was just no plan for the navy boys, I guess, in all the confusion."

At they talked, the large Red Cross banner was unfurled for the occasion, not far from the circular drive where Filipino stewards polished the running boards and cleaned the windows of President Roosevelt's Packard. Before the ceremonial greeting started, Bill said, "I am so grateful to you for this information, to know that that you saw him alive." And then: "Our mother will be overjoyed to hear these things. This is a feast of news compared to what we've had so far."

11

★ ★ ★

MIDWAY

BOLSTERED BY THE BRILLIANT success of USN Task Force 16 and Colonel Doolittle's Tokyo raid, military intelligence worked furiously to break JN-25, the Japanese naval code. There was no doubt in anyone's mind that the surprise invasion had enraged the enemy and shaken their confidence. A strong Japanese answer to the humiliating home-island strike was expected somewhere, and soon. No foreign power had successfully attacked Japan in more than four hundred years, and its military had assured the civilian government that Japanese skies and surrounding waters were protected and safe. The Japanese, it was soon learned, were formulating a grand reprisal.

Navy cryptanalysts at Pearl Harbor and in Washington scrutinized hundreds of intercepts a day and worked around the clock. The only other Pacific intercept stations—in Guam and the Philippines—had been lost, placing particular pressure on the already shorthanded Station Hypo, Oahu's Naval Intelligence operation.

JN-25 was formidable. It consisted of approximately forty-five thousand five-digit numbers, each representing a word or phrase. For transmission, the five-digit numbers were superenciphered using an additive table. Cracking the code first required intense mathematical analysis to strip off the additive, and then analysis of patterns and sequences to determine the meaning of the five-digit numbers. Under Commander Joe Rochefort, Station Hypo's brilliant, if eccentric, head, the staff made slow but steady progress—thanks to JN-25's rote use of the additive tables.

In May, Hypo cryptanalysts picked through thousands of radio intercepts between enemy ships with intensifying interest. There had been a spike in Japanese naval communications in the Pacific, and each bit of decrypted intelligence from that heightened traffic flow offered tiny clues to the Japanese Navy's whereabouts and intentions. In the White House Map Room, Bill Mott logged the code-cracking progress reports and then presented the eyes-only summaries to the White House inner sanctum and FDR himself.

Bill's own training in codes and ciphers enabled him to follow Station Hypo's progress with knowledge and precision. By the second half of May, Rochefort felt sure that a major enemy strike was in late-stage planning, though the coded traffic had so far revealed little more. Hypo's staff was still deciphering only fractional bits of JN-25 at a time and understood 10 percent to 15 percent of the overall code, at best. Still, a persistent clue from recent intercepts was emerging: the term or location "AF" was mentioned repeatedly.

Meanwhile, *Enterprise* and *Hornet* had been abruptly called back to Pearl Harbor from reconnaissance patrols in the Central Pacific. The cryptic cable from Admiral Halsey to CNO Admiral Ernest King was of far greater weight than the sum of its words:

```
Have Ordered Enterprise and Hornet to Expedite Return.
```

```
                    Halsey
```

Bill never feared more for Benny's life. American naval strength against Japan was at an all-time low, and the enemy knew it. Not only was the battleship fleet crippled, the carrier *Lexington* had been sunk in early May at the Battle of the Coral Sea, where an eight-hundred-pound bomb had also ripped apart USS *Yorktown*'s insides. It was unclear whether *Yorktown* could be repaired, and her sister carrier, USS *Saratoga*, was still in dry dock from the broadside torpedo it took at the Gilbert and Marshall Islands.

Official Washington pondered this paltry flattop arithmetic as the clocks ticked down toward a certain enemy assault on beleaguered US naval forces somewhere in the Pacific. Five carriers minus *Lexington* and *Yorktown* equaled three. Three minus *Saratoga* equaled two, leaving only *Enterprise* and her new sister, *Hornet*, which had never engaged in battle. Two carriers to hold the Pacific against an all-out assault by the Imperial Navy?

As the new storm clouds gathered, Station Hypo's wildcatter analysts struck a cryptographic gusher. Acting on a hunch that "AF" was the JN-25 designation for Midway Island, Hypo directed the commanding officer at Midway to send a message in the clear indicating a malfunction at Midway's water distillation plant and that fresh water was needed urgently. Shortly after, Hypo intercepted a Japanese intelligence report indicating that "AF" had a water problem. This breakthrough not only confirmed the identification of "AF" as Midway, but also verified that Hypo had broken JN-25, the General Purpose Code used by the Japanese Navy.

This electrifying revelation also meant that the opportunity for a surprise attack had just reverted from the Japanese to the Americans; they now had a shot at ambushing the enemy's incipient ambush. But even with this powerful advantage of surprise, the engagement still carried long odds for the handicapped US Navy. Intercepts revealed that as many as seventy enemy ships and sixteen submarines were priming to launch against Midway, including at least four, possibly five, aircraft carriers brimming with superior planes and experienced pilots. And the fateful rendezvous was fast approaching, according to Station Hypo; the Japanese assault on "AF" was slated for the third or fourth of June.

Heeding Halsey's curt order, *Enterprise* and *Hornet* churned back to Pearl in late May, and the heavily damaged *Yorktown* hobbled to drydock for repairs. The plan was to refuel and reprovision the first two and to repair *Yorktown*—in four days, not the three months considered minimally necessary. The warships would then sail west and lie in wait northeast of Midway for the approaching Japanese armada.

JAPAN'S DECISION TO ATTACK Midway was based on a grand misperception that would ultimately change the course of the Pacific War. The enemy picket boats that Benny had sighted on April 17—and that *Nashville* torpedoed just before Colonel Doolittle and his men took to the skies—never did get the word to their Japanese superiors that the planes over Tokyo had launched from an aircraft carrier. When queried by the press after the attack, President Roosevelt said with a smile that the B-25s had flown from "Shangri-La"—the mythical city in James Hilton's popular novel *Lost Horizon*. But the Japanese believed they had launched from Midway, the closest American land base to Japan's home islands. As a result, Japanese high command decided to revise its war strategy and attack and occupy Midway to prevent future raids on its home soil.

Admiral Yamamoto had advocated securing Midway, understanding the power of his adversary. He had attended Harvard University and traveled extensively in the United States as a young officer. "I fear we have awakened a sleeping giant," he was rumored to have said after coordinating the successful Pearl Harbor attack. He stood alone among victory disease-ridden commanders in his belief that Japan could succeed against America only if it knocked out its battleship *and* carrier strength early in the war, before the country's mighty shipbuilding industry could mobilize to replace them. This would give resource-starved Japan enough time to seize the oilfields of the Dutch East Indies and Malaya and strengthen its own arsenal before any Allied counterattack.

Only after the humiliating success of Doolittle's surprise Tokyo raid did Yamamoto's superiors yield to his view—and his imperative that the Japanese attack and occupy Midway Atoll, strategically situated 1,300 miles northwest of Honolulu and 2,500 miles east of Japan. Wresting Midway from the Americans, he persuaded, would limit their ability to defend Hawaii, thwart their resistance to Nippon conquests in the entire region, and protect Japan proper. Seizing the objective in an overwhelming surprise attack would further allow the Japanese Navy to annihilate the remainder of the US Pacific Fleet. Under Yamamoto's ambitious Midway annexation plan, the Pacific Ocean would soon become one large Japanese fishpond.

ON THE COOL SPRING evening of May 26, 1942, Bill Mott stood outside the Oval Office with an urgent intelligence update for Admiral Ernest King, chief of naval operations (CNO). King was behind closed doors with President Roosevelt, a relative rarity. Despite King's accurate reputation as generally irascible, Bill respected him for his unalterable—if minority—view that America's interests were best served by allocating more men, money, and materiel to the battle in the Pacific. In a world war in which British and other European interests competed with this priority, the navy's senior flag officer was consistently obdurate on this point.

To his core, King was suspicious of what he saw as British attempts to divert resources from his ability to fight Japan—not just to save their homeland but also to preserve their colonial holdings in the Pacific. The CNO wasn't isolated in this opinion: the Allies' joint South East Asia Command (SEAC) was mordantly nicknamed "Save England's Asian Colonies" by his sympathizers. King was also well known for his rants against MacArthur, using unprintable adjectives to describe his disgust at the general's failures in the Philippines as well as his "absurd" demands on the US Navy. Bill didn't hate that about the CNO, either.

While he waited to speak with Admiral King, Bill chatted with Grace Tully, the president's secretary, all the while nervously fingering the envelope, stamped "Top Secret," in his hand. Grace finally told him she would ring the Map Room as soon as King emerged from the Oval Office; their meeting seemed to be taking longer than expected. Still clutching the envelope, Bill retreated down the cavernous West Wing hallway, now quiet at the relatively late hour of seven o'clock.

The Map Room was tense, hushed, and smoky. Barely audible above the teletype was the murmur of gathering brass conferring over the same eyes-only document that Bill Mott had presented to them a half hour earlier. The communication was from Admiral Chester Nimitz, commander in chief of the Pacific Fleet (CINCPAC). It revealed the shattering news that Admiral Halsey was too sick to engage in the "next operation" and had to be practically forced off the *Enterprise* to be hospitalized at Pearl Harbor, fuming and cursing every step of the way.

To his crew and top Washington brass, the seemingly irreplaceable Halsey was now unable to lead the charge in this next—and most critical— sea battle of the war. The diagnosis was a severe case of dermatitis compounded by exhaustion, for which there was no quick or easy cure. Worse yet, Halsey had apparently decided, with minimal consultation, that a little-known rear admiral by the name of Raymond Spruance was to take his place.

Spruance! The news took Bill by surprise. As if Benny and the crew weren't in enough danger, now subtract the revered, fearless, battle-hardened Halsey and install a cruiser commander—who wasn't even an aviator and who had never commanded an aircraft carrier? Respected? Yes, but untested, and Spruance had never even seen sea-air battle!

War Secretary Stimson said nothing as he reviewed the onionskin paper containing the news. In the uncomfortable silence that followed, Bill walked along the Pacific wall map and inspected the updates. Not one of the men voiced concern about Spruance, as though to do so would have placed a hex. But the discomfiting news hung in the air as palpably as the layer of smoke from Stimson's cigarette.

The facts were these: Admiral Halsey had worked with Raymond Spruance—currently in command of a cruiser division—for more than a decade and had tremendous faith in him. Halsey regarded Spruance as a brilliant tactician with a reputation for making quick, masterful, and precise decisions under pressure. Admiral Nimitz also liked and respected Spruance, but, more importantly, he had immeasurable faith in Halsey's judgment in such matters.

When Admiral King was finally apprised of Spruance's selection to replace Halsey for the Midway operation, he too concurred. He was certainly not about to challenge either Nimitz or Halsey on the eve of battle, from a distance of six thousand miles. Thus the closed society of top brass had spoken by barely speaking. The selection of Rear Admiral Raymond Spruance, cruiser commander, for tactical command of the upcoming Armageddon of the Pacific was not reversible.

ABOARD THE USS *ENTERPRISE*, when the ship and air crews learned of Halsey's illness and the substitution of Spruance, the reaction was seismic. "Spruance! He was against sending Doolittle to Tokyo!" Benny hollered across the wardroom as the men ate their dinner. "I know that for a *fact*."

"He thinks aviators are for the birds, that's what I heard," came a reply. "The pilots are mad as hell!"

These and countless other such conversations reverberated throughout *Enterprise* just hours before the men were to put to sea for certain battle. The crew were stunned and gloomy when they heard about Halsey. Some cursed and fretted, others prayed. With little else to go on in the last six months, they'd placed every ounce of hope, faith, and pride in their feisty and indefatigable admiral. In their heart of hearts, the *Enterprise* crew was in the fight as much for Halsey as they was for their country.

At daybreak on May 28, 1942, *Enterprise, Hornet,* and a rudely patched-up *Yorktown* slipped from their Pearl Harbor berths, followed by an abbreviated band of weary-looking cruisers and oilers. There was a keen sense among all of them that David was trudging to meet Goliath, though the precise details of their mission had not yet been announced.

Early rumors aboard *Enterprise* were that they were on their way to repel an all-out Japanese assault—complete with planned troop landings—on the Hawaiian Islands; it was dramatic, if wildly inaccurate. By early morning May 29, however, the convoy was three hundred miles north of the Hawaiian island of Kauai, a distance at growing odds with rumors of a land attack in the other direction. At 0505 that same morning, just after the ships' sirens wailed general quarters and the men took to their battle stations, a message from Admiral Nimitz was read aloud over the ships' loudspeakers:

"In the cruise just starting, you will have the opportunity to deal the enemy heavy blows. You have done this before, and I have great confidence in your courage, skill, and ability to strike even harder blows. Good hunting and good luck."

Then came Captain Murray's voice:

"We have reason to believe the Japanese may attempt to occupy Midway Island. We are, therefore, moving into such position to counter such an attempt should it develop."

Lastly, the voice of the little-known Admiral Spruance came through:

"An attack on Midway Island is expected. Enemy forces include all combatant types, four or five carriers, plus transport and train vessels. If we remain unknown to the enemy, we should be able to flank attack from a position northeast of Midway. Should our carriers become separated by enemy aircraft, they will attempt to maintain visual contact. The successful conclusion of operations now commencing will be of great value to our country."

Benny leaned back in his seat in the wardroom and let out a long, low whistle. "Jesus, Mary, and Joseph! Four or five carriers and how many escorts? Against what? About two and a half of us?" He turned to face Captain Randall. "I think I'd better go write my mother," Benny said with disdain.

But since *Enterprise* had embarked from Pearl, Admiral Raymond Spruance, a wiry, energetic man whose low-key manner belied a hefty intellect and tremendous self-confidence, had paced several miles on *Enterprise*'s flight deck. Senior officers took turns walking alongside him, briefing Spruance and answering questions. The tenor of these conversations was always the same. They were laser-focused, intense, to the point. Almost like a relay race, when one ambulatory meeting concluded, another officer took his place by the admiral's side, Spruance's gait never slowing.

The admiral would question, listen, question, listen, and question some more. He had inherited Halsey's capable, battle-hardened staff, and in these walking meetings, Spruance processed every detail and committed to memory every critical aspect of the upcoming mission. A strategy was developing in his head.

By the last day of May, *Enterprise* and *Hornet* had assumed striking position northeast of Midway—on the flank of the enemy's anticipated thrust. Submarine reports confirmed that the Japanese attack force was approaching from the northwest, as expected. A low cloud cover and poor visibility so far favored the Japanese, because that made it all the harder for the Midway defenders to spot and repel their approaching ships and planes.

For the first three days of June, Benny slept fitfully. His sole comfort those lonely and anxious nights was that he was moving closer to Barton. He would remind his mother of this because he knew it would comfort her—assuming he survived the next two days.

During that same seventy-two hours, the American force maneuvered continuously to avoid detection, then reversed course to arrive at "Point Luck"—code name for the rendezvous point northeast of Midway—on June 4. At 0330 that morning, *Enterprise* reveille sounded, followed by the loud, clangorous general quarters summoning crew to battle stations.

Anticipation coursed through the ship like a high-voltage electrical current. From stem to stern, from flight deck to bridge, in all departments and at all levels, the USS *Enterprise* prepared for action.

Benny made a final gunnery check at each antiaircraft mount. Guns of every caliber and on every level of the ship, port and starboard, were as ready as they would ever be. Planes were also armed and primed for launch. Together with seventeen-year-old Texas sharpshooter Wayne Barnhill (who'd lied about his age to enlist and serve with his older brother), Benny stood in Sky Control, poised for certain action. Wayne was in charge of the sound-operated telephone used to communicate Benny's rapid-fire orders to the gunners throughout the carrier during battle.

Wayne's brother, photographer James Barnhill, nicknamed Barney, set up his action camera on the 0-2 level, halfway down the ship, to capture battle scenes for newsreels to be dispatched to Washington. Though Wayne chose not to speak his mind, he wished his brother would move a little farther back from the rail toward the camouflage draped against the ship's side. When Wayne winced for Barney's safety, Benny understood in a way he could barely express. He slapped Wayne on the back, momentarily holding his shoulder. In a rare act of informality between an enlisted man and officer, he looked him in the eye and said, "Look at it this way, son: he'll have a terrific view!"

Word shot through the ship an hour later that Japanese planes had begun their attack on Midway. The enemy flotilla was two hundred miles northwest of the base and the US convoy the same distance to the northeast. Of the forty-three American planes that launched in the first four hours, only six returned. Forty attacking Zeros had shot the others out of the sky like so many skeet clays. Benny barely took his eyes off the flight deck as the hours ticked away, trying to conceal building unease. The sense of impending disaster pervading Sky Control seemed to confirm the worst-case fears leading up to the Halsey-less mission.

But despite the dearth of returning planes, the American Navy's luck was about to turn. *Enterprise*'s flight leader, Lieutenant Wade McClusky, had inadvertently flown off course to find nothing but vacant seas. Disheartened and low on fuel, he prepared to turn his squadron back toward *Enterprise* when, through a peephole in the clouds, he spied a lone Japanese destroyer heading northeast at flank speed. On a hunch, McClusky ordered his air group to pursue the unsuspecting destroyer instead. Within ten minutes, the hunch paid off. Dead ahead was the entire Japanese striking force, replete with four carriers and a dozen support vessels, including battleships, destroyers, and cruisers.

Benny was so startled to hear McClusky's voice break radio silence over the crackling ship's radio that he spilled his coffee all over Wayne Barnhill. He quickly turned the knob just in time to hear McClusky's staccato delivery of stunning news: not only had they sighted the Japanese carriers, but also their first round of attack planes had just returned from Midway for refueling. Eureka!

Fuel hoses crisscrossed the Japanese carrier decks, and stacks of munitions were piled for reloading in plain view as the *Enterprise* squadron—and, shortly after, *Yorktown*'s fighters—came hurtling through the clouds. From ten thousand feet, McClusky and his thirty-seven bombers bore down on the Japanese anchorage at a seventy-degree angle. In less than thirty minutes, they had handily sunk two of their four carriers and wiped out half their airpower. By sundown, *Yorktown* pilots had torpedoed a third carrier. By the time the planes returned to *Enterprise*, *Kaga*, *Soryu*, and *Akagi* were nosing toward the ocean floor.

The fourth and last Japanese carrier, *Hiryu*, had not been located, but its pilots, seething with revenge, had discovered the American ships' position northeast of Midway and were heading straight for them. Although *Yorktown* and *Enterprise* were steaming less than six miles apart, *Yorktown* was closer to the approaching Japanese fighters. Benny watched enemy dive bombers roar toward *Yorktown* like a swarm of angry bees. Her antiaircraft gunners responded with furious intensity—but their efforts were futile.

With *Enterprise* beyond gun range, Benny and his megaphone were of no use to *Yorktown*. He could only watch helplessly from Sky Control as three bombs and two torpedoes all found their deadly marks. Seconds later, *Yorktown* was belching flames and smoke. Barney Barnhill swept his camera back and forth, back and forth, duty-bound to record the horrific scene. Only a fixed grimace hinted at his internal turmoil while he recorded hundreds of burning sailors jumping into the water. Soon the listing ship's outline blurred into a fireball after which only an urgent water rescue operation was left to film.

The jubilant return of *Enterprise* planes to the flight deck was tempered by the grim spectacle. They were soon followed by *Yorktown*'s fighters—orphaned by the fatal blows to their mother ship. But there was no time for the *Yorktown* pilots to grieve the certain loss of so many shipmates. Within minutes, they refueled and were again airborne, charging at *Hiryu* to exact their own revenge. *Hiryu* soon joined the three other Japanese carriers on the Pacific floor.

FOR BILL MOTT IN the White House Map Room, the suspense—listening moment to moment for the teletype to begin its clicking report of agonizing defeat, failure, and loss—was like waiting for as many pulls on a pistol trigger. The lopsided match between twenty-four American ships and an enemy armada four times that size had him on heart-hammering edge, hour after hour, waiting for Midway's battle status to come across.

Over the course of the three-day engagement, the crowded Map Room was efficient but hushed. Frequently the only sound that could be heard was the semicircular protractor scratching around a table map dotted with two- and three-inch ships. When the dispatch arrived about the loss of *Yorktown*—in advance of any news on the fate of the Japanese carriers—Bill braced for the rash of casualty reports.

When word then came through of the *Enterprise* squadron's brilliant air strikes and the enormity of *enemy* losses—and, best of all, that Japanese firepower was eliminated before it could retaliate against *Enterprise*—Bill threw a celebratory fist in the air and joined in the party-like atmosphere that had fully erupted in the Map Room. Similar celebrations were breaking out throughout the War Department and on Capitol Hill.

Admiral Spruance was forthwith crowned the navy's newest wunderkind. As it turned out, his painstaking preparation, tactical brilliance, and calculated risk of launching all task force planes ahead of schedule to ensure the crucial element of surprise—worked. His strategy not only achieved complete surprise and devastated enemy forces, but also prevented the deadly nighttime counterstrikes at which the Japanese excelled. In a rare moment of cheerful self-deprecation, Admiral King was overheard saying, "I see now that I am only the second-smartest man in the United States Navy!"

The reduction in Japanese Fleet strength wrought by the American Navy at Midway seemed almost too good to be true. Japan had lost four carriers, a heavy cruiser, and well over three hundred aircraft, not to mention its most experienced pilots. The Battle of Midway marked a strategic reversal in the Pacific War; America was now the aggressor, and Japan on the defense.

Admiral Nimitz immediately recalled the remainder of the Midway task force to Pearl Harbor. The mood aboard *Enterprise* was a strange mix of relief, exhilaration, and mourning. They had won and won big, but *Enterprise* had lost numerous pilots and air crews. There had not even been an opportunity to pay last respects on the fantail at a burial at sea service. The airmen had crashed to their Pacific graves without so much as a final salute.

Admiral Spruance came over the loudspeaker and delivered the following message as *Enterprise* steamed to port:

"I wish to express my admiration and commendation to every officer and man of the *Enterprise* and especially to the pilots and gunners for their splendid performance . . . The personnel losses are most regretted, but it is felt that these gallant men contributed materially in striking a decisive blow against the enemy."

The ship's radio buzzed with congratulatory messages. They poured in from President Roosevelt and Allied commands and officials from around the globe. There was also an awkwardly translated and wildly inaccurate report from Radio Tokyo, claiming victory for Japan's navy:

"Japan's forces carried out fierce attacks on Midway Island, inflicting heavy damage on fleet reinforcements in that area, also damaging naval and air installations . . . Japanese sank carrier *Enterprise* and *Hornet* and shot down one hundred twenty enemy aircraft."

Benny allowed a wide grin as he listened to the message. This was the second time the Japanese had reported sinking the *Enterprise*: the first was after the Gilbert and Marshall Islands raid in February. When the translation was read gleefully over the ship's loudspeakers, crew on every level stamped their feet approvingly. It was getting to be a good omen. Admiral Halsey's sobriquet for his beloved flagship, the Galloping Ghost of the Oahu Coast, had been well earned.

On the afternoon of June 13, 1942, every soldier and sailor in Pearl Harbor lined the docks to welcome *Enterprise* home. Deafening cheers and waving flags greeted the task force as it approached. The beginning of a forty-eight-hour congratulatory liberty found Benny and hundreds of other boisterous *Enterprise* celebrants crowding the bar at the Royal Hawaiian Hotel. None of them paid for their own drinks that night.

Over the ukuleles, laughing, and back slapping, one comment made the rounds countless times: "That Spruance! Brilliant, by God, *brilliant!*"

12

★ ★ ★

UNDER SIEGE: JN-25

WHILE SLIGHTLY HUNG OVER the morning after *Enterprise*'s victorious return to Pearl from Midway, Benny penned a reply to two letters from Bill that awaited him:

                                    June 14, 1942

Dear Bill,

    I haven't had much time to write, as you might imagine, but many thanks for your welcome words of encouragement. Your letters always give me something to look forward to. I would very much like to talk with you right now--I'm sure we could find many things of mutual interest to discuss without the veil of censorship.

    We've been lucky so far--the line has been held once

again. But there is such a thing as riding a good horse to death. I am bone tired. The situation remains grave however and there will be no respite, as you know.

To be honest, the thing that keeps me going are thoughts of Bart. After four years at sea they say I could stay and work ashore for a month or so, recognizing that one does need some rest to be of any use. But I feel the worse because when he came through here, he knew conditions were bad, and I told him not to worry too much, as we would be out there, ready and waiting if anything broke. I want to make good on that assurance before it's too late.

As for how badly you want to go to sea, Bill, I want to say again I think you can do more and serve better where you are. I know how you feel about Bart, but I believe if I could see you and have a talk with you I could convince you of that . . .

Well Bill, that's all for now except I have some good ideas I wish I could talk over with you so you could pass them on to the right people.

                         Do your best always,

                         Love,

                         Benny

BILL READ AND REREAD Benny's somewhat disjointed response to his letters. He was relieved to finally get direct word from his brother, and for the moment dismissed the usual admonition about his desire to go to sea. Right now he was focused on a different phrase Benny had used: "veil of censorship." Bill had just learned that an unbelievable tear in that veil had occurred, quashing his jubilant mood over the victory at Midway. The breach could potentially endanger Benny and his crew as much as any incipient Japanese assault.

The Midway task force had just prevailed because of a combination of intelligence work, skill, and luck in breaking the Japanese naval code. Even better, the Japanese were unaware that their code had been cracked; they continued to use JN-25 after Midway to encrypt naval messages. But the work of one Stanley Johnston—World War I veteran, champion sculler, and heady Australian war correspondent for the *Chicago Tribune*—had potentially reversed Station Hypo's crucial code breaking gains.

Johnston had distinguished himself while on assignment covering the Coral Sea Battle back in early May. When the *Lexington* received her fatal bomb blow during that engagement, Johnston, in the heat of battle, heroically rescued burning sailors from "Lady Lex's" doomed hold. He was one of the last to leave the ship. Then, while the crew members thrashed desperately in the oily water, Johnston, a strong swimmer, was further credited with saving a number of lives by helping them to land into lifeboats.

Both *Lexington's* skipper and his executive officer, M. T. "Mort" Seligman, were so impressed by Johnston's actions that they recommended him for a navy heroism citation. In fact, their experience of surviving the harrowing *Lexington* disaster forged a bond between Johnston and Seligman, who shared a cabin from the Coral Sea back to the States aboard the navy transport *Barnett*. During that voyage, a secret dispatch containing the decoded Japanese order of battle for the upcoming Midway engagement was selectively distributed.

As *Lexington's* XO, Seligman received a copy of the classified dispatch, its blue lines standing out from the other papers on his desk. Versions vary on what happened next. One is that Johnston, being a good reporter and sleuth, observed the document and took note of its contents. Another holds that Seligman shared the very interesting top secret document with

Johnston, whom he now considered a close friend and confidant. Either way, Seligman would soon be in very hot water.

On return to the States, Johnston caught the first flight to Chicago, his priority to finish and file his story on the Coral Sea drama in which several men, including Mort Seligman and himself, were cast as heroes. But Johnston was also roughing out another story on his L.C. Smith & Corona Standard—bearing the electrifying draft lede that the US Navy had broken the Japanese naval code.

On June 7, while the Midway battle was still in progress, the *Chicago Tribune* presses cranked out hundreds of thousands of copies of the day's broadsheet, with Johnston's article appearing on page A1, above the fold. The headline: "Navy Had Word of Jap Plan to Strike at Sea." The story also appeared in other newspapers that subscribed to the *Tribune's* newswire, including conservative Cissy Patterson's *Washington Times-Herald*.

The opening lines of the article, which carried a Washington dateline, soon had jaws dropping all over the capital:

```
Washington, DC, June 7--

The strength of the Japanese forces which the Ameri-
can Navy is battling somewhere west of Midway Island
in what is believed to be the war's greatest naval
battle, was well-known in American naval circles, re-
liable sources in Naval Intelligence disclosed here
tonight.
```

The story named the four carriers of the Japanese striking force and listed the Japanese order of battle. It further noted that all American outposts in the Pacific had been given the advance warning. The Washington dateline on the story was designed to conceal that Johnston in Chicago was the source of the breach, implying instead that the leak was from Naval Intelligence in Washington.

As news of the catastrophic leak settled in, military and political leaders began vying for first blood. An enraged Roosevelt threatened to send marines to Chicago to shut down Tribune Tower, home of the loathed newspaper, which he viewed as a thinly disguised organ of the Republican Party. Roosevelt already famously despised its publisher, Colonel Robert McCormick, a conservative and vocal anti–New Dealer—and old nemesis of the president's, going all the way back to their boarding school days at Groton School.

The navy went straight to work to rout the leaker. Astoundingly, the article had managed to clear censorship channels, with the critical nature of the contents somehow eluding the readers at the US Office of War Information (OWI).

The Japanese had only to read the *Chicago Tribune* to find that their codes had been compromised! Admiral King was said to be in "a white fury" that months of exhausting, round-the-clock effort to break JN-25—a singular feat on which the tide of the Pacific War had just turned—could soon be for naught. For days, Bill shuttled endlessly between the White House and the Navy Department as the navy and administration attempted to understand how this crucial secret had been compromised—not to mention how such a story could have slipped through the censors' fingers.

The investigation quickly confirmed that Commander Morton T. Seligman, the *Lexington*'s XO, had shared a cabin with correspondent Johnston, "in which the reporter observed the classified documents, including a JN-25-C decryption containing the Japanese order of battle at Midway." Whether Seligman intentionally shared the information or Johnston obtained it by sleuth, the result was the same. Seligman's naval career was effectively over. Still, more bloodletting was sought.

This was one of many instances in which Bill was grateful that none of his White House associates were aware of his Republican background. Burning with partisan rage toward McCormick, Roosevelt and other prominent Democrats demanded a grand jury investigation; party loyalists on both sides lined up to watch the goring. Roosevelt was not interested in Stanley Johnston's resignation or censure of the hapless Seligman. He wanted Colonel McCormick's scalp.

Miraculously, however, in the first week following the initial news leak and its subsequent coverage, the Japanese barely tweaked JN-25. Navy cryptanalysts began to wonder: Was it possible that no Japanese sympathizers or spies had read the article or its reprint in any American newspaper? Code breakers scrutinized new intercepts with bated breath, expecting at any moment for them to become indecipherable. But only small, manageable changes to JN-25 were detected. This wasn't necessarily unusual—minor code modifications happened all the time. But was Johnston's article the reason? Only the Japanese knew the answer to that.

BILL FOLDED BENNY'S LETTER and put it back in his briefcase. He was now trying to absorb the latest development in the crisis: a White House visit earlier that day by his old friend "Saffo." US Navy Captain Larry Safford was the brilliant, low-key head of OP-20-G, the code breaking division within the Office of Naval Intelligence. Saffo had come to Bill with an idea and a request. He hoped Bill might impart his thoughts to higher-ups and tame the hysteria.

The last thing Captain Safford wanted was a long-drawn-out grand jury investigation, trial, and more publicity than had already been generated by the original article. He fretted this would *ensure* the Japanese would learn that their naval code had been compromised, if that hadn't happened already. "Bill," Saffo had said, "we think that with no more publicity on this thing, we can crack the changes the Japs have made to their code since Midway. I'm telling you, they make changes all the time. But if this thing doesn't go away, we are going to have a much, much bigger problem. You've got to stop this lawsuit."

Bill looked at Safford, mouth agape. "Who, *me*?" was all he could muster. "Come on, Saffo, I can't do that." The old Roosevelt-McCormick political rivalry had overshadowed all reason. "You don't know how much these two people hate each other."

Safford shook his head. "Well, Bill," he said somberly, "if this story gets any bigger, if that grand jury gets going, we'll never be able to break the Japanese naval codes again. *Never.*"

Before Bill left the White House late that evening, he put the finishing touches on a memo to Captain McCrea explaining Safford's grave concerns and recommendations. He had promised Saffo he would give it a try, using his best legal and personal powers of persuasion—and not only because it was the right thing to do for the United States Navy and the war in the Pacific. Almost certainly, Benny stood to gain or lose in the outcome.

Several weeks later, JN-25 was still being used by the Japanese, with only minor changes. Admiral King wasted no time barring Commander Seligman forever from promotion and made sure the only vessel he would see thereafter was an "LSD": a large steel desk. Stanley Johnston's award for bravery at the Battle of the Coral Sea was disallowed by the White House. But, inexplicably, the grand jury investigation of the *Chicago Tribune* was abruptly dropped. No concrete reason was ever given to the press by William Mitchell, the special prosecutor in the case.

13

★ ★ ★

TO DAVAO: *EN AVANT!*

CONDITIONS AT CABANATUAN IMPROVED from dire to grim over Barton's first three months there, from a loss of 1,300 men in June and July 1942 to fewer than 300 in August. This was primarily due to prisoner-generated solutions to waste management disposal and control of malaria-carrying mosquitoes. Though mistreatment by their guards had not abated, these and other morale-building improvements helped the prisoners beat back despair.

The men were heartened as well by persistent rumors of American gains in the Pacific. Despite strict Japanese rules against dispensing war information to prisoners, news accounts managed to trickle in—primarily via Filipinos working at or near the camp.

But when a draft of 400 Cabanatuan prisoners was abruptly shipped to Japan as laborers for the Nippon war effort, the remaining POWs had fresh cause for apprehension. They loathed Cabanatuan in every respect, but shipment to Japan was by far their biggest fear. The prisoners assumed little chance of survival on enemy home soil. So when word leaked of Japanese plans to ship a second, much larger detail out of Cabanatuan, tensions spiked.

Lieutenant Colonel Mori ended their speculation by announcing that a thousand "able-bodied" prisoners would be selected for relocation to a prison farm on Mindanao, the southernmost Philippine island. The "able-bodied" designation disqualified a wide swath of prisoners suffering from various diseases, including dysentery, pellagra, and diphtheria.

The news sparked an outbreak of optimism—despite nagging suspicions that this could be a Japanese trick to get them to depart peacefully and then route them to Japan. But once a knowledgeable senior American officer confirmed—after conferring with the Japanese—that this was not the case, men rushed to volunteer in a rare display of enthusiasm. A move from Cabanatuan but not to Japan was regarded as improving their chances of survival.

The new place, named Davao Penal Colony, became a beacon of hope. It brought the imagined prospect of better food and improved living conditions, plus the psychological benefit of its southern location: nearly a thousand miles closer to Allied-held Australia. Cabanatuan prisoners of all stripes eagerly signed up for the Davao draft; in the end, hundreds were crushed to learn they'd been turned down.

JUST BEFORE SUNRISE ON October 25, 1942, the first of two groups selected for Mindanao was awakened, fed a small breakfast of tea and rice, and ordered out on foot. Barton and Charles and the rest of the first five hundred prisoners marched the several kilometers back to Cabanatuan City in the now-familiar four-abreast formation. With many barefooted and their bodies wrecked and undernourished, the hours-long march proved the most difficult one so far. But they pressed on, eager to appear fit for the journey lest they be removed from the draft of "able-bodied" prisoners. All along the way, local Filipinos flashed their signature V signs and tossed fruit and other victuals to the grateful prisoners.

The next leg of the long southbound journey to Mindanao meant reboarding the dreaded narrow-gauge boxcars that would carry them back to Manila. Barton checked his incipient panic when he saw that the cars had been cooled by hours of overnight rain. Better still, the guards agreed to leave the cars' sliding doors ajar so the men might get fresh air. Whether this was a rare show of goodwill or a reflection of the guards' disdain for handling suffocated corpses upon arrival in Manila mattered little to the prisoners.

The prospect of distancing themselves from the much-loathed Cabanatuan had the prisoners actually smiling as the train jerked to life and began rumbling toward Manila. From there, they would board a ship to Mindanao. They chatted quietly, calmly among themselves, swapping yarns and talking, as always, of family.

A locomotive's rhythmic movement had always had a somnolent effect on Barton, and he eventually dozed off as he so often had on the late train home from the city. Did he hear the stationmaster's insistent calls in his slumber? *"Red Bank! Perth Amboy! Hoboken! Long Branch!"* And was that Mother? Out the window on the platform? Scanning faces in the passing windows? But the train in all his dreams would pass right through those familiar stations without so much as a pause.

The long, low screech that brought the prison train to a halt awoke Barton with a start. His attention was redirected to the sound of Filipinos gathering on the station platform of a small barrio. Suddenly rice balls, bananas, and bits of fried chicken were being tossed toward the boxcar openings. Only a few reached their car, but Barton let out a signature barrel laugh after fielding a chicken leg and a fat, sweetened rice ball. When the train resumed, he divided his spoils into impossibly small portions and distributed them to those who had failed to score.

At the next station, the group of local well-wishers was even larger and better prepared. More food was handed to the prisoners through the boxcar openings, but the larger gift was a chorus of young boys at the far edge of the platform humming a melody. They dared not sing the words for fear of enraging the guards, but the familiar tune "God Bless America" could be heard loud and clear throughout the train compartments. The strengthening effect this had on the prisoners was at least equal to the proffered foodstuffs. "Victory, Joe!" one young boy called out as the train pulled away. Two of his small, dirty fingers were fixed in a defiant V.

Hours later, the men arrived at Manila—hot, tired, and thirsty. Without respite, they formed up and marched back to the familiar intersection of Azcarraga and Quezon. Just before they passed through Bilibid's gates, one of the men, "Ship" Daniels, collapsed. He had been placed on the Davao roster by a well-intentioned superior hoping that Mindanao's climate might improve his failing health. Fellow prisoners looked on helplessly as repeated beatings by the guards failed to revive him. Ship was finally picked up and carried into Bilibid. He died later that night.

The returned Cabanatuan prisoners were kept in cramped quarters at the northern end of the Bilibid compound, sequestered from the other inmates. Despite the discomfort, they prayed for only one thing that night: that tomorrow's voyage wouldn't prove a ruse for shipping them to Japan.

The next morning, Barton and Charles stayed close as the prisoners assembled into groups of one hundred and began yet another march past throngs of careworn Manilans. Women wept openly at the sight of the diminished, half-clad American soldiers and sailors. But defiant V flashes were also spied and murmurs of "*Mabuhay*," or "Long life," were heard all along their route to the waterfront.

This would be Barton's third such post-capture stroll, again past the Manila Hotel, the high commissioner's residence, the Manila Polo Club, and his onetime home, the Manila Army and Navy Club. Despite the many months away, it still stung to see a large Japanese flag flying atop its flagpole.

Its gardens were weedy and unkempt, but the club had so far been spared the destruction that surrounded it; bomb rubble, boarded-up shops, and piles of debris now defiled the once-pristine Dewey Boulevard.

The terminus of their march was Pier 7, another familiar landmark. The loading of so many prisoners onto the awaiting ship, an old coal-burning vessel named *Erie Maru* (which the Japanese had requisitioned from the Americans before the war), took several hours in the hot sun. Enthusiasm diminished as the men were packed tightly into nightmarishly dark holds thick with coal dust. The sleeping bays were three feet high, five feet wide, and ten feet deep, and twelve prisoners were crammed into each one. Worse, they were met in the holds by a tenacious new enemy: millions of tiny, crawling body lice, well established in the deep coal dust. Soon virtually every man's skin crawled with them.

A competitive game developed: prisoners tallied and compared the number of lice on their bodies. When Charles's grousing did not improve with the game, Barton urged him to count his blessings instead—for their ever-widening distance from Cabanatuan.

On October 27, 1942, the *Erie Maru* cast its lines and moved out of Manila Bay. They were all attentive to the ship's course, nervous that a turn north would confirm their worst fears. But when *Erie Maru* heeled to port and turned south into the South China Sea, there was collective relief: here was irrefutable confirmation that they were not going to Japan.

The ship proceeded to follow a nine-hundred-kilometer zigzag, hugging the Philippine shoreline as closely as its captain dared, demonstrating an early Japanese fear that American submarines might be lurking off the coast. The prisoners were confined belowdeck at night but were allowed topside during daylight hours. After the second day of the journey, Barton, Charles, and a fortunate group of other naval officers somehow negotiated to remain topside for the balance of the voyage. Free of the desperate confines of the past ten months, they luxuriated in the healthy dose of sea air. Even Charles remarked positively on this development.

Better yet, the food aboard ship was a feast compared with anything since their capture, despite the rueful observation that several of the chow containers bore a "US Navy Base Cavite" stamp. But three meals a day, variously of cabbage soup with any combination of pork, spinach, meat, milk, dried fish, corned beef, and squash, had most of the men feeling much improved almost immediately—particularly in the absence of harsh camp labor to dissipate their new energy stores. Such allowances alone made their *Erie Maru* overseers seem more humane than those at Cabanatuan. Could this be a harbinger of better treatment ahead?

More heartening still was the explanation for their prolonged layover at an anchorage on the island of Panay. A Filipino stevedore at the Iloilo City docks tipped off the prisoners: a fierce sea battle between the Japanese and Allied navies raged near the Solomon Islands. As a result, the *Erie Maru* was ordered to remain at Panay until further notice. "Japanese Navy *losing!*" the stevedore exuded in a triumphant whisper. This was a shot of adrenaline for Barton, who thrilled at the prospect that Benny was there in the Solomons—thousands of miles closer to the Philippines than he could have imagined—directing fire from *Enterprise.*

When the *Erie Maru* finally departed Panay and steered east through the Surigao Strait and into the open Pacific, Japanese crew and guards warily donned life jackets. Fear of American submarine strikes loomed even larger as word had circulated of hit-and-run strikes on Japanese shipping in the area. Not one of the Japanese transports that had been struck—whether carrying goods, munitions, or people—had seen its presumed American attacker. That the *Erie Maru* bore no markings as a prisoner-of-war transport made her fair game.

During the wait at Panay, Barton had become acquainted with a number of the older naval officers in the Davao draft. One, Commander Melvin McCoy, had been two years ahead of Benny at Annapolis, a connection the two men enjoyed exploring for days on end. But when McCoy's talk turned to the possibility of the naval officers taking over the ship, Barton declined comment. Reprisals for a failed mutiny attempt would be severe—likely resulting in the torture and death of many innocent friends, if not all of them.

Strengthened by the improved rations, McCoy and others had whispered the possibility of charging the ship's crew and commandeering the *Erie Maru* to Australia. Philippine constabulary troops were also aboard and, although under Japanese control, they were presumed to be sympathetic with the prisoners' plight. Barton was relieved when the would-be conspirators concluded the odds were too great to risk so many lives, and the matter was dropped.

Despite obvious uneasiness among the crew, the *Erie Maru* sailed unmolested all the way to Davao Gulf at Mindanao. On November 7, eleven days after departing Manila, her lumbering engines finally downshifted and the ship dropped anchor by a simple wooden pier. The place was called Barrio Lasang, a tiny logging anchorage northeast of Davao Harbor.

After the lines were secured, an American voice boomed from the rusted loudspeaker: "Now hear this. Now hear this . . . We are to disembark [at Barrio Lasang] and march to Davao Penal Colony, a distance of twenty-seven kilometers (sixteen miles). Food will be distributed at the end of the gangplank. When you leave the ship, form a column at the far end of the pier. That is all."

After a meal of rice and *camotes*, however, the prisoners were ordered to sit in the midday sun for several hours without explanation. The men had come to call this familiar exercise the "sun treatment," which they believed the Japanese guards deliberately employed to weaken them so they would be easier to control.

They were finally rousted to their feet in the peak-afternoon heat, assembled into columns, and directed up a narrow jungle road that cut through dense vegetation. The prisoners marched deep into the night, and by the wee hours, the road had tapered to a steep, deeply rutted trail. Visibility was practically nil, despite bright flecks of moonlight filtering through the rainforest canopy.

Several fell out from sheer exhaustion as the going grew more difficult. But unlike earlier marches where they might have been slapped, bayoneted or shot for the same transgression, collapsing Davao-bound prisoners were loaded onto a truck trailing the columns and driven the rest of the way. Approximately halfway to the camp, Charles was loaded onto the truck. By then, Barton's world had narrowed to the dirt path directly in front of him, and he managed to make the entire trek to the promised land on foot. It ended at 0400, after nine grueling hours.

Barton was among the first to stumble into what initially seemed like a jungle clearing, but once his eyes adjusted to the dim, a tidy compound of barracks and other outbuildings spread out before him. In the predawn glow at least, Davao Penal Colony appeared as hoped for: a significant improvement over Cabanatuan. The prisoners were herded into a large warehouse-like building. After the order "Fall out. This is the end of the line," an exhausted Barton Cross curled up on the floor alongside a thousand other hopeful arrivals and surrendered to a deep and welcome sleep.

DAVAO PENAL COLONY, OR DAPECOL as it was called, was a maximum security prison established by the Philippine government for habitual and incorrigible prisoners. Its location—still marked "Unexplored" on a 1940 map—was in the middle of a rain forest barely north of the equator. But to the prisoners from Cabanatuan, it seemed the answer to so many prayers. It had acres of rice fields, and crops of coffee, papaya, and mung beans. It also boasted pig and chicken farms, a lumber mill, carpentry shop, hospital, and chapel. Though rough and unpainted, the tin-roofed barracks were water tight, alone a substantial improvement over Cabanatuan. The prisoners felt the promise of survival.

After inspecting the new arrivals, however, DAPECOL's camp commander, Major Kazuo Maeda, complained angrily to the assembled group that they resembled walking corpses. He had been told, he said, that he was being sent the strongest of the POWs for his mission of running the farm to supply food to Japanese soldiers in the Philippines.

Nonetheless he proceeded to deliver the following speech, with his *l*s replaced mostly with *r*s—the prisoners' scant and only source of humor for the day: "You have had soft, easy life since your capture. All that will be different here. You will learn about hard labor. Every prisoner will work unless he is in hospital. Punishment for malingering will be severe."

14

★ ★ ★

AND THEN THERE WAS ONE:
USS *ENTERPRISE* VERSUS JAPAN

IN MID-OCTOBER 1942, THE USS *Enterprise* was again poised to move out of Pearl Harbor's narrow channel, bound for the South Pacific. The ship had been in drydock for two months, undergoing repairs from three bomb hits she'd received in August at the Eastern Solomons battle. One hit alone had killed thirty-eight men in the gun gallery on the carrier's aft starboard side.

Benny worked with navy dentists for hours following to help identify his dead gunners. The boys' clothes were vaporized by the initial blast, and identification was made harder yet by the furious gunpowder-fueled fire that ensued. Like uncovered remains at ancient Pompeii, a number were frozen in the stances they'd held on impact: one still seated, leaning into his sights, training his gun on an incoming plane; another handing over a powder keg, the hands of both giver and receiver still outstretched; pointers and trainers were hunched over in their seats as though resting. Benny had the further unhappy task of writing to the families of the fallen men. His heart heaved with each note, knowing how his own mother might receive such news.

Stories of the fierce clash in the Solomons had been fully reported by the time mutilated *Enterprise* limped back into Pearl Harbor for repairs. Waiting for Benny was a hastily composed and badly typed letter from Bill:

```
Dear Benny,

    The suspense I have gone through since hearing from
you last has been terrific. If you do get this letter which
Praise God you will, call me collect at the White House at
your earliest opportunity, sometime between the hours of
eight and twelve in the morning or five to seven at night. I
have told the White House operators that you might call, so
they will be expecting it. The times given above are Eastern
War Time which is the same as Zone Plus Four.


                              Devotedly,
                              Bill
```

Benny placed the call immediately. As he waited for the White House operator to put him through to the Map Room, he tore open his one other piece of mail: a legal notice indicating that his wife Jeannette had requested that his life insurance policy eliminate Helen Cross as a joint beneficiary and name her as sole beneficiary. The explanation given was that she would need all the proceeds to support herself and their daughter, given the high probability that something would happen to her husband. Benny was crushed.

He set aside the rude shock when Bill's voice broke in on the line.

"Jesus, you had me worried this time!" Bill said, trying to sound jocular, but his voice was thick with emotion.

"Yup—well, this one was a nail-biter, I don't mind telling you," came Benny's reply, also tinged with forced cheerfulness. "Thanks for your note. I just got it. Matter of fact, we just got in."

The two brothers spoke at length of their shared relief that Benny had survived another terrifying ordeal, the details of which Bill already knew well. *Enterprise* had pulled through again, if barely, this time listing and afire, spewing black smoke and loaded with charred bodies. Benny had lost many friends, and he admitted to Bill he was badly shaken. "Worst one yet, this one—for me, anyway." Benny let out a disconsolate chuckle before sharing the contents of his other letter. "Nice homecoming present, eh? Guess she was hoping I was one of our casualties."

Bill assured Benny he would assume the task of responding to Jeannette's shabby request and that "two-bit lawyer" she had engaged even as her husband had steamed toward battle. When they hung up, Bill heaved a deep sigh and scrolled a piece of White House letterhead into his typewriter. In an instant, he went from enormous relief to a controlled state of rage. Still, rigorous legal training had taught him to hew to the facts. He was pleased to report, he began, both as Commander E. B. Mott's brother and now his legal representative, that Benny had survived the recent engagements in the Pacific, rendering Jeannette's concern over his life insurance policy premature.

In any case, the policy was indeed being revised, Bill continued coolly— by giving Helen Cross, the existing joint beneficiary, special new powers. Her role would be to see that any amounts that might at some future point be due Jeannette would instead be placed into trust for young Jeanne Marie. Bill could be contacted at the White House if the lawyer misunderstood any of the foregoing. Only on the last line did Bill yield to temptation, concluding the missive with the following remark: "I cannot understand for the life of me why any woman would want to torture and make miserable the life of anyone who is already giving so much for his country, but I guess this war has shown there are a lot of things about human nature that are inexplicable."

As Bill saw to Benny's painful marital matters, Benny returned to urgent ship business. While *Enterprise* was under repair, he'd managed the critical installation of powerful and more precise 40-millimeter quad-mounted guns, plus new mounts to the bow of the ship on the forecastle. Forty-six new 20-millimeter guns were installed as well. In all, the carrier now had much more powerful and protective antiaircraft batteries than in the Eastern Solomons, and Benny was confident they would do valiant service in upcoming battle.

With customary good rapport, the Gunnery and Air Departments worked together to train the ship's gunners—both green and veteran—on the new equipment. Benny and *Enterprise*'s air officer, Commander John Crommelin, met on the flight deck each morning for target practice with the new guns. The two officers worked closely together on the complex carrier minuet that combined air combat with sea fighting. Thousands of lives and survival of the ship itself depended heavily on the quality of their cooperative efforts.

During these exercises, Crommelin would order a group of planes to fly over the ship so that the gunners could practice training their gun sights onto enemy aircraft. Benny would then give commands over the flight deck bullhorn to commence and cease fire. They would conduct these exercises for hours at a time.

Whenever the men called for a break, Benny, with the quick, flat wit of a train conductor, would issue the following over the bullhorn: "Boys," he said, then sighed and paused for effect, "I'd like you to think about something on your little break. There are two kinds of people in gunnery. The quick and the dead."

That usually made the point that the long, hot practices were crucial. In battle, the time a gunner had to train his artillery on a dive bomber and then fire on it was between five and eight seconds. In that minuscule flash of time, the attacking plane would have to be downed or the aim of the pilot spoiled if the ship was to be spared. Only practice improved those odds.

★   ★   ★

ON OCTOBER 16, 1942, *Enterprise* departed Pearl Harbor for certain battle. After six days at sea, she merged with the USS *Hornet*'s convoy and several new crew members zipped over to *Enterprise* via high line, a conveyance cable suspended between support and troop vessels and warships. Benny and Commander Crommelin interrupted their morning rehearsals while the new recruits came aboard. Both men commented on the questionable wisdom of adding inexperienced crew members so soon before battle.

Their musings turned from concern to salty invective when a smiling young ensign swayed and dangled on the high line between the troopship and *Enterprise*, and then dropped to the deck with golf clubs slung over his shoulder and carrying a tennis racquet.

Other newly boarded men would distinguish themselves in a different way. One was a naval aviator named Robert Emmett Riera, a 1935 Annapolis graduate who had also worked in gunnery before attending flight school in Pensacola, Florida. Riera was joining *Enterprise* from his first Pacific piloting assignment with Scouting Squadron Sixteen. Benny naturally liked the fact that Riera knew gunnery and was also an Academy man—particularly with so many novice pilots joining the fight. This was the type of naval aviator that rose quickly in rank in officer-starved 1942, assuming he continued to make good decisions.

The brutal work ahead for the *Enterprise* crew was the continuation of what they had begun in August in their harrowing foray to the Solomon Islands. Their mission then was to assist in the landing of the First Marine Division on a little-known island called Guadalcanal. It had been a deadly two months since. The protracted air, land, and sea battle to control that remote but strategically invaluable jungle outpost was showing no sign of letting up.

It all began in July with a tip from hidden Australian coastwatchers that the Japanese were building an airfield on Guadalcanal. Admiral King reacted immediately. Not only did Guadalcanal mark the outer perimeter of mainland Japan's defense, but King instantly understood that an enemy airfield there would also give long-range Japanese bombers a launch pad for decimating US-Australia shipping and supply lanes. With Roosevelt's direct support, King ordered an immediate naval counteroffensive.

When Admiral Nimitz asked for Seventh Fleet ships to assist with the campaign, General MacArthur registered his fury with Washington. Alleging that the "navy cabal" was attempting to relegate him to a subordinate role in the Pacific, he claimed Nimitz had violated the divided command structure by not going *through* him to request access to the US Navy's Australia-based ships. And, he declared, any US Navy offensive to seize Guadalcanal was a further "breach," as Guadalcanal was part of the Solomon Islands chain, the dividing line between his command purview (Southwest Pacific) and Admiral Nimitz's (Central Pacific).

In a radiogram to both the War Department and the White House Map Room, MacArthur alleged:

"IT IS QUITE EVIDENT . . . THAT NAVY CONTEMPLATES ASSUMING GENERAL COMMAND CONTROL OF ALL OPERATIONS IN THE PACIFIC THEATER, THE ROLE OF THE ARMY BEING SUBSIDIARY AND CONSISTING LARGELY OF PLACING ITS FORCES AT THE DISPOSAL OR UNDER THE COMMAND OF NAVY OR MARINE OFFICERS."

The incoming rant raised plenty of eyebrows in the Map Room, but at the Navy Department, the veins in Admiral King's neck reportedly bulged at the news. Imagine his having to request permission from General MacArthur for access to the navy's own ships! MacArthur's petulant missive thus effectively reignited the Washington turf battle over which service would take overall command of the Pacific theater of war. As the command scuffle was thrashed out in Washington, the Japanese made handsome

progress toward completing their airfield on Guadalcanal. Many senior
navy officers were implacably hostile toward MacArthur forever after.

THE ISSUE OF OVERALL command in the Pacific had been simmering between the army and the navy since war was declared seven months
earlier. To CNO Admiral King, the matter was simple: the battlefield in question was a multimillion-square-mile expanse of open ocean—emphatically
and logically suited to naval command. Army Chief of Staff General George
Marshall, however, argued in favor of awarding command of the Pacific to
General MacArthur—himself a onetime army chief of staff and already on
duty in the Philippines. Marshall was not about to let MacArthur become
subordinate to naval command.

Admiral King, just as adamantly, refused to allow the precious remaining ships of the Pacific Fleet to be placed under Army General MacArthur.
This was not only because King disliked and mistrusted MacArthur—whom
he considered a megalomaniac—but also because MacArthur's knowledge
of basic naval operations was critically deficient. King's own solution for
overall Pacific command was, to him, the obvious choice: the commander
in chief of the Pacific Fleet (CINCPAC): namely, Admiral Chester Nimitz,
who was also at the ready in Pacific-bounded Hawaii.

Unable to reach consensus on either the army's or the navy's proposal,
the Joint Chiefs of Staff (JCS) elected to *split* Pacific command between
MacArthur—by then in Australia—and Nimitz. The command area dividing line was drawn along the Solomon Islands chain. MacArthur was named
commander in chief of the Southwest Pacific Area (SWPA) and charged
with subduing the Japanese at Port Moresby, New Guinea, and then driving
his forces north from Australia to the Philippine archipelago.

Admiral Nimitz was named commander in chief of the Pacific Ocean
Areas (POA) and charged with advancing easterly across the Cen-
tral Pacific—clearing enemy resistance in the Marshall Islands and the
Marianas—and ultimately converging with MacArthur's forces in the

waters off the Philippines. The combined Allied force would then retake the Philippines, beginning logically with Mindanao, its southernmost island, and then make its final move against mainland Japan.

Under the Joint Chiefs' agreement, if either service happened to be operating within the other's command area, they would become subordinate to that area's theater commander, even if interservice radio channels were poor or nonexistent—a risk at any time, but particularly during war. The JCS's imperfect resolution solved the immediate spat but seemed destined to produce fractured communications, a disunity of effort, and enormous loss of life. Moreover, it had only temporarily solved the Pacific command scuffle.

MacArthur's petulant objections delayed the urgent Guadalcanal counteroffensive for weeks while a revision to the command geography was hammered out between General Marshall and Admiral King. The resulting amendment nudged the dividing line westward, placing the lower Solomons—including Guadalcanal and nearby Tulagi—under Admiral Nimitz's command. The agreement also allowed General MacArthur to lead future Allied moves against Rabaul, New Guinea, as well as New Britain, located northwest of Guadalcanal.

Finally, in early August, carriers *Enterprise*, *Wasp*, and *Saratoga*—and a cobbling together of nearly every available support naval vessel in the Pacific, including Seventh Fleet ships from "MacArthur's Navy"—had pressed toward Guadalcanal at flank speed. They were carrying a landing force of 19,000 marines. The mission was named Operation Watchtower, but a nickname quickly circulated among Washington military planners: "Operation Shoestring."

The stakes were high for both sides. The Allies could not allow a completed enemy airfield on Guadalcanal, especially since the Japanese could use it to attack all remaining Allied bases in the South Pacific—as well as Australia and New Zealand—with land-based bombers. The Allies also wanted Guadalcanal, the "unsinkable aircraft carrier," as a launching point for their own land-based bombers. Neither side could afford to lose it to the other.

The First Marine Division was landed on Guadalcanal and Tulagi, but nearly everything else about the operation's launch went badly. In this very first amphibious landing of the Pacific War, the newly named amphibian force commander, Admiral Richmond "Kelly" Turner, was forced to withdraw his ships prematurely "in view of heavy impending air attacks." The aircraft carriers—commanded by Admiral Frank Jack Fletcher—had withdrawn first, denying Turner's supply vessels crucial air cover. Turner was forced, therefore, to order withdrawal of *all* remaining ships, which had not yet unloaded armaments, rations, and medical supplies—and a thousand-man reserve force. In one of the proudest chapters of Marine Corps history however, the food-and-supply-strapped Corps on Guadalcanal still managed to seize the airfield, which they promptly rechristened Henderson Field in honor of a fellow marine killed at Midway.

Loath to lose the strategic benefits of the Guadalcanal airstrip, the Japanese staged a series of counteroffensives to repel the US Marines and retake the island. For the next two months, both sides poured blood and treasure into their dueling claim for that malarial speck of jungle in the Central Pacific. On October 22, the Japanese, supported by a forty-warship naval force, launched a massive ground offensive, with the additional objective of striking a decisive blow against approaching US naval forces, especially her aircraft carriers. For four days and nights, outnumbered, underfed, and exhausted, the marines continuously beat back the strengthened attack force at the airfield perimeter. Incredibly, on October 26, when *Enterprise*, *Hornet*, and their escorts arrived to assist with the counteroffensive, the marines still held Henderson Field.

THAT MORNING, *ENTERPRISE* STOOD west of Guadalcanal, just north of the Santa Cruz Islands. At first light, Admiral Halsey's order came through from his island headquarters at Nouméa, New Caledonia, 5,700 miles southwest of their location. The radiogram required no signature to identify its sender: "Attack. Repeat, Attack."

At 0630 Benny was in Sky Control, squinting eastward through his field glasses. Tense and expectant, he had just learned that one of *Enterprise*'s PBY scouting planes had been spotted by the Japanese. Suspecting their position, the enemy naval force had turned north to confront the American convoy. All was ready for certain battle; now only the dreadful wait.

"Guad-al-*canal*." Benny had sounded it out the first time he'd located it on a map—the largest of the Solomon Islands on the northeastern approach to Australia. He'd never heard of it, but nor had a single US Navy admiral until July when the vigilant coastwatchers first reported the landing of laborers and heavy construction equipment there. Since then, loss of life and limb had mounted nonstop—by the troops battling ashore, by the sailors at sea, and by scores of carrier pilots all seeking to both attack enemy positions and defend hard-won ground.

The sun had barely cleared the horizon when *Enterprise* got its next scouting report—another disappointing one. A sizeable Japanese air squadron had launched and found *Hornet*. Benny focused his field glasses astern. *Hornet* was at least ten miles away, but he had a clear view of the evolving battle.

Through fiftyfold magnified lenses, Benny could plainly see one after another of *Hornet*'s planes getting shot down—then, worse, a bright orange geyser of flames erupting from the ship itself. He'd witnessed a similar sight just ahead of *Yorktown*'s incineration at Midway. By the size of this explosion and the profusion of smoke, he knew *Hornet* was also doomed. Within seconds, Benny was notified that *Hornet*'s crew had been ordered to abandon ship and her remaining planes redirected to *Enterprise*'s flight deck.

Meanwhile, both *Hornet* and *Enterprise* fighters had scored hits of their own on two of the advancing Japanese carriers. But the carriers had still managed to launch their Zeros and were steaming toward *Enterprise* like wounded, raging bulls. In a flash, Benny calculated the shrinking distance between the ship and the incoming planes and relayed firing instructions to his AA gunners with the urgent, rapid articulation of an auctioneer.

Bullets ricocheted off Sky Control's metal overhang, and for the first time since the war's outbreak, Benny understood the sudden mortal grip of fear. Only adrenaline and the repetitive rigors of years-long training kept him from seizing up.

He was not one to forget the timeworn aviator creed that flyers were a ship's first line of defense; her antiaircraft guns, a close second. Seaborne radar had risen in value and accuracy since Pearl Harbor, but at the moment, it offered little defense against the sky itself. *Enterprise* radar units had detected the Zeros closing in, but low clouds limited pilot visibility to less than five feet. As a result, neither the *Enterprise* pilots aloft nor the ship's AA gunners could get an early fix on the Japanese planes.

Suddenly a second wave of planes, this time Aichi Val bombers, dropped from the clouds, and Benny, following their course through his binoculars, alerted his portside gunners to the planes' position. The gunners whipped their weapons to a seventy-five-degree angle and, in a split second, unleashed a torrent of hot lead on the Val bombers bearing down on the ship.

From his summit post, Benny had a commanding view of the unfolding battle. Perspiration drenched his khaki uniform as he stood in the open aft section just forward of the stack. He gripped his bullhorn with one hand and the railing with the other as the ship zigzagged violently to spoil the multiple attackers' aim.

Jack Rountree and Roger McCabe, Benny's spotter and phone talker, were with him, both battle hardened from *Enterprise*'s August clashes in the Eastern Solomons. When either sighted a plane, Benny hollered the bearing and elevation over his bullhorn, and Rountree repeated it over the ship's sound-operated telephone. Later he couldn't remember whether the plane or the new 20-millimeter portside gun had fired first during this wave of attacks, but he remembered his amazement at the tremendous burst of fire from the new equipment.

Twenty-millimeter tracers soared over the stack, thirty feet aft of Sky Control. The leading aircraft crumbled in flames and dropped to the sea. A simultaneous whoop went up in Sky Control and the portside gun gallery.

Japanese Val bombers dove in a shallower pattern than their American counterparts, generally about a fifty-degree dive. They bore down expertly on *Enterprise*, one after another after another. As each plane closed in, anti-aircraft batteries opened up, and a barrage of tracer shells riddled the planes. Benny, Rountree, and McCabe watched in a combination of horror and admiration as exploding shells hit their marks over and over, and enemy planes became so many flaming shards slamming into the sea.

Every time Benny barked out the bearings, he reminded his gunners to *lead* the plane, which they did with repeated success thanks to those count-less hours of mind-numbing rehearsals. If the plane kept steady in its dive, the pilot would likely be killed and the bomb not released. But even if the pilot tried to "jink" out of the cone of fire from the ship, time-tested the-ory had shown that the bomb would still miss the ship because the tracers would follow and heckle the plane. Benny had always contended that the main function of antiaircraft fire was to throw off the pilot's aim; planes shot down were a bonus.

Line after line of fifteen-plane air groups continued to drop below the cloud cover and hurtle toward *Enterprise*. After each wave, there was just enough time to reload the burning-hot AA guns before the next phalanx came at them in a glinting, buzzing fury. Gone was Benny's fear now; it had been replaced by pure competitive instinct—and anger as hot as a spent tracer shell. *Goddamn it, this one's for those boys I lost in the Eastern Solomons.*

Benny's bullhorn was wet from the spit of his orders, but his voice came through strong and clear. The gunners processed his staccato directions almost simultaneously and threw plane after enemy plane off target. Vic-tory was beginning to feel possible—even imminent. At this point, Benny greeted Associated Press correspondent Eugene Burns, who'd made his way up to Sky Control for a better view of the action. Jubilant, Benny clapped Burns so hard on the back that Burns winced in pain. "Ha, you think that's bad," Benny said in a moment of dark humor. "Stick around!" But the jovial moment was short-lived.

Rountree tapped Benny on the shoulder and pointed at the first airplane in yet another wave of bombers. At eight thousand feet, it punched through the bruise-colored cloud ceiling and, with steely accuracy, bore down at 120 degrees toward *Enterprise*'s starboard beam. In a split second, Benny shouted coordinates into the bullhorn. The ship jerked radically to throw off the pilot, but this time it also threw off the gunners' aim. Their tracers only glanced the attacker, and the pilot managed to release his deadly load. Seconds later, the bomb tore through the flight deck and exploded just off the stern; an earsplitting explosion of fuel tanks followed.

The rest of the planes in that wave were either shot down or they missed badly, except for one near miss that violently rocked the ship—even as repair and rescue crews raced to the initial explosion site. While they triaged among the wounded and dead and trained fire hoses on the burning flight deck, another squadron of fifteen Japanese dive bombers lowered toward *Enterprise*. This time the five-inch-gun batteries found their targets, again and again. The first shell hit an incoming plane in the engine. The bomber disintegrated eerily before Benny's eyes and then dropped silently from the sky in a series of spare parts. Thirteen more were either shot down or their aim was thrown off. But *Enterprise* was not to be spared. The last plane in the attack wave came screaming in, astern of the ship, its machine guns strafing and winking at Sky Control as it dove.

Bullets clicked and bounced off the overhang like a hailstorm. Benny ducked but managed to keep his sights on the plane and continued shouting instructions. But he knew as soon as its bomb was released from the bay that it would hit the ship. He gripped the railing and braced for impact.

Enterprise rocked and shook with repeated explosions as the bomb pene-trated deep into her infrastructure.

The report came up that the bomb had exploded in the ammunition-handling room, instantly killing its entire gunnery and damage-control group. The forward aircraft elevator was on fire, too, and more than thirty officers' rooms below were destroyed.

In the brief lull that followed, Benny spotted movement in the water a few hundred yards out. Two Japanese pilots were clinging to what appeared to be an aircraft wheel and tire. Thinking they should be taken as prisoners for interrogation, Benny made the announcement over the loudspeaker. He was horrified in the next instant when all the automatic weapons on the starboard side opened up on the clinging pilots. He shouted, "Cease fire at once!" but not soon enough to save them. Burning grief and rage over lost comrades and a desire for revenge had overwhelmed the gunners, who had fired almost in unison.

Seconds later came another shock. Rountree hollered to Benny and pointed astern of the ship: *another* fifteen torpedo planes were charging at full throttle and low over the water, this time bearing down on both sides of the bow, intent on ensnaring *Enterprise* whichever way she zigzagged. The bow gunners went right to work on them, as did gunners from *Enterprise*'s screening vessels, just as the attackers opened their payloads for a devastat-ing double-sided strike.

But at once from amidships, port, and starboard, every gunner started firing at the incoming planes. Despite the raw terror of what they'd just been through, their aim remained intact. The most remarkable strike was made by a forward port gunner. He had fixed his sights on the nose of the plane but due to a slight deflection, he hit the tail instead. The plane flipped back-ward into the sea as if lassoed by an ace cowboy's rope. More than half this group of planes was neutralized, but the last two managed to release their payloads, sending two more torpedoes plunging deep into the ship. Fire and rescue crews raced toward multiple sites of concussive explosions and horrific carnage.

As suddenly as it began, after sixty planes in four waves of continuous attacks, in what became known as the Battle of the Santa Cruz Islands, was over. It had lasted one hour and fifteen minutes, the longest sustained aerial attack ever on an American ship. Smoke from the fires and the reek of cordite from untold thousands of rounds of expended ammunition hung like a pall over bloodied *Enterprise*. But at least the Japanese had failed in their mission of the day; the air and seas around Guadalcanal remained under Allied control, and *Enterprise* remained afloat.

Other ships were not so lucky. Just over the horizon, fires continued to rage aboard the doomed *Hornet*. The pocked and burning deck from which Colonel Doolittle had valiantly launched his Tokyo-bound squadron of B-25s was slanting toward a certain descent to the ocean floor, three miles down. She'd been in service a year and six days, and would be at the bottom of the Pacific by the next morning.

Drained and weak from exhaustion, Benny slumped against the railing to catch his breath as wounded *Enterprise* retreated to the Allied base at Nouméa for urgent repairs. His chest tightened at the prospect of the impending sea burials, the gunners he would need to replace, the grieving mothers he would need to write.

But here again, *he* had survived. For what? His resilience now ripped away, he felt a deep and unshakeable loneliness. But then came the answer: for his daughter, Jeanne Marie, of course. It was her future he was working to protect out here, no matter what her mother did to hurt him.

WHEN FINALLY RELIEVED FROM Sky Control, Benny felt his way along dim, watery passageways to the forward handling room, in ruins from the first bomb hit. He waded on, navigating in the knee-high water by patting his hand along the passageway wall. With the aid of a flashlight, he located where his quarters had once been. Ajar from the blast, the warm

metal door creaked open. He took one tentative step inside to test the footing, and then ventured another. His old surroundings were barely recognizable; the room was a smoky tumult of wet, scorched debris.

The impact of the blast, the leakage, and the heat from the nearby fires
had each wrought damage. Benny poked around the compartment as long
as he dared, recovering only a dented box containing the remains of his
white dress hat and his Naval Academy sword, still warm from the heat of
the blast and bent in a semicircle.

It would never again be extracted from its sheath, but somehow that
didn't bother him. He fingered the scabbard's ornamental filigree, and
then tucked the ruined weapon under his arm and continued down the
dim passageway. His next stop would be the battle dressing stations and
his next task identification of his dead gunners. He paused on the hangar
deck in front of a large, defiant sign erected by crew members, still wet with
industrial-grade paint.

"Enterprise vs. Japan" was rendered in large, uneven letters. The reality
stunned: at the conclusion of the Battle of Santa Cruz, the USS *Enterprise*
was now the only operational American aircraft carrier in the hostile waters of the Pacific. One by one, every other prewar flattop had either been
lost in battle or forced to withdraw for lengthy repairs. *Lexington* had gone
down in May at the Coral Sea battle. *Yorktown* was lost at Midway less than
a month later. On the last day of August in the Eastern Solomons, *Saratoga*
had taken a second devastating torpedo hit and retired to drydock at Pearl
Harbor. *Wasp*, en route to Guadalcanal two weeks later, was fatally struck by
three torpedoes. And now *Hornet*'s pyre burned over the horizon.

Over the course of 1942, *Enterprise* had been struck a total of six times
by Japanese bombs or torpedoes and had suffered hundreds of casualties.
The painted sign reflected both the grimness of the situation and the grit
of a determined crew: this sole surviving American aircraft carrier in the
seventy-million-square-mile Pacific war front was in no mood for backing
down.

15

★ ★ ★

THE OTHER WAR: ARMY-NAVY FOOTBALL

ON NOVEMBER 1, 1942, a mangled USS *Enterprise* staggered into Nouméa, New Caledonia, for repairs. Compared with other war-darkened Allied outposts in the Pacific, Admiral Halsey's Nouméa headquarters was ablaze with lights, as hordes of Seabees—the navy's skilled construction and engineering battalions—worked around the clock. With so few ships and *Enterprise* now the only functional carrier, the urgency of nighttime repair work outweighed security concerns.

The Santa Cruz attacks on *Enterprise* were the fiercest ever launched against a single vessel in the war, and the damage was extensive. The forward section of the hangar deck—from the number one aircraft elevator clear to the quarterdeck—was a grotesque collage of charred and twisted metal. The powerful blasts had also recast the hangar deck into a bizarre configuration of mountains and valleys. Every inch of it had to be cut, flattened, and rewelded.

The number one elevator shaft was so badly damaged that it was beyond repair entirely. The only positive note was that it was stuck in the upright position at the flight deck level, and so wouldn't hinder launching of aircraft. The officers' living quarters had to be pumped dry, repaired, and resealed to be usable. In the meantime, makeshift sleeping quarters were created by stringing up curtains in open areas to provide a modicum of privacy.

Seabees from the repair ship *Vestal* boarded *Enterprise* at her docking. The foreman estimated it would take three weeks to repair the damage, but Admiral Halsey made it clear that was three weeks he didn't have—they would have to get it done in ten days. For those living aboard the carrier, there was no respite from the spark and sputter of the welders' arcs.

Benny called Bill shortly after the ship arrived.

"I'm not sure if it's worse for you there," Bill said, "or me here, waiting for word—over and over again—whether you made it through! Jesus!" Bill had read the Santa Cruz dispatches about the damage *Enterprise* had sustained, and the casualty estimates. But there had been no casualty list, only word that losses to gunnery had been particularly high. He was electrified when the call came through and grateful beyond words that his brother had survived yet again.

"Listen, Bill," comforted Benny, "in the things that count, we're getting the upper hand. If they want to trade some more, well, let 'em. I think they'll find the exchange even less in their favor going forward."

"Anybody taking furloughs while they fix her up?" Bill asked. The abrupt topic shift reflected his concern about discussing too much war information over the phone lines. Nouméa was a free French island and friendly port, but it was known to have its Axis sympathizers. From half a world away, he couldn't be sure that Benny was safe from determined eavesdroppers. But the subject change was not unwelcome.

He could hear the wistfulness in Benny's voice. "My God, wouldn't I love that! I'd hoped to get out of the trenches for the holidays, but it's not looking that way now. You'll have to have a few good eggnogs for me, I guess."

"You do know the big game is on, don't you?" said Bill. "It'll be different this year, of course, but wish we could go together like the old days."

"Are you actually *going*?" Benny asked in a raised voice tinged with envy. "Are you going to the army-navy game?" he repeated, now hollering into the phone. Last Benny had heard, Congress was pushing for the game's cancellation. "Well, I'll be there in spirit, you can count on that—wish I could lend you my topside megaphone!"

The rest of the conversation centered on the game's executive level rescue, relocation, and various other war-related adjustments—and, lastly the odds, a ritual the brothers had held dear for years. The distance between them closed with time-honored bets on score spreads and game stars before they reluctantly said their good-byes.

With the tireless vigilance of a surgical team bent over a life-support patient, the Seabees labored day and night so *Enterprise* could return to the urgent contest for Guadalcanal. Tipped off by coastwatchers and confirmed by scout planes, Halsey knew the Japanese were returning with an armada to strengthen their garrison and regain control of Henderson Field.

Enterprise had scarcely arrived at Nouméa before being ordered out again, taking the hard-working Seabees and their thrumming pneumatic drills with her. *Enterprise* hastened out of Nouméa on November 11 and made straight for the treacherous waters off Guadalcanal. From November 13 to 15, the solitary carrier and her escorts resumed their offense—an increasingly dangerous mission as fewer and fewer screening vessels were available to provide cover. At least eighteen American warships had already gone down off Guadalcanal, giving Savo Sound at the island's southern end its nickname "Ironbottom Sound." Japanese ship losses were even more numerous.

Finally, on November 15, Halsey received word that the Japanese Fleet was retreating to the north. Given the rapid attrition of its ships, planes, and pilots, it appeared—at least for the time being—that the enemy had quit the scrum for Guadalcanal and Henderson Field.

There was a collective sigh of relief among a mourning *Enterprise* crew. Several more screening vessels had gone down protecting her this time and taken scores of good friends with them, compounding the crew's battle distress. Every officer, pilot, and sailor aboard needed a respite from months of near-constant battle.

Admiral Halsey ordered the ship and a grateful crew back to Nouméa. *Enterprise* had survived multiple attacks over the past two months, and the Seabees needed to complete urgent repairs from the devastating Santa Cruz strikes. This time the ship would be there for weeks of sorely needed overhaul—and rest for her crew.

IN MID-NOVEMBER THE MAP Room teletype barely rested as it spit out obituary after obituary of sunken American ships in Savo Sound. On edge, Bill watched and waited. When confirmation came through on November 15 that the enemy was in retreat and Guadalcanal was secured, cheers went up. With this, Bill's relentless anxiety over Benny's safety got a temporary reprieve. He also had a cautious sense that better intelligence about Barton might be coming through soon. For the first time since the fall of Bataan and Corregidor, intercepted messages from unsurrendered individuals in the Philippines were providing concrete intelligence. Station KFS, a powerful commercial San Francisco station that also furnished relay services for the military, was now forwarding them to Washington with some regularity.

The senders were scattered Filipino guerrillas using contraband radios. Several had managed shortwave contact with MacArthur's headquarters in Australia as well. The messages were clear: "We are resisting the Japanese. Can you hear us? Can you help us?"

Equally intriguing was the startling news about one naval reserve officer, Lieutenant Charles "Chick" Parsons, who cloaked his American naval identity after Manila fell by assuming the guise of his onetime role as Panamanian consul. After persuading the Japanese of his diplomatic status, he secured passage out of Manila.

When he showed up unannounced at Naval Intelligence in Washington, Parsons caused quite a stir. Not only had he eluded capture, he had secreted out with him high-value intelligence on everything from the state of the burgeoning guerrilla movement to the treatment, status, and location of Allied prisoners of war. Parsons's escape, attendant story, and detailed documentation of activity behind enemy lines had jaws dropping all over Washington.

Lieutenant Parsons confirmed that the intercepts picked up in Australia and by station KFS were not Japanese feints; they were from guerrilla bands cropping up all across the islands. But he had more. From the shadows of occupied Manila, he had taken dozens of pages of detailed notes on the occupiers' cruel crackdown. Before he and his family gained passage out of Manila on a Red Cross ship, he had fully chronicled meticulous details on the new puppet government, food supplies, enemy troop strength, torturous interrogations by Japan's ruthless Kempeitai, guerrilla espionage potential, and the condition and movement of prisoners of war. He presented a fifty-one-page document complete with underground contact names and places and other crucial intelligence. Navy officials were stunned.

Built like a boxer, Parsons was five feet seven inches and tanned to a deep umber. He could easily pose as Filipino on one mission and a Panamanian on the next. The Tennessee native spoke English without a drawl, Spanish like a native, and numerous Tagalog dialects without a trace of an accent. And from his years of running a Manila stevedoring business and marriage into a well-respected Filipino family, he knew the islands cold.

During his Washington debriefings, Parsons volunteered to return to the Philippine war zone. His potential for high-value intelligence gathering and bolstering the developing resistance movement were considerable. Parsons ticked off a list of what he could accomplish: evaluate guerrilla assets such as leadership, armaments, and personnel; set up intelligence networks; and establish additional coast-watcher stations, which would be positioned on key islands so as to track enemy shipping and monitor war prisoners' movements. He could also smuggle in personnel and supplies and generally advise Filipino citizens on best methods for resisting their occupiers. Parsons wasn't offering to undertake the high-risk mission for just the navy's or even the Allies' sake—he had powerful personal motives as well. He had left behind an extended family, a thriving business, and his entire life savings.

But since the lieutenant was navy and the Philippines war zone was now under General MacArthur's control, returning Parsons to Manila under US Navy auspices could be complicated. As it turned out, however, MacArthur's attitude toward Parsons would be different, despite his usual antipathy toward anything concerning the "damn navy." Some interservice bartering—instead of bickering, for a change—would be in order.

The navy proposed to MacArthur that Chick Parsons go to Brisbane under the tutelage of Captain Arthur "Mac" McCollum USN, the Seventh Fleet's intelligence officer. The officials bristled at the Seventh Fleet's new nickname, "MacArthur's Navy," due to its anchorage within SWPA, but with respect to Parsons, it served their purposes perfectly.

It was no secret that MacArthur craved control over the widening Pacific War, particularly with respect to the Philippines—the command he had lost under humiliating circumstances. Getting the general's headquarters to forward their guerrilla-derived intelligence to anyone in Washington had been nearly as difficult as getting the guerrilla transmissions past the Japanese.

This was because the Office of Strategic Services (OSS), the powerful, Washington-based secret intelligence agency, was operating in every Allied theater of war except SWPA. MacArthur had firmly and repeatedly declined OSS assistance; instead, he elected to use the services of Australia's Allied Intelligence Bureau (AIB), which was now under his full control.

Underlying this choice was that MacArthur did not want any of his GHQ (General Headquarters) functions brought under the War Department's or any other Washington-based agency's purview. OSS director William "Wild Bill" Donovan expressed concerns about the depth and quality of AIB, yet his offers to send experienced field agents to MacArthur were all in vain.

But Parsons was different. He wasn't a Washington insider or even a navy insider. A longtime expat, Parsons had married a Filipino woman, started a family, and had managed and grown a thriving Manila business for more than a decade.

In fact, Parsons's naval career began only when he was awakened on December 8, 1941, and told that his entire Luzon Stevedoring Company— personnel, equipment, and ships—had been taken over by the US Navy. Admiral Hart swore him in the same day. Freshly minted lieutenant Charles Parsons, USNR, was as unsullied a naval officer as a navy-hating army general would ever find. MacArthur, it turned out, was interested.

In late November 1942 the navy's proposal to send Parsons to Brisbane under the tutelage of Captain McCollum and the Seventh Fleet received an affirmative response from MacArthur. "Send Parsons," wrote the general himself, with uncharacteristic brevity.

ENCOURAGED BY NOVEMBER'S DEVELOPMENTS, Bill took a rare Saturday off for a beloved cause: the army-navy football game. Though the Cabinet and Congress had both debated cancelling the time-honored match to conserve rubber and gasoline for the war, Bill's navy-football-loving boss FDR ended the debate by personally ordering that the game be played.

Annapolis coach John "Billick" Whelchel and assistant coach Edgar "Rip" Miller generously credited Bill Mott with nudging the decision, but he insisted their gratitude was undeserved. While Bill had weighed in enthusiastically during the official bickering, the leader of the free world had already made up his mind. The army-navy gridiron face-off was key to morale at both academies, Roosevelt declared, and good for the country, too. Game on.

The game was relocated from Philadelphia's traditionally neutral ground to Thompson Stadium at Annapolis, and wartime travel restrictions would limit attendance to mostly local spectators. How Bill Mott got around the ten-mile radius restriction may never be known, but exceptions were in fact made. He might have happily volunteered to chauffeur one or more Washington-based sweethearts of fourth-year middies—all of whom were allowed to attend.

Since West Point's Corps of Cadets, Army's traditional cheering section, was not allowed to make the trip, another novel accommodation was made. The Academy's third- and fourth-year midshipmen were ordered to sit behind the Army bench and cheer for the visiting team. The 1942 match grew more unique by the hour.

Newsmen in attendance wrote enthusiastically about Army's Navy-populated cheering section. Midshipmen braying the Corps cheer was living proof of interservice comity, they reported. Even the touchdown-starved Army players expressed their gratitude to the cheerleaders, despite their 14–0 loss in a match they had been heavily favored to win. The 1942 game would be Navy's fourth consecutive victory over West Point.

Game attendance may have been a tenth the size of the usual hundred thousand Philadelphia sellout, but President Roosevelt had correctly gauged the broad national interest in the match. An unprecedented forty million Americans tuned in to the live radio broadcast. The defiant, patriotic fervor at Thompson Stadium compensated for the reduced spectator size. From the emotional opening remarks to the extra staccato in the last stanza of the Annapolis school song, "Navy Blue and Gold," fans wept, cheered, and sang themselves hoarse on their country's behalf.

Bill always belted out his alma mater anthem with gusto, and always off key. It was impossible not to recall doing the same with Benny and Barton at his side in 1937, the last time all three Jersey brothers attended the match. Today, Bill surely sang it for them instead of with them.

Rip Miller wrote Bill after the game, thanking him for his "splendid work in keeping the navy football team before 'the big head coach.' I don't know where we could do any better for our cause here than what you have made possible for us."

Bill continued to refuse credit, but he was so pleased by the overall turn of events that he started advancing the idea of sending the game reels to Admiral Halsey's men in the Pacific. As it happened, the garrulous Admiral William "Windy" Calhoun, commander of the Service Force of the Pacific Fleet, was in town to meet with officials from the White House, State Department, and War Department in the days following the game. Bill was assigned as his escort.

During their banter to and from the meetings, Bill mentioned that he had seen the army-navy game films and casually suggested sending them out to the Pacific. Calhoun's eyes widened. "Terrific idea, Commander! Great for morale!" He clapped Bill on the shoulder and asked for copies of the reels to take back to Pearl Harbor with him. Bill savored the prospect of telling Benny he'd had a hand in dispatching the films to the war front, particularly given Navy's shutout victory.

16

★ ★ ★

HAPPY DAYS AT THE
PENAL COLONY

WHEN THE PRISONERS AWOKE to their new home at Davao Penal Colony in November 1942, there was universal agreement: the move had been an open-and-shut case of divine intervention. Housing and sanitation were a dramatic improvement over Cabanatuan, and the rations, while still spare, were double the size. They knew the purpose of the latter was to strengthen them for heavy farm labor—logging, sawmill operation, field and railroad work—but the quantity and quality of the food was measurably better than at any previous Japanese accommodation. With the addition of vegetables purloined on farmwork details, Barton, Charles, and the other ensigns began to regain weight and strength.

Still, Davao was a prison camp. Scurvy was rampant, and the men despaired at the sight of wild citrus rotting beyond their reach or being devoured by bands of plump parrots. And there were trillions of disease-carrying mosquitoes that bred in the swamps of the surrounding rain forest.

Dark, whining clouds of them feasted on the prisoners as they toiled in the fields, and cases of malaria skyrocketed.

On the other hand, prisoner details were lightly guarded, a marked shift from the oppressive oversight at Cabanatuan. Major Maeda believed that heavy guarding at Davao was unnecessary because it was surrounded by impenetrable, alligator-ridden jungle, not to mention by roving bands of Moros, Mindanao's reclusive but fierce Muslim tribe, widely feared for their head-hunting practices. Another surprising bright spot at DAPECOL was its corps of Filipino convicts. When Barton's draft arrived, 80 percent of the camp's existing inmates were convicted murderers serving life sentences. These men understood all aspects of the farm operations better than the guards or camp administrators, and they were ordered to train the Cabanatuan newcomers.

The cutthroats, who dubbed the new arrivals "gentlemen prisoners," promptly got to work instructing them on the primitive sugar and sawmill operations and the dangerous business of bringing down massive mahogany trees and processing the lumber. They also taught them how to harness caribao and Brahman steer and guide them to the fields. The convicts were friendly, helpful, and seemingly pro-American. The POWs were uniformly sorry when these kindly mentors were rotated out of DAPECOL for lack of space.

BARTON, CHARLES, AND ANOTHER Cabanatuan colleague, Ken Wheeler, made several new friends at Davao—mostly young naval ensigns like themselves. They spent nearly all their time together as their Davao overseers also quartered prisoners by service and rank and usually applied the same groupings to work details.

Together these friends shared the smallest of pleasures: a contraband banana, a fistful of coffee beans, a captured lizard—executed, cooked, and cut up—or a tin of canned fish extracted at a dear price from the camp's black market. Even seeds from a withering tobacco plant discovered on a work detail were a source of shared entertainment. They planted the seeds underneath their barracks, and the yield of bitter green leaves was "cured" on short poles. The greatly anticipated first smoke from the pathetic harvest became a deep and happy memory.

Decision-making also became unusually communal. When the prisoners learned that they would be allowed to write one postcard (of no more than fifty words), they debated at length who they would write (parents? wife/girlfriend?) and shared many a joke about the disfavor they would earn from those not selected. But despite generous advice, Barton stuck with his first choice. Even as a prisoner of war on the other side of the world, he had no appetite for the imagined rebuke; he knew he must write his mother.

"Am hoping the time draws near when we may see each other again," he wrote, somewhat stiffly. "Think of you all constantly, and also of William's many accomplishments in the culinary department."

On some level, Barton knew this bit of humor would telegraph that, despite his unfortunate circumstances, he was intact mentally. He was prohibited from disclosing where he was, what had happened to him, and very nearly anything else of a personal nature. Beneath the section of the card marked "Health," he underlined "fair" (versus "good" or "under treatment").

This was likely due to the recurring infection of his shrapnel wound, thanks to its daily exposure to mud and muck on the rice detail. He and Ken Wheeler had also contracted vicious cases of malaria. It made them shaky and weak, but the malady was so commonplace it was not sufficient to excuse them from the fieldwork. Every hand was needed during peak rice planting season.

Each rectangular paddy measured thirty-five by forty yards. A rope with knots spaced at six-inch intervals was laid across the short end of each tract, and a planting team of twenty-eight prisoners was then distributed along the rope. Standing midhip in mud with the rope in front of them, each prisoner took six seeds from his satchel and plunged them deep into the mud, bare-handed. They then stepped back a precise eight inches and repeated the process. So when the opportunity to switch to the carpentry detail "to build a new prisoner barracks" arose, Ken and Barton—despite some uneasiness that they would instead be assigned to rumored local Japanese airfield construction—were among the first to volunteer.

To qualify, they were marched to the DAPECOL carpentry shop and quizzed on the identity and use of such tools as saws, hammers, and planes. A chorus of wisecracks followed Barton's proud performance on the carpentry exam. "Who knew I had this aptitude?" he joked. He and Ken bonded all the more on their new detail. The work was hard, but it was on dry ground, in the shade, and infinitely more interesting than planting rice. And they did indeed build a new barrack, as well as a new prisoner galley— the men took great satisfaction in the finished products. Their next work detail was even better.

An interpreter came into their barracks one evening and asked for "four navy men" to run a boat. After a hurried conference, Ken, Barton, and two more senior officers stepped forward. The four happy sailors were taken via hand-cranked cart over the prison's narrow-gauge railroad to a place called Anebogan, on the Tuganay River. The very smell of the water excited them, and they eagerly scanned the dock area for their new vessel. When Ken spied the dangerously listing diesel tug, he quietly scaled back his dream of engineering a possible escape. The rusted, leaky hauler would not be capable of making an open-sea trip.

Still, working on a boat was infinitely better duty than toiling in the rice fields or in a wood shop. The men were first charged with repairing the tug, and then towing supply barges from Davao City upriver to the prison camp and small Japanese outposts along the way. They got right to work. Because the boat had B. P. stamped on the bow—for Bureau of Prisons— they cheerfully nicknamed their new command "Bo Peep."

After days of patching, caulking, and engine tinkering—and prodigious use of the kind of language that gives "sailor mouth" its name—they coaxed a belch of black smoke from the tug's engine and it sputtered to life. They then nosed *Bo Peep* into the Tuganay River under the careful scrutiny of four guards—one per man. The sailors divided their shipborne duties quite professionally and were pleased to find they had largely retained vital seafaring skills—including how to bail bilges, which they did frequently, even after plugging a number of newly discovered leaks with flattened tin cans.

The break from tedious prison routine was a true pleasure, and it felt good to be on the water again. The river breeze offered reprieve from DAPECOL's mosquito swarms, and the guards had brought along more and better food than they'd received inside the camp. There was also unexpected entertainment along the way: the jungle-lined shores were a *National Geographic*-worthy movie reel of iguanas, frolicking monkeys, and baboons by the hundreds. A veritable orchestra of animal and bird sounds filled the air—as surely a salve for the prisoner soul as the water itself.

When *Bo Beep* approached the mouth of the river and egress to open sea, the guards became especially attentive to their charges. There were ample disincentives for escape· heavily armed guards, a vessel that was hardly seaworthy, and head-hunting aboriginal tribes in the jungle. But if *Bo Peep*'s crew had known what lay ahead for them, might they have attempted escape anyway?

IN DECEMBER 1942, DAPECOL was full of anticipation. To the prisoners' universal surprise and pleasure, they were notified that they would be allowed to hold a Christmas service. Every man who was able took part. The preparation was earnest and intense, and the result was a rare and emotional evening that brought together the prisoners, local Filipinos, and even the camp's Japanese overseers.

The service was scheduled for seven o'clock on Christmas Eve and was held in the camp mess hall-turned-chapel. A light rain fell that afternoon, but it did little to dampen local spirits. The room filled to capacity quickly—and while the prisoners were carefully sequestered from the local Filipinos, smiles and eye contact between them reflected a tacit solidarity.

Lieutenant Yuki, a Christian camp official, served as interpreter and master of ceremonies. Barton's a cappella group was the first to perform, and the crowd hushed as the forty-strong choir assembled. Barton stood proudly in the front row, not only because of his size but also because of his role as lead tenor. It was a fleeting moment of pure joy, doing what he loved and did well before a very special group of friends.

He and the two other ensemble leaders then issued a synchronized hum in middle C. The chorus followed in unison, during which the hall went completely silent. Only the evening sounds of the rain forest could be heard in that brief lull before the group burst into "O Holy Night."

By the last stanza, Barton and the rest of the singers had tears in their eyes, and most in the audience were openly weeping. But then the pace picked up, and laughter replaced tears as the chorus broke into Hoagy Carmichael's popular tune "Stardust." The crowd chimed right in, alternately clapping and humming along. The refrain was bittersweet:

> Sometimes I wonder why I spend
> The lonely nights
> Dreaming of a song
> The melody haunts my reverie
> And I am once again with you.
> When our love was new and each kiss an inspiration
> But that was long ago, and now my consolation
> Is in the stardust of a song.

On cue several members of the chorus then paired off and gave brief but hilarious demonstrations of the jitterbug, rumba, and tap dance as the singing continued. The crowd clapped with delight. The hours of rehearsal were evident as bass, tenor, and alto sections harmonized perfectly. At the closing note, the crowd jumped to its feet, wild with whistles and applause.

The choristers joined hands and took a deep bow. This wasn't the *Radio City Christmas Spectacular* in which Barton had once fantasized taking part. But if one measure of success in life is a moment of contentment derived from deep fellowship and hard work, the evening's performance easily surpassed that dream.

A group of local Filipinos took the stage next. They performed a series of traditional island dances and sang native folk songs. The prisoners whooped and hollered in approval. Then, to the surprise of all present, an ensemble of Japanese soldiers rose and crooned a series of classic Oriental tunes followed by an elaborate sword dance demonstration. Next up was another group of Americans who performed Indian sun dances of the Iroquois, Sioux, Navajo, and Pueblo Indians—thanks to generous prisoner representation from Texas and Oklahoma.

Cigarettes and small gifts were passed around at the end of the revue, and the hall was alive with conversation, laughter, and general goodwill. While the stage was converted to an altar for the service that would follow, the Americans and Filipinos mingled, speaking in English, an unusual opportunity that was not interrupted by Major Maeda. For the duration of the evening, in fact, the differences between foe and friend were put aside.

After the break, the audience returned to their seats for the Christmas service. A manger and crude but recognizable nativity scene—created by children in Davao City—now adorned the brightly lit stage. A small group of Catholic and Protestant chaplains officiated together. They opened the service by thanking Major Maeda for allowing the important Christmas observation, and also Lieutenant Yuki for serving as translator and master of ceremonies.

A simple but deeply moving homily followed readings from the New Testament and a few liturgical prayers.

"Tonight we celebrate the birth of Jesus in a place far from home, far from your loved ones, mothers, fathers, brothers, sisters, wives, and children. We celebrate tonight in an entirely different way from your various traditions. Whether you are from the North, South, East, or West, you miss such familiar scenes—for me it is snow and the sound of bells . . . But let me lead you for a moment away from those cares and toward a place called Bethlehem. There a child was born this very night that we may forget our earthly sufferings."

Communion, the last rite of the service, was taken simply and silently by nearly all attendees, no matter their denomination. The majority of prisoners had experienced some form of spiritual awakening during their incarceration, and the Christmas service carried unusual significance as a result. Many tried unsuccessfully not to cry. Barton surely understood this—his own unbidden religious renewal had sustained him, from Christ School on, in ways he could not have imagined at the time.

As the prisoners filed out of the building and moved toward their barracks, guards were already posted with fixed bayonets; camp life had quickly returned to normal. Barton and a gaggle of choristers sang rounds of "Oh Christmas Tree" while they walked, as if in mock challenge to the alien surrounds of mahogany and palm trees.

Their upbeat chorus likely drowned out a quiet exchange between two marine lieutenants, also heading toward the barracks. Trailing the others, they talked intently and in low voices all the way. The gist from one of them, a Texan, was that this was going to be the last damn Christmas he planned to spend as a prisoner of war—a resolution that would have a far-reaching impact on his fellow residents at Davao Penal Colony.

PART
TWO

17

★ ★ ★

WINTER'S GRIEF

CHRISTMAS OF 1942 AT Lilac Hedges came and went, slowly and painfully. Helen confided to her diary: "A different Christmas this year. A tiny tree, subdued decorations, no Barton. We all tried to be cheery as he'd like to think us."

Even Bill's letter confirming that Barton's name remained absent from the most recent casualty lists was only enough, she wrote, "to keep dinner from sticking in our throats on Christmas Day."

The dining room at Lilac Hedges had long since become its own well-appointed Map Room. The mahogany table was covered with Pacific maps, maps of the world, and maps of the Philippines, all variously marked up. International Red Cross reports and Bataan Relief Organization newsletters littered the floor, and several colored pencils, a ruler, and a magnifying glass could reliably be found on one or another of the dining chairs. Locations in the South Pacific were circled or had notations or question marks beside them, and pads of paper with daily notes were permanent fixtures alongside the sterling tea service, long in disuse.

After Christmas dinner, Helen wasted no time reverting the dining table—which had been cleared for the first time in a year—to Map Room status. It had become all important for her to walk into the room at any hour, pore over her maps, or look down at the red circle around the Philippines and "visit."

On the day after Christmas, she was off to participate in another such ritual, this one at the local chapter of the American Red Cross. Here mothers, wives, daughters, and sisters donned aprons and gloves and lined up at a conveyer belt to pack boxes for prisoners of war in the Pacific. Before turning off her bedside lamp that night, long after Arthur had nodded off, Helen picked up her diary and pen.

> *Packed boxes for prisoners all afternoon at the Red Cross. Seven thousand of them rolled by me on the conveyor belt and who knows? One may be going to Barton! I found myself caressing the contents before packing them in, as though sending my love and prayers along with the food stuffs. God be with him!*

IN WASHINGTON, TOO, CHRISTMAS of 1942 was barely a footnote as war operations ground on. The new year, 1943, dawned icy, cold, and gray, but the frigid weather didn't delay the January opening of the massive new War Department headquarters in Arlington, Virginia. Dubbed "the Pentagon" for its five-sided shape, the building was ready for occupation after only sixteen months of construction—right on schedule. In addition to their other duties, Bill Mott and his Map Room staff now had to retool a number of procedures to adapt to the daunting relocation of the army and the navy, soon to be across the river instead of a short walk down Constitution Avenue.

In early January, they were also busy coordinating the president's imminent and very secret meeting with Prime Minister Churchill in Casablanca, Morocco. Preparations included the assembly of dozens of briefing binders as well as the execution of an elaborate series of ruses to preserve the secrecy of the meeting location. They also needed to fabricate a foolproof story on FDR's whereabouts during his White House absence.

At midnight on January 9, Bill allowed a sigh of relief as President Roosevelt, Harry Hopkins, Captain McCrea, Admiral McIntyre (as FDR's physician), and the rest of the covert entourage finally departed the Executive Mansion for the first leg of the seventeen-thousand-mile journey to Morocco. Bill was exhausted, and looked forward to a respite from the frantic activity of the past several days.

But on the evening of January 12, the Map Room telephone shattered the relative calm of the previous seventy-two hours. Bill answered it on the first ring, his custom, and stiffened when he heard the voice on the other end of the line. The caller was Lieutenant Commander Randall Jacobs, head of the Navy Casualty Section. Bill braced for what surely was news of one of his brothers. Why else the unusual late-night call?

He was uncharacteristically quiet for nearly the entire call. "Good God," he said finally. Then, "Yes, I see, yes, all right . . . Of course . . . Right away," and replaced the heavy black receiver.

A flurry of press calls followed on the same subject; they were on deadline and pushing for details. The horrific story took Bill some minutes to absorb, and his own anxieties on behalf of his family suddenly paled in comparison. He simply couldn't imagine his own mother absorbing such news.

Bill handled each media inquiry deftly, with promise after promise of a return call. But first things first. He sat down at the typewriter to compose a memorandum for Captain McCrea and the president for immediate dispatch to Casablanca:

The White House

Washington

January 12, 1943

Memorandum for: the President and Captain McCrea

Lieutenant Commander Jacobs from the Casualty Section of
the Bureau of Naval Personnel has just called to say he is
preparing a letter for the President's signature regarding
the death of five brothers, the Sullivan boys, in the
sinking of the light cruiser Juneau off Guadalcanal.

These boys were the sons of Mr. and Mrs. Thomas F.
Sullivan, 98 Adams Street, Waterloo, Iowa. They enlisted
in January 1942 contingent on the Navy's promise that they
could serve together. Every effort was made to dissuade
them from this course both at the time of their enlistment
and after they joined the Fleet. However these efforts were
of no avail and they all went down with their ship. Only
one of these boys was married. His wife is Mrs. Albert Leo
Sullivan, 2228 Hawthorn Street, Waterloo, Iowa.

The parents were notified today by the Lieutenant
Commander [Truman Jones] in charge of the Navy Recruiting
Station at Des Moines, Iowa. The press is anxious for a
story on this, but the Department is reluctant to give
any details, such as the name of the ship, because of the
significant publicity on these five brothers when they
first enlisted together. The thinking is that a letter from
the President would make good copy and they are anxious to
get one signed as soon as possible.

I have told them nothing, of course, about the

President's whereabouts, but will forward their proposed
letter to you by the next pouch.

    You may recall that President Lincoln once had to write
the same kind of letter and did such a good job of it that
all students of composition have been using the same as a
model ever since.

                        Very Respectfully,
                        W. C. Mott

The Sullivan brothers' ship, USS *Juneau,* had been one of *Enterprise's*
protective screening vessels in the deadly seas around Guadalcanal. Bill
couldn't help but feel this one a little deeper in the gut. He sat back to review the memorandum, but his mind was still on the conversation with
Commander Jacobs.

Jacobs told Bill that when Lieutenant Commander Jones and two other
officers approached the Sullivans' front door in Waterloo, Iowa, the boys'
father, Thomas Sullivan, greeted them.

"I have some news for you about your boys, sir," Jones had said.

"Which one?" asked Thomas.

"I'm sorry, sir," Jones replied. "All five."

18

★ ★ ★

ESCAPE: CRIME AND
PUNISHMENT

BY PRISON CAMP STANDARDS, the Christmas festivities had been a high-water mark, but the best day at DAPECOL came a few weeks later, in January 1943. The men were already buoyed by news relayed by a friendly Filipino working near the camp: the American Navy had held in the long struggle for Guadalcanal, meaning Australia was safe and that the sea-lanes between it and the United States were protected. The good news was confirmed by broadcasts over a contraband shortwave radio occasionally tinkered to life by one fearless inmate.

Moods swung higher still when word circulated that the International Red Cross had shipped gift boxes to the DAPECOL prisoners via the *Gripsholm*, a Swedish goodwill vessel. The boxes had arrived at Davao City! It was their first official acknowledgment that the Allied world knew where they were, knew they were in need, and that they cared. The effect on prisoner morale was profound.

On January 12, 1943, Barton, Ken Wheeler, and *Bo Peep* commander

Alan McCracken made their way to Anebogan with two Filipinos and three Japanese guards. Full of anticipation, they boarded *Bo Peep* and set a downriver course to *Gripsholm*'s anchorage.

Bo Peep's ad hoc crew were the first Americans to see the huge stacks of lovingly packed boxes, each stamped with the reassuring and familiar Red Cross insignia. It took hours to transfer the precious cargo from *Gripsholm* to the waiting barge, but it was more thrill than labor.

The smiling *Bo Peep* crew navigated the tug upriver, blowing smoke rings from the Lucky Strikes their guards had filched out of a box and magnanimously shared. They were in a fine mood that afternoon, and not only because of the Red Cross boxes; *Gripsholm* had also off-loaded several sackfuls of mail—the first word from home since their capture.

Assembly of the Red Cross boxes had been a true Allied effort. They were filled by volunteers in Canada, South Africa, Britain, and the United States. Inside each box was a variety of precious goods: evaporated milk, hardtack and cheese, vitamin pills, soap, shoe polish, a container of cocoa, cans of corned beef and pilchards, chocolate bars, sugar, orange concentrate, instant coffee, dried soups, pudding and tea (British), and Roy and Lucky Strike cigarettes (American). The boxes were uniform in size, and each weighed eleven pounds. The prisoners all got a good laugh out of the shoe polish; few of them still had shoes. Their primary foot protection at this point consisted of crude wooden slats called "go-aheads," which they strapped to their feet. But the very sight and smell of familiar American goods made their eyes well up.

Agony replaced delicious anticipation as neither the boxes nor the mail was distributed on arrival at DAPECOL. A Japanese Special Service Unit intercepted the treasure-laden trucks as they rumbled through the camp gates. The unit's purpose was to "inspect" the shipment and "censor" the mail. The men on the truck detail, including Charles Armour, were ordered back to the barracks empty-handed. Charles quickly reverted to his grumpy self, theorizing that "the goddamn Nips" were sore about the war news and jealous over the contents of the boxes.

Several anxious days later, two boxes were finally distributed to each prisoner. Though they had been rifled through and some original contents were missing, the men were thrilled nonetheless. Impromptu trading posts popped up in every barrack as the men swapped for favorite items. Medicines, sugar, and many of the coveted cigarettes had been lifted by the Japanese, but the remaining Red Cross box contents nourished body and soul and undoubtedly saved lives.

It took days longer for the Japanese to "sort" the equally priceless mail. The men knew it had arrived, and the wait seemed interminable. Finally, one by one, names on the envelopes were read aloud and the mail distributed. Several of Barton's barrack mates received two and three pieces of mail in that shipment; they wept as they read and reread the reassuring missives from mothers, fathers, wives, and girlfriends. Barton agonized over who his mail might be from. Had the lovely Eve—that distant erotic memory from his visit to Pearl Harbor—cared enough to inquire how to write him? He hoped they wouldn't *all* be from his family, though he could hardly wait for word from them. Rosemary? Bill? Benny?

But Barton received no mail in the January 1943 shipment of ten thousand letters to Davao, nor any in the next shipment two months later. By that time, some of his colleagues' letters numbered a half dozen or more. Did everyone think he was dead? he wondered. Had they simply given up? He tried to make light of it and joke about it, as he had with so many other adversities he'd endured over time. But this hurt Barton more than all the privations and insults in his long, dark months of incarceration, and it was obvious to his close friends.

Charles made every effort to convince him that it was the goddamn Nips' fault. Those letters were out there for him—*somewhere*—his friends insisted, and they went to great lengths to take Barton's mind off his pain just as he had done for them so many times. But whatever the cause, the inexplicable silence from home caused a sharp prick of sadness in Barton, and a tinge of resentment, too. The next precious card the guards allowed him to write went not to his mother or father but to a Chapel Hill classmate, whose postal address, remarkably, he still remembered. Let his parents hear of him from that, he thought.

ON THE EVENING OF April 3, 1943, Major Maeda arranged for movie night at Davao. That night's feature was a Japanese propaganda film on the bombing of Pearl Harbor. Over the past few months, Maeda had grown anxious that the prisoners might become troublesome if they learned the details of steady American gains against the Japanese at sea. He was also nervous about the strengthening guerrilla presence in the jungles around the penal colony. Lightning-quick hit-and-run raids on local roads had resulted in the gruesome slaughter of a number of Japanese soldiers.

Some guerrillas had been apprehended and punished brutally, but many more had notched deadly blows against the occupiers. Maeda knew that the local guerrilla movement—with both American and Filipino elements—had grown in strength and size and that they were in contact with distant Allied commands. Weeks earlier, Japanese planes had dropped pamphlets over Mindanao, warning of mortal consequences for collusion with the guerrillas.

Central to Maeda's concern was that Mindanao was the closest Philippine island to Australia—an obvious first step in any Allied move to retake the Philippines. In view of the looming threat, anything the major could do to dampen prisoner morale—reduce rations, impose longer and harder work details, or feature a movie on the decimation of Pearl Harbor—was a worthy countermeasure.

The men sat quietly through the pummeling of the USS *Arizona*, understanding well the wisdom of not provoking their captors with sneers or catcalls. Still, as they watched the guards struggle with changing the reels on the projector, Barton couldn't resist whispering a mock dare to Charles (now widely known as "Ensign Goddamn"): "Okay, who wants to ask if we can watch the bombing of Tokyo next?"

Despite Major Maeda's concerted efforts to the contrary, camp morale *had* improved. Enough war news had leaked through to boost prisoner confidence that chances for their eventual rescue were improving, if they could just keep themselves alive. The evening's film feature had a particularly galvanizing effect on one small contingent in the audience. These men were poised for a long-planned escape—scheduled for the very next day.

THE MORNING OF APRIL 4, 1943, began as most Sundays did at Davao: stifling, dreary, and overcast. Reveille pierced the air, but since it was Sunday, only a few voluntary work details were scheduled to go out. Sometimes prisoners signed up for these out of boredom; others went hoping to score an extra piece of fruit or a few husks of rice. Beneath their mosquito nets, Barton and Charles took little notice as two of their barrack mates roused for Sunday detail. They likely gave no thought as to whether either might be a member of his shooting squad.

Ten Americans—eight officers and two enlisted men from all three services—lined up at the camp gate, initially in separate groups. They were heading out on routine details: a few to build a rain shelter; others to feed and water the animals used to haul a bull cart that carried tools and supplies around the colony. In plain view of sentries toting machine guns, the men walked calmly out the gate and down the road as though it were just another workday.

Once out of sight of the sentries, they left the road and crept noiselessly through tall cogon grass toward a prearranged rendezvous point; there they recovered hidden supplies and met their guides, two Filipino convicts who had left the prison camp on a separate work detail. The DAPECOL system of rotating guards to work details rather than assigning all-day overseers to each group was critical to the plan's success. The expanded escape party then proceeded into the rain forest, unobserved, and began their dash to freedom.

The escape had been planned for months, each element precisely thought out. The jungle-wise and more savvy Filipino convicts were recruited to guide them through thick and dangerous forest and swampland. Supplies needed to survive outside of camp were gradually stockpiled at a secret location over a period of several weeks. The choice of a Sunday, in hopes they wouldn't be missed until they did not return at the end of the day, would give them a full day's lead over certain pursuers.

In fact, it was not until evening *tenko* that the numbers failed to add up. "*Ichi, ni, san, shi . . .*" At first, the Japanese thought they had miscounted and ordered the some two thousand prisoners to stand for a second, hours-long count. When it, too, came up short, but by a different number, Major Maeda flew into a rage and ordered a third, fourth, and fifth tally, each with varying results but all still short of the previous evening's count. It was after midnight by the time the ten missing men were identified. Mr. Shusuke Wada, the perpetually angry hunchback interpreter, reminded the prisoners of the shooting squad rule with a sneer. "For every man who escape, nine die!"

Search parties were immediately dispatched with orders to shoot on sight. Fearing a mass prison break coordinated with a guerrilla attack on the compound, Maeda also placed guards in each barrack and set up a perimeter defense around the camp. The men from barracks five through eight, where the ten escapees had variously lived, were particularly fearful of the ten-for-one death-sentence trigger. Which would it be? Shot? Bayoneted? Beheaded?

Every occupant of those four barracks was taken to Japanese headquarters for questioning. While the men waited their turn, arguments over prisoner escapes were renewed. Some spat curses, while others reminded the group that they were duty-bound by military doctrine to attempt escape if captured. "Even if we're held by fucking barbarians who ignore the Geneva Convention?" came a bitter response. "To hell with your goddamn doctrine. It's no good to me dead."

From that day forward, nothing was the same at Davao Penal Colony.

Guards who had been friendly were reassigned. Those who remained were mistrustful, hostile, and quicker to punish with slaps, kicks, or rifle butt strikes. Rations were cut drastically. Religious services were again forbidden; any prisoner gathering had the potential for collusion.

On April 11, as the frantic search for the escapees lengthened into a second week, residents of barracks five through eight were marched to a maximum security pen at the north end of the compound. The grim enclosure was surrounded by guard towers and three concentric rings of barbed wire fencing. Inside the cramped prison within a prison, Barton spent the next day—his twenty-fifth birthday—fighting claustrophobia and a creeping fear of inevitable execution.

Between interrogations, the sequestered men were kept in wire-screened, double-decked cages resembling rabbit hutches, alive with bedbugs. Nesting rats scurried beneath them. Their rations were cut to rice only, twice daily, brought in by oxcart. They were forbidden to speak to one another and ordered to "meditate" on their wrongdoing.

Instead, they contemplated their dimming prospects for survival. What would the final punishment be? All signs pointed to a mass execution. They wrote wills and last messages and buried them in tin cans during latrine breaks—the only times, other than for interrogation, that they were let out of the cages.

The incarceration lasted for a month. In mid-May, they were marched outside the guardhouse and ordered to line up. Trembling, they obeyed and braced for the worst.

19

★ ★ ★

FAREWELL TO THE
WHITE HOUSE

SPRING AND SUMMER OF 1943 found Bill Mott busier than ever, increasingly besieged by both personal and professional concerns. His wife, Romie, had been restricted to bed rest due to complications with her second pregnancy. At the same time, Map Room personnel were providing critical support to Trident. This third strategic conference of Allied leaders was taking place in Washington, with meetings at both the White House and the Federal Reserve Building. Prime Minister Churchill was again in residence at the White House, and he and his entourage had Bill and the Map Room watch officers hopping day and night, with demands both official and unofficial.

In this same time frame, Bill was also waiting for a response to his request for release from White House duty so that he could go to sea and join the fight. Impatient, he could no longer bear standing by while the enemy held his brother, particularly in light of recent intelligence regarding Japanese treatment of POWs in the Philippines. The new information shocked the senses, even in a wartime context.

The first dispatch came from Luzon in February 1943. MacArthur had radioed the information to Washington:

> A guerrilla leader on Luzon confirms reports from Filipino escapees that at Camp O'Donnell . . . deaths of American and Filipino prisoners by execution or disease, numbered 23,000 by November 1; Executions daily for such causes as disrespectful or insubordinate attitude or inability to work, deaths by disease resulting from dysentery, malaria, influenza, beriberi, pneumonia in order of importance; no medicine and two Red Cross trucks with medicine doctors and nurses from Manila refused entrance; meals consist of cold rice twice daily, sometimes with rotten camotes; no sanitation; for every prisoner that escapes, the Japs shoot five [sic] hostages; attempts by loyal Filipinos to smuggle in food, medicine punished by rough treatment and shooting; also prisoners had no blankets and only their original shoes and clothing.

Bill chafed at the "No Action" recommendation on the circulated radiogram. He knew the reason, of course. This was very bad, but not a priority to resource-strapped war leaders.

Then another, more significant dispatch came through concerning a different prison camp, this one on the island of Mindanao. The highly classified memorandum reported that a group of American officers, including at least one naval officer, had escaped from the very same camp where Bill felt sure Barton was being held prisoner. His heart had jumped at the news.

The men had escaped in early April and were now safe in the hands of Mindanao guerrillas. Thanks to Chick Parsons, arrangements to get them to Australia by navy submarine were in process. Bill was acutely disappointed to learn that Barton was not among the escapees, but apparently these men had quite a story to tell—one that would make all previous reports pale in comparison. Horrific details were trickling in via the Filipino guerrilla unit protecting the men. He would know more once the escapees arrived in Washington.

Bill was hopeful that they would bring concrete news about Barton, but another thought also nagged him—one that always crossed his mind with good news from the Pacific, as with the recent downing of Admiral Yamamoto's plane over Bougainville, the largest of the Solomon Islands. He had a recurrent, consuming anxiety that any Allied gain—whether the elimination of a revered Japanese admiral, a victorious sea battle, or a large-scale escape from an Allied prison camp—could trigger enemy retribution against the war prisoners under their control.

Around this time, the White House had new senior naval aide: Admiral Wilson Brown—the same Wilson Brown who'd been Naval Academy superintendent the year that Barton was forced to withdraw from Annapolis. Captain McCrea had departed to command the USS *Iowa*, the first of the new "fast battleships" churning out of American shipyards. Bidding farewell to his important mentor and friend was difficult for Bill. But Captain McCrea had also been driven to take part in the fight—on the war front instead of from inside the secure marble confines of the White House.

This was Admiral Brown's fourth stint as White House naval aide; the previous three had been under Presidents Calvin Coolidge and Herbert Hoover, and an earlier iteration (in the 1930s) under FDR. Despite their sizeable age difference, Bill and Admiral Brown found a quick and easy rapport. They had strong common ground in their mutual devotion to Annapolis (including its gloried football lore).

They swapped stories throughout the days and evenings as their work allowed. Brown savored one story in particular—likely with a twinkle in his eye—during an afternoon lull in the Map Room. Apparently Helen Cross's 1938 letter dressing down the Naval Academy for its "unpedagogic methods" had left quite an impression on then superintendent Brown. Bill shook his head and held up his hands in mock surrender, as though in belated apology on the family's behalf.

But Admiral Brown recalled Barton's situation sympathetically. Even when Academy rules didn't make sense, his job was to enforce them, he offered, in half apology. This was the first that Brown had heard of Barton's post-Annapolis reentry into the navy (he thought the boy had pursued a singing career) and of his wounding and capture in the Philippines. From that point forward, he asked frequently about both Barton and Benny, touching Bill more than he ever let on.

When the timing seemed right, Bill summoned the courage to ask Admiral Brown to endorse his waiver request regarding his nearsightedness. Doing so, he explained, would greatly improve his chances to get to the Pacific front. Though Bill's eyesight was now correctable with something called contact lenses, only a formal waiver would clear him for sea duty.

Brown worried that finding a qualified replacement to run the Map Room could be as big an obstacle as the waiver request, but Bill pointed out that the able and well-liked Lieutenant George Elsey—whom Bill had hired back at ONI and subsequently brought over to the White House— could assume his responsibilities seamlessly. Not only was Elsey familiar with Map Room operations, the president liked and trusted him. Bill had learned to spot discretion and talent, he assured the admiral, and Elsey possessed both. Brown agreed.

After conferring with the president, Wilson Brown penned an enthusiastic endorsement of Bill's formal request to the chief of naval personnel.

Two days later, three bells sounded outside the Map Room door, the all-important signal that the president was on his way. Bill and the duty officers readied themselves quickly for the day's briefing and question-and-answer session that always followed. When the door opened, Mott took the wheelchair handles over from the president's valet (who was not allowed in the room) and carefully steered Roosevelt into position for the briefing.

Before it started, Roosevelt turned to Bill, now beside him, affixing his blue eyes on Bill's own. "William," he said, "Admiral Brown spoke to me of your request to leave us and go to sea. You must know, I was reluctant. Eleanor was most disappointed to hear it, too. We don't want you to go."

Bill was a combination of stunned, pleased, and embarrassed, wondering all the time that Roosevelt was speaking how to respond appropriately. When the moment came, his answer poured out.

"Thank you, Mr. President. I am deeply honored, but you know how when you first come into this room and look on the maps for your sons' ships—even that of your Hyde Park butler? Well, sir, every day I look at the postings of the *Enterprise* and then the Philippines where my little brother is a prisoner of the Japanese. I feel compelled to go, to fight."

The president nodded somberly, already having turned his gaze to the Pacific wall map, scanning for the USS *Wasp* on which his son John was serving. "Yes, son, I do, I do understand," he said. By then, his mind seemed half a world away from the conversation.

Optimistic, Bill wrote Benny of the development:

> You know I have been trying for some time to get some
> kind of sea duty, but my every way has been blocked because
> of my eyes . . . Admiral Brown recommended me to the course
> at the Naval War College at Newport, which coupled with the
> President's approval, will mean, I hope, that orders will
> come through soon . . . Please don't blow me a blast about
> leaving my nice soft job in the White House, because it
> means a lot to me to become one of the fighting brothers . . .
>
> I visited both Rockaway and Oceanport last week
> and found things in pretty good shape. Mother of course
> grieves over Barton, and as could be expected, is slightly
> irrational on the subject. She can't understand why we
> don't turn all our effort into the Pacific in order to
> avenge the heroes of Bataan. Emotionally, I agree with her,

```
but realize the Combined Chiefs of Staff are the people
to make that decision. Incidentally, we have had a very
interesting guest at the White House in the last few weeks,
as you probably have heard.
```

When Prime Minister Churchill arrived for the Trident Conference, he rejected the Queens' Bedroom, named for the many royal White House guests it had hosted in the past. Instead, he took over the more comfortable Rose Bedroom, also on the second floor, just as he had during his June 1942 stay. Churchill also brought along his legendary traveling map room. But when its director, the tall, handsome, and very proper Captain Richard Pike Pim, saw how sophisticated the White House Map Room had become, he proposed to Bill that the British contingent move in with them. Maintaining separate maps would be inefficient and superfluous, Pim insisted.

So Pim and Churchill made full use of the Map Room—morning, noon, night, and very late night. Bill built on the convivial rapport established during the PM's previous visits. In addition to inaugurating an afternoon tea ritual, the Map Room watch officers supplemented their regular daily map postings with incoming war cables from the Admiralty and London's War Office.

Churchill made himself very much at home, often appearing at the Map Room door in the wee hours. He was always in his Royal Air Force jumpsuit, usually barefoot, and never without a lighted cigar. One such evening during Trident, the Map Room sentry admitted the prime minister, this time carrying both a cigar and a snifter of brandy. "Good evening, my boy," the PM said to a startled Bill Mott as the door closed behind him, and he began to pace its perimeter thoughtfully. "How's Hitler?" he growled, pausing at the European map, then, drawing himself up, "the *bah*-stard."

On occasion, Bill delivered dispatches and briefing materials to the Rose Bedroom. On such visits he was often asked to pull up a footstool and read the material aloud or provide an impromptu summary of the world naval situation while the ample, pink-fleshed Churchill listened pensively from the bathtub. The naked prime minister, ringed in cigar smoke, always responded with insightful and impeccably phrased questions.

On Wednesday morning, May 19, 1943, Bill escorted Churchill to another recently converted White House coat room, this one into a movie theater. They took their seats to watch the latest war newsreels and the film to be premiered at the upcoming White House dinner honoring the prime minister. The documentary *The Battle of Britain* was the latest in Frank Capra's popular series Why We Fight. Halfway through the feature, however, the president's butler, Alonzo Fields, stepped into the darkened, smoky theater and tapped Bill on the shoulder. Given his charge, Bill might have been annoyed by the interruption had Fields not said immediately, "Congratulations, sir. It's a girl."

The prime minister's eyes grew wide, and an impish smile spread across his face. The onscreen fighting for country momentarily lost its audience. "Goodness, William," said the PM, "you are too modest! Congratulations indeed!"

That afternoon, a generous bouquet of pink roses and a charming note of congratulations arrived for Romie Mott and hours-old Janie (Jeannette Baker) Mott, causing quite a stir in the Garfield Hospital maternity ward. The card was signed in elegant script, "Winston S. Churchill."

BILL HAD SEEN LITTLE of his wife during the final days of her pregnancy, thanks to late hours in the Map Room and Trident's long, contentious Combined Chiefs of Staff meetings. Unlike the easy Anglo-American Map Room camaraderie, these sessions laid bare the mutual suspicions between the respective Allied countries' senior representatives and their aides.

Admiral King's reflexive exhortations about the dearth of resources going to the Pacific always flustered the London brass, sparking fresh concern of a possible US defection from the Europe First policy. Nor did the

American delegation hide its uneasiness that Britain might drop out of the Pacific War once Britain was made secure by Germany's defeat. Battle lines on maps were drawn and redrawn as the meetings themselves seemed to teeter on the brink of hostilities.

But just as Romie endured a long and difficult labor to productive end, the quarrelsome Trident Conference ultimately bore a fruitful resolution: Allied forces would launch a cross-Channel invasion of Europe in May 1944. A stepped-up campaign against the Japanese was also approved, as was accelerating the development of a devastating new weapon that harnessed atomic energy, possibly for use against Japan to speed her surrender. Though details were few, Bill found the last two decisions personally encouraging.

NOT LONG AFTER THE conclusion of Trident, a thick envelope addressed to Lieutenant Commander William C. Mott was delivered to the Map Room along with the morning's locked pouches full of classified documents from the War Department. When Bill first spied the manila envelope, stamped "BUPERS" (Bureau of Personnel), his heart jumped. He was sure the envelope contained orders that would either change his life completely by allowing him to go to sea or indefinitely tether him to his present course. He slipped the sealed envelope into his briefcase. He would open it at home, where he could react in relative privacy.

Meanwhile, Romie and a seven-pound, twelve-ounce, pink-blanketed Jeannette, forever after called Janie, had finally been released from Garfield Hospital and returned to 7 Newlands Street. Friends and neighbors streamed through, bearing good wishes and all manner of pink gifts and posies. Romie had been unwell for the last month of her pregnancy, and the fact that both mother and child were in good health and home was cause for neighborhood celebration.

Bill was not so unwise as to open the BUPERS envelope on arrival home that evening, though he ached to know its contents. The first order of business was to greet his weary wife and new baby girl, who was already demonstrating strong vocal cords, and reassure a slightly bewildered three-year-old Adam.

When the family finally retired for the evening, Bill engaged in a quiet ritual, rarely enjoyed of late. He walked into the kitchen and turned on the tap, letting the water run while he opened the glass-paned cabinet and retrieved his favorite cut-crystal tumbler and bottle of Old Grand-Dad. He poured until the glass was a third full and then held his finger under the tap stream, staring out the kitchen window as he waited for it to cool.

Stirring the drink with his finger, Bill walked back into the living room toward the stuffed briefcase slumping against his easy chair. He paused to savor the charm and tranquility of his surroundings with a new perspective— of one who might be taking leave of its comforts—and confines—for an indeterminate period. How many men, he wondered, would lunge for his position, the excitement, the prestige, the proximity to power and safety from harm—and count themselves lucky? Here was a beautiful wife and family, a lovely home, a terrific job. Was it right to want to go?

But reading daily about Benny and *Enterprise*'s brilliant and daring exploits and worrying hourly over Barton had worn him down, leaving him feeling more and more a useless bystander in the world's titanic struggle against determined enemies. He had to do this.

Bill sank deep into the armchair and placed his bourbon and water on the polished mahogany side table. The first letter was from his mother, which had also arrived that day.

Billy dear,

   A censored letter I wrote as secretary of my Club came back to me after months yesterday. Perhaps this is why mail is so slow now; I do hope you get this note in better time! We are all thrilled about baby Jeannette and that Romie is improving . . .

You now have one more good reason to stop this talk of going to sea—it seems to me that you are doing very useful work where you are—God knows we need badly some men with brains in Intelligence work! When I think of Benny and Barton and such stupidity at the top—whee! But these Pacific island attacks have been glorious haven't they? I suspect Benny was right there...

It would be such a comfort to hear directly from Barton; I know something unusual prevents it... I am proud of them both out in the thick of it, and of you too, trying to carry on at home. I hope you won't go to sea unless really needed. I do need one son left and you have more to lose than either Benny or Barton, the truth be told. One has hardly lived at all and the other has had enough mental suffering so that action might well help him right now.

Maybe you can slip up here for a rest very soon—we will make it a real rest for your nerves, away from Washington entirely. We think often and fondly of you, Bill. You are dear to me, my son.

Mother

Bill's first reaction to her letter was a wince at the praise for Benny—"out in the thick of it"—and her pride in "those glorious island attacks." These things stood out as though she had written nothing else, uppermost were they already in his mind.

He folded her letter and put it back in the powder-blue envelope with "Lilac Hedges" embossed on the back and collected himself. The BUPERS envelope rested on his lap. With his recent bid for orders that would take him to sea, he had played his last best card. If a recommendation from Admiral Brown—who had cleared it with the president—had not done the trick, there was no higher appeal short of Almighty God. Should the contents of this envelope prevent it, he could be sure that was the final answer.

Certainly the sleeping inhabitants of this house would prefer that outcome. But again, he told himself, in that endless quarrel between head and heart, what good was he to his family if he didn't join the fight and do what he was trained to do? Or stand aside with a lifetime of halfhearted explanations ahead—that it was his *eyes* that prevented him from fighting, not a shortage of courage or ability?

Bill finally tore open the envelope and pulled out a sheaf of papers, flipping through the pages, scanning the contents from the first to last. He then reread the cover memorandum:

```
From: The Chief of Naval Personnel
To: Lieutenant Commander William C. Mott
Office of the Naval Aide to the President,
The White House


Subject: Change of duty.


When directed by Admiral Brown, you will regard yourself
detached from duty at the White House, Washington, DC, and
from such other duty as may have been assigned you; you
will proceed to Newport, Rhode Island and report to the
President, Naval War College, for duty under instruction.
     You will be assigned government quarters in one of the
officers' dormitories of the Naval Training Station. These
quarters are not adequate for your dependents.
```

He might well have imagined a divine light shining down on him in the dimly lit living room. After tucking his new orders back in the envelope, Bill allowed a measure of relief. This would be difficult news to break to his family, but his prayer had surely been answered. With luck, he would finish his training at the Naval War College in Newport and be in the Pacific by year's end.

★   ★   ★

A MONTH OF HASTY preparations followed, interrupted in late May by a whirlwind trip to Pearl Harbor with a planeload of navy luminaries for a very special ceremony. If Bill needed any additional visuals to seal his resolve, his happy reunion with Benny on the occasion of *Enterprise's* receipt of the Presidential Unit Citation—the first ever awarded an aircraft carrier—certainly did.

Bill had stood in the oval office as FDR signed the executive order. He'd barely been able to contain himself when the president—knowing, of course, that Benny was *Enterprise's* gunnery officer—then suggested Bill attend the ceremony.

A battle-scarred USS *Enterprise* had returned to Pearl Harbor to receive the award and also, after nine hard months at sea, to undergo a major structural overhaul. Benny was grateful for the chance to catch his breath and savor Bill's surprise visit. Here was a long-deferred reunion in which a pent-up checklist of items that could only be shared in person—the war, Lilac Hedges, Barton, their complicated parentage, their own marriages and children, Bill's decision to go to sea, and Benny's weariness of it—would be covered in an adrenaline-charged conversation in Sky Control preceding the citation ceremony.

Bill was particularly excited to relate the recent intelligence that a group of men had escaped from Davao Penal Colony on the island of Mindanao. He was sure, he said, that this was where Barton was being held. Benny was incredulous. "Are you saying Barton was one of them? Oh my God!"

"Sadly, no," Bill replied. Barton wasn't among the escapees, but this was still an encouraging development, he insisted, even as his brother's disappointment registered. It was the first and only contact with any captured American since the fall of Bataan and Corregidor. The navy was going to send a submarine to rescue the escapees, who were under the protection of

Mindanao guerrillas. He would know more after they were safe in Brisbane and could be debriefed.

He repeated that the escape was good news. "One," he said, holding up his index finger: "The men got out alive. Two"—he raised a second finger—"word is, there's a navy commander in the group; an Academy graduate. If they were at the same camp, and I'm fairly certain they were, he had to know Barton and will have news of him. Three, these men will have other dope on the prisoners in the Philippines—plenty of it."

Knowing this last could be a mix of bad and good news, Bill elected not to speculate. "Meanwhile," he said, shoring himself up with some emotion, "you're safe! Amazing what you've been through, what you've accomplished. Honest to God. You have been getting closer to Barton in your own right."

He was referring to *Enterprise*'s relentless westward foray against one after another enemy-held islands in the Pacific. Every battle, it seemed, had brought *Enterprise* a thousand miles closer to Manila. "Between the two of us," Bill said, "we'll get through to him."

Benny sighed. "Well, I sure as hell hope you're right, Bill. To tell you the truth, I wouldn't mind some new orders myself, but then it's hard to think about much else. Even though we're lickin' 'em, they're still holding Bart in a pen somewhere. That keeps me going on the worst days."

With that, band music sounded, and their precious time together was up. Top brass had begun to assemble on *Enterprise*'s flight deck, and Bill would have to return to Washington shortly after the award ceremony. Taking his place behind a phalanx of captains and admirals, he watched with patriotic and familial pride as Benny and the crew, in dress whites, stood at attention.

The flags on *Enterprise*'s yardarm snapped in the stiff Pearl Harbor breeze as Admiral Nimitz, CINCPAC, stepped forward to read the Presidential Unit Citation. Poignantly, he stopped just aft of the patched-over impact point of the bomb that had wiped out Repair Crew II at Santa

Cruz, and a few feet forward of the new starboard quarterdecking where Benny's thirty-eight gunners were incinerated by the bomb blast in the Eastern Solomons.

Admiral Nimitz cleared his throat, leaned into the microphone, and began his address to the white-clad assembly. The text before him was a large ceremonial document signed by President Roosevelt:

> For consistently outstanding performance and distinguished achievement during repeated action against enemy Japanese forces in the Pacific War area, December 7, 1941, to November 15, 1942. Participating in nearly every major carrier engagement in the first year of the war, the Enterprise and her air group, exclusive of far-flung destruction of hostile shore installations throughout the battle area, did sink or damage on her own a total of thirty-five Japanese vessels and shoot down a total of a hundred eighty-five Japanese aircraft. Her aggressive spirit and superb combat efficiency are fitting tribute to the officers and men who so gallantly established her as an ahead bulwark in the defense of the American nation.

The admiral then listed action after heroic action, all which the ship's crew recalled well, if painfully.

Enterprise's current captain, Samuel Ginder, followed Admiral Nimitz. His every booming syllable echoed off the ships moored along a restored Battleship Row and drew cheers from hundreds of sailors manning those rails. Captain Ginder smiled and turned to acknowledge the rising crescendo of admiration and gratitude before continuing. "Your record has never been even remotely approached by any ship of this or any other navy."

Captain Ginder then proceeded to read a telegram from Admiral

Halsey, now commander of all South Pacific naval forces, but once and for-ever *Enterprise*'s symbolic leader and champion:

"It is with deep pride and gratification that I learn of the Presidential Unit Citation for *Enterprise*. This eminently deserved award expresses the appreciation of a grateful people for your outstanding accomplishments in this war.

"Keep fighting, ever mindful of the glorious traditions you have estab-lished. My heart is always with you."

At this the crew could not help, to the last man, grinning so hard it hurt.

Bill was left nearly wordless by the serial superlatives his brother's ship had earned. For eighteen months, USS *Enterprise* had been to him a thimble-sized marker that he had moved, always carefully, thoughtfully, around a map inside a window-blackened room six thousand miles away. The force of finally being aboard her with Benny, at such a charged and his-toric moment, was overwhelming.

After exchanging words of encouragement and a crisp salute—though they both would have preferred a hug—Bill said his last good-byes to Benny and boarded the waiting military aircraft.

The Washington-bound plane lumbered off Ford Island's runway into graying eastern skies. Pearl Harbor and a storied Oahu sunset retreated into the distance through a porthole-sized window. This day's experience made all the clearer the chasm between the insulated world of the White House Map Room and life aboard a ship at war. He would come to appreciate all the differences soon enough. What was that niggling feeling this realization gave rise to—was it fear?

ON HIS LAST DAY at the White House, Bill made the rounds, bidding farewell to the close-knit staff who had become a surrogate family to him. There was a perceptible sense among all of them that they might never see Bill again. The somber White House staff was still grieving over the recent loss of Daniel Callahan, another well-liked Roosevelt naval aide who had been drawn to the front. He was killed in the action off Guadalcanal.

Eleanor Roosevelt's farewell was especially unnerving, though Bill didn't let on. She clasped his shoulders with her hands and looked directly into his eyes, as though trying to memorize his features in case he didn't return. She had taken to him during his tenure there, always asking about his family and producing the occasional plaything for his young son. Her affection had been returned in kind by a young man who'd experienced too little maternal warmth and attention.

Bill's last stop was the Oval Office. Grace Tully pressed his hand in her own, said good-bye, and then opened the president's door. Roosevelt was sitting in his wheelchair beside his desk instead of behind it, his Scottish terrier Fala lounging at his feet. "Good afternoon, Mr. President," Bill said. "I've come to say good-bye and to thank you for your many kindnesses."

"Well, William," the president said, and then paused and leaned forward. "You know you really should stay here." The comment seemed more a gesture of affection rather than reproof, and Bill took it that way.

"Well, sir, the Japs have my brother in a prison camp, as you know. I really feel I must go."

Their eyes met, and the president nodded.

After a few minutes of small talk, Bill finally said, "Well, Mr. President, I hate to leave, but you may be sure I'll be back for the peace conference." Roosevelt's ice-blue, half-hooded eyes again met Bill's gaze. Then he looked away. The dark circles beneath them had deepened in recent months, and he had clearly lost weight. And though it was June, he still had a wool cape draped over his shoulders.

"Well, son," the president said, "I'm not sure there will ever be one."

20

★ ★ ★

A TALE OF ATROCITIES

THE FIRST THREE OF the escaped Davao prisoners to be rotated out of Mindanao by submarine were William Dyess (army air corps), Melvin McCoy (navy), and Steven Mellnik (army). When they arrived in Perth, Australia, two could barely walk, and the third emerged through the sub hatch on a stretcher. Within hours, all three received a stern summons from MacArthur's Brisbane headquarters: proceed to GHQ for debriefing as soon as physically able. They were also ordered, in no uncertain terms, to otherwise keep their mouths shut:

> Do Not, Repeat, Do Not, Discuss Experiences with Anyone.
> Imperative You Arrive in Brisbane Soon as Possible. Have
> Notified Your Family of Safe Arrival.
>
> MacArthur

The ex-prisoners got a warm reception in Brisbane, however—especially Steve Mellnik, who had served on General MacArthur's prewar staff in Manila. They were particularly surprised when the general pinned Distinguished Service Awards on their very new uniforms. While accepted graciously, all three men commented to the assembled brass that the real heroes—both dead and alive—were those they had left behind.

After the awards, the gathered officers and their note takers listened, mostly in silence, alternately horrified and entranced as the escapees told the tale of their capture, the grisly methods used to exterminate thousands of prisoners of war, and the particulars of their escape. Except for their repeated expressions of gratitude and respect for the Mindanao guerrillas who had rescued and delivered them, the details were relentlessly grim. The AIB's Colonel Allison Ind paused the proceedings every twenty minutes or so, as much for the weakened officers as for the weeping stenographers.

Dyess, Mellnik, and McCoy chronicled the marches that killed tens of thousands, the beatings and bayonetings, the burying of men alive, the starvation and gruesome torture—all carried out with bland and unemotional Japanese efficiency. This was the very first report to the outside world of the Bataan Death March and the savage abuses of daily prison camp life that followed. The men spoke haltingly at first, and then with more energy and animation, likely motivated by reawakened outrage.

There was particular interest in their method of escape, which had been months in the planning. Key to their success, they explained, was the Japanese practice of sending out unchaperoned details on Sundays; they stressed that DAPECOL was lightly guarded compared with Bilibid, O'Donnell, and Cabanatuan—the prison camps on Luzon.

The lax oversight gave the incipient escapees the opportunity to preassemble food and essential equipment, including a compass, precious canned goods from their Red Cross packages, a sextant, quinine tablets, and maps of Mindanao and sea routes to Australia. They gradually removed the vital supplies from the camp on a bull cart used for hauling and hid them near the jungle perimeter until Sunday, April 4.

The Brisbane audience was also intrigued by the critical assistance provided by two longtime Filipino convicts, both in for murder. In fact, among the escapees' first requests was that MacArthur arrange for President-in-exile Manuel Quezon to formally pardon these criminals. This had been the bargain the American prisoners had gladly struck with the convicts early in the planning.

The two men, Benigno de la Cruz and Victorio Jumarong, had risked their lives—or worse, recapture and torture by the Japanese—to aid the Americans in a life-threatening, weeks-long ordeal, during which the escapees had hiked, half starved, across more than sixty miles of dark jungle, treacherous swamps, and rugged mountain ranges—nearly always within whispering distance of enraged Japanese search parties. Only with the convicts' help had the men miraculously made good on the escape.

Even with the convicts' knowledge of the jungle, they encountered difficulty from the start. After initially losing their way, they had unwittingly doubled back toward the prison camp, potentially squandering their all-important head start. With Japanese troops in hot pursuit, they narrowly avoided recapture.

Weakened by days on the run, wading chest deep through snake- and alligator-infested swamps, their rations running short, and the Japanese close on their heels, the escape party was finally picked up by Mindanao guerrillas, who promptly led them to safety. The guerrillas fed and clothed them, and treated their malaria, skin ulcers, and other raging ailments. Guerrilla-protected villagers even threw fiestas to celebrate the Americans' newfound freedom. These events, in further display of Filipino loyalty to the American cause, featured platters of food, flowing *tuba*, an alcoholic beverage coaxed from jungle vines, and music and dancing.

There had been one significant exception to the escapees' positive guerrilla experience, however: "Colonel" Wendell Fertig, an unsurrendered American mining engineer who had muscled his way to leadership of the various Mindanao guerrilla bands. Fertig had treated them with suspicion and arrogance and initially resisted their request that he radio authorities in Australia and notify them of their escape. Only when McCoy, Mellnik, and Dyess confronted Fertig and displayed a gun they had acquired did he relent and allow the encrypted message to be sent to GHQ receiving stations in Brisbane.

After this part of the story was told, General Charles A. Willoughby, MacArthur's intelligence chief, launched into an explanation. "Colonel Fertig was with the Corps of Engineers working to construct airfields on Mindanao when hostilities broke out," Willoughby began. "He fled to the hills and later came down, gradually assuming control of local guerrilla units, which were struggling to oversee food distribution to the local villages and generally maintain civil control. Fertig then established radio contact with us here in Brisbane, and when those units understood he was in contact with us and had accorded him rank, they gradually allowed him to organize and oversee all the guerrilla bands on Mindanao. We understand his drawbacks, but he's done a decent job distributing supplies and providing intelligence. He's set up a number of radio 'stations' on the island—including the one from which your dispatch was relayed—as well as formalized a coastwatcher network that monitors enemy shipping.

"His personality has grated on more than just you; I'm not sure the guerrilla leaders on the island fully trust Fertig. After all, he assumed control over indigenous units that they had organized. But they ceded control because of his power to distribute supplies, not his leadership ability. The local leaders probably pay him lip service in proportion to what Fertig can furnish them.

"That said, it's our impression he didn't quite know what to do with you initially—I believe he meant no harm. Fertig desperately needs skilled men to help him, and he probably saw you as potential recruits! We are aware that he is egotistical and difficult, but he has been helpful to us in many ways, including resolving power skirmishes between the guerrilla bands. They are no good to us if they are fighting with each other. That is why we granted him the temporary senior rank of colonel—so he can assert Allied authority. We need Fertig to organize those bands into a cohesive military operation on Mindanao for when we *return.*"

General Willoughby emphasized the final word, echoing MacArthur's famous pledge.

WILLOUGHBY WAS PLEASED TO have the opportunity to demonstrate his command of Mindanao's state of affairs before such an attentive audience. He was senior in rank and experience to Courtney Whitney, who had recently arrived in Brisbane and become his chief rival for MacArthur's attention. Willoughby had been in charge of Philippine affairs until MacArthur appointed Whitney to head GHQ's new and semiautonomous Philippine Regional Section (PRS). PRS now oversaw all Philippine operations for MacArthur, including guerrilla operations. To Willoughby's further chagrin, Whitney was now also the GHQ liaison to the navy's Seventh Fleet—and thus in control of Chick Parsons's covert submarine supply operation as well.

The clever Courtney Whitney had risen in stature at GHQ thanks to a steady stream of glowing, ingratiating praise of General MacArthur. It is said that a fool flatters himself but a wise man flatters the fool, and from the moment of his arrival at GHQ, Whitney had proven himself a master among masters at manipulating his new boss. It began with comments he had made on MacArthur's draft press statement to be broadcast on the anniversary of the fall of Bataan.

"This is superb," Whitney wrote to MacArthur. "It has the classical quality of imperishable statements. I predict that someday it will be carved in stone on monuments in the Philippines. I predict a tremendous emotional effect. American history is shot through with the power of such words and slogans. Like 'Remember the Alamo' . . . it has the dignity of distinguished literature."

Whitney's stature at GHQ soared following this early and memorable exchange, and his meteoric rise was vexing in the extreme to General Willoughby—especially because he'd lost command of Philippine affairs. Now it was the ambitious Whitney who controlled the guerrilla leader Wendell Fertig and who was charged with bringing MacArthur's iconic "I Shall Return" pledge to fruition. Whitney would control the vain Fertig with similar tactics—by implying that his own place in history would be secured by following Whitney's lead.

Willoughby was furious that the potential of Mindanao's twenty-two-thousand-strong guerrilla movement was now being undermined by Whitney's politically motivated tolerance of Fertig's limited leadership skills and poor people skills. Even Fertig's principal aides, American captains Ernest McLish and Clyde Childress, regarded him as paranoid and consumed with personal ambition. They did not like or trust him.

Willoughby had continued to push for trained military personnel and intelligence officers to be sent to Mindanao to take over operations from the one-time mining engineer, but Courtney Whitney had blocked him at every turn, preferring his tight control over the vain, inexperienced Fertig. Whitney liked the arrangement just as it was.

STEVE MELLNIK LISTENED AND nodded quietly during Willoughby's explanation, while also watching the body language—including that of the inscrutable Whitney—of all present. The experience brought back pre-capture memories of all the petty rivalries that had animated MacArthur's Manila headquarters before the war. It was one of the very few things, he realized, that he had not missed during captivity.

The conversation moved quickly beyond the escapees' interactions with Wendell Fertig. The men continued in their high praise of the other

Mindanao guerrilla leaders, whose operations they'd had plenty of time to observe in the nearly two-months hiatus between their escape and submarine rendezvous with Chick Parsons. One leader stood out: Captain Claro Lauretta, head of the Davao region guerrillas and the first with whom the escapees had come in contact. Lauretta's operational ingenuity and sophisticated level of organization, particularly given his primitive surrounds, had especially impressed them.

The GHQ audience showed intensified interest. They were hungry for well-sourced details on how the guerrilla units functioned, their living conditions in the jungle, their morale, their ability to gather enemy intelligence, and the extent and nature of their interactions with the Japanese. The escapees filled in the many blanks with hard facts.

Numbering several thousand, the Mindanao guerrillas were tough and smart. They knew the terrain like the backs of their hands, enjoyed widespread Filipino loyalty and support, and dealt ruthlessly with the Japanese, who increasingly feared and avoided them. The Japanese garrison on Mindanao persistently underestimated their strength and cunning. Not only had the guerrillas inflicted hundreds of Japanese casualties, but their very presence tied down thousands of other Japanese troops who could have otherwise been deployed elsewhere. Whenever the Japanese tried to attack them, the guerrillas melted expertly into the jungles and mountains, taking their food, supplies, and radios with them.

When the stenographers' work was finally done, MacArthur sent the word-for-word transcript to the White House by special air dispatch, on orders of President Roosevelt.

After the debriefing, General Willoughby said, "I'm convinced the guerrillas will play a major role during the liberation. Their potential for intelligence and sabotage is enormous. We need someone familiar with their operations to help us develop that potential." Looking at Steve Mellnik, whom he remembered well from prewar Manila, Willoughby then announced to the group, "Steve will need to take off for several weeks' debriefing in Washington, but when he's through, I'd like him to return and join our staff." Only after General MacArthur nodded in agreement did Courtney Whitney concur quietly.

Mellnik could not have been more pleased. Though he didn't say it at the time, he was already envisioning another role for the Mindanao guerrillas, one in which he might now play a critical part: as facilitators of a mass rescue of the two thousand remaining prisoners at the Davao Penal Colony.

21

★ ★ ★

AUGUST 1943: ALLIED WAR
SUMMIT, QUEBEC, CANADA

WHEN IT WAS DECIDED that a fourth major Allied war summit was to be held in August 1943, Washington's stifling summer heat was rejected in favor of Winston Churchill's suggestion that they meet in cooler climes: Her Majesty's Quebec, Canada. That he might have the honor of hosting the president at the British Empire's largest North American fortress, the Citadel—proudly overlooking the site where the British defeated the French in 1760 to claim the spoils of all of Canada—was reason alone for the prime minister to favor the location.

But in addition to the historic Citadel and Canada's infinitely superior summer weather, Quebec also boasted a large, comfortable, and secure château-hotel where the Allied leaders' sizable military and civilian staffs could hold their "pick-and-shovel" sessions, the detailed meetings that converted the war leaders' big decisions into workable plans. So on August 1, 1943, some three thousand reservations at the famed Le Château Frontenac, the magnificent Gothic Revival edifice perched high above the rushing

Saint Lawrence River, were abruptly cancelled. Preparations for the war conference began immediately. Secrecy shrouded the arrangements, and rumors regarding the unexplained cancellations abounded. The two most remarkable were that Pope Pius XII was leaving war-torn Italy to set up temporary Vatican headquarters there, and that the storied hotel was to be converted to a military hospital.

In two weeks' time—with the addition of several miles of barbed wire, portable antiaircraft batteries, and armed sentries—the site's conversion to a first-rate world war summit location was complete. Hundreds of American, British, and Canadian officials began descending on Frontenac: from senior staffs, to secret service agents, to military intelligence officers, to Signal Corps communications specialists. President Roosevelt and Prime Minister Churchill took up official residence within the Citadel's elegant residential quarters, an ideal environment for informal and confidential discussions, as well as for high-level meetings.

The priority at Quadrant was to refine the timing and strategy for Operation Overlord, the seminal cross-Channel Allied landing in France that would launch the all-out assault on "the Axis in Europe." Still to be addressed were the sticky details of "combined" commands over American and British land, air, and sea forces, as well as other turf-related Overlord logistics.

Also vying for attention at Quadrant was the simmering intra-Allied battle over strategic next steps in the Pacific. Whenever the discussion turned to that topic, the British delegation appeared more focused on approaches favoring its lost imperial colonies—Hong Kong and Singapore in particular—than on prioritizing men and ships for an attack on Japan's home islands.

From Day One at Quadrant, the Anglophobic Admiral King pressed relentlessly for more aggressive action against Japan—and sooner rather than later—with George Marshall voicing his strongest support yet for King's position. Building on his Casablanca and Trident fulminations, King turned up the heat at Quebec, all but alleging that Britain lacked serious commitment to defeating the Japanese once Europe was liberated from the Nazis. The meeting room quieted at the accusation.

British representatives grew red with irritation whenever Admiral King opened his mouth. King was brilliant, but even on his best days, his personality was like a blowtorch. It wasn't that he was singling out the British for especially harsh treatment—he treated just about everyone that way. General Dwight Eisenhower, in charge of the US Army's European operations, once confided to his diary: "One thing that might help win this war is to get someone to shoot King. He's the antithesis of cooperation, a deliberately rude person . . . [and] a mental bully."

But popularity seemed utterly unimportant to Ernest King. In fact, by all accounts, he held dear his tough, lionlike defense of the United States Navy. When he was tapped to replace Admiral Harold Stark as CNO in the post–Pearl Harbor shake-up, he said famously, "You see, when things get tough, they call in the sons of bitches."

To Admiral King, the Pacific War—in which America and her navy had the greatest stake of all the Allies—had always come first. He pressed inexorably for the American Navy's needs and priorities, no matter the venue. At Quebec, he reminded the august assembly of the US Navy's string of Pacific victories, earned despite a paucity of men, ships, and materiel—a paucity not only compared with enemy assets but also compared with those being allocated to the European front.

King's clear implication was that the navy's heavy casualties in the early battles were greater than they *should* have been and a direct result of misplaced priorities of higher-ups. This was particularly true of sailors of the surface fleet, among whom the Guadalcanal toll alone was more than 5,000 young lives—a stratospheric number even when compared with the much-publicized losses by the US Army and Marine Corps during the protracted struggle ashore. That casualty estimate stood at 1,592.

In fact, Pacific naval commands had been appallingly underfed in the past two years compared with commands in Europe, arguably because of the time it took to convert US industrial capacity to a dedicated output of war goods. But here it was August 1943, King argued, and *still* only 15 percent of the supplies pouring out of converted American plants and factories were designated for the Pacific War. Moreover, the number of troops deployed to battle the Nazis was double that sent to the Pacific, which occupied a larger and more complicated theater of war.

In what one British representative deemed "very undiplomatic language," Admiral King demanded an agreement at Quadrant that more ships and personnel be sent to the Pacific front. King had already assigned the shrewd and equally irascible Admiral Kelly Turner as commander of Pacific amphibious forces. Recalling that Guadalcanal had been nicknamed Operation Shoestring, what Turner needed now, King exhorted, were the men, ships, and equipment to win the decisive next rounds of amphibious assaults as they closed in on Japan's home islands. With proper resources, Admiral Turner would get the job done.

At Quadrant, King's and Marshall's exhortations for stepped-up aggression against Japan seemed to have a greater urgency than at previous summits. The reason was that both men—as well as President Roosevelt—had very recently read the sworn statements of the escaped Davao prisoners. In addition to being outraged, they wanted an accelerated action plan agreed to by Allied war leaders at Quebec ahead of the inevitable release of these atrocity reports to the American public.

ON THE NEXT-TO-LAST DAY of the conference, as a final punctuation to their position throughout the week, King and Marshall won President Roosevelt's approval to have one of the escaped POWs' sworn statements read aloud to the combined military chiefs.

And so on August 23, with Major William Dyess's affidavit in hand, General Marshall rose from his seat in Le Château Frontenac's elegant Salon Rose Room, a circular space with rose-colored walls and floor-to-ceiling windows affording sweeping views of the Saint Lawrence River. Just outside the meeting room, lunch was waiting to be served. Perspiring pitchers of ice water and lemonade were perched next to a grand silver service of steaming coffee and tea. Beside the beverage table was a brimming buffet of fresh fruits, salads, breads, and platters of chicken, beef, and Canada's fine smoked salmon.

General Marshall began:

At daylight, 10 April, 1942, we started marching on the National Road off Bataan . . . This march is referred to by American prisoners of war as the Death March of Bataan. Had the Americans or Filipinos known the fate in store for them, though beaten, hungry, and tired from months of hardships, never would they have surrendered to our dishonorable foe . . . It was a terrifically hot day as we marched along the road without food, cover, or water.

We frequently passed men lying on the side of the road. Many had been run over by Japanese trucks and flattened. The next day, still with no food or water, we were marched twenty-one hours continuously. Men started falling out frequently, but the guards did not allow us to aid them. We could hear gunshots behind us. The Japanese had clean-up squads marching behind us, killing those who had fallen out . . .

At three a.m. we were placed in a barbed-wire bullpen that might have ordinarily housed two hundred men. In this pen were at least two thousand men. Human filth and maggots were everywhere . . . Three Filipinos and three Americans were buried alive, and one of the guards went so far as to make one of our own American sergeants hit one of the men in the head with a shovel when he tried to get out of the grave. Many of the men went crazy, and several of the delirious were dragged out and shot.

The secretary of the army cleared his throat as he read the statement, so replete with gruesome bayonetings, beheadings, and descriptions of mass starvation, brutality, and disease that some of the meeting attendees seemed to be fighting nausea. Still, General Marshall read the document in its entirety, pausing periodically so that the full impact of the narrative could be absorbed by even the most ardent Pacific Second advocates in the room. Dyess's closing statement, however, seemed to draw the greatest attention:

> "In my opinion, it is not only advisable, but absolutely necessary, that all civilized people of the world know the conditions of the Japanese prison camps and the atrocities against American prisoners of war."

When the meeting broke, the sumptuous buffet lunch outside Salon Rose was hardly touched. Admiral Ernest King had suddenly become the least of the meeting attendees' concerns.

At the conclusion of the weeklong Quadrant, a weary President Roosevelt was wheeled into his temporary office next to the Citadel residence's drawing room, a bright, windowed space with river views on three sides. Roosevelt settled in for a day of reading and responding to accumulated correspondence that had been dispatched from Washington.

The president's secretary, Grace Tully, had developed a fine sense over the years of what was urgent, what could wait, and what could be responded to adequately by someone else. With four thousand letters a day pouring into the White House since the beginning of the war, Tully culled to a fraction the mail that actually reached the president. In further efficiency, she always attached a brief note summarizing each piece of correspondence. Letters of a personal nature were decorated with a red tag.

So marked was a letter atop that morning's tidy pile, written on powder-blue stationery. In a long, sweeping hand, the linen envelope carried a return address of Lilac Hedges, Oceanport, New Jersey. In the cover note attached to the letter, Tully had written:

> Letter from Mrs. A. Barton Cross. Her son was an officer
> in the White House (Lt. Com. Mott), has another son, Chief
> Gunnery Officer on aircraft carrier, a daughter--an
> officer in the WAVES, and third son is a Japanese prisoner.
> Is grieved over her youngest son in the Philippines. Was
> John's [Roosevelt] classmate at Harvard. Asks the President
> if these prisoners are forgotten as he never mentions them
> in his [speeches] etc. . . . Since Mrs. Roosevelt is away and
> this is addressed to both the President and Mrs. Roosevelt
> and is from Commander Mott's mother, perhaps you would care
> to answer.

Roosevelt read Grace's note and the letter itself, which he was told Eleanor had already seen and urged be sent on to him. No doubt the president paused before penning his reply. The escapee depositions sent him by MacArthur had stunned him. Their sworn statements stressed the dire circumstances these men had escaped, but perhaps the most haunting assertion was William Dyess's: "If any American could sit down and conjure the most diabolical of nightmares, he might come close to . . . the tortures and horrors that these men are going through." Roosevelt was surely also mindful of the personal note he received from MacArthur just prior to his departure for Quebec:

> [O]ur quiescent policy with respect to the Philippines . . . is
> in no small degree responsible for the unfolding of a drama
> the stark tragedy of which has no counterpart in American
> history. Our prisoners of war are being subjected to slow and
> deliberate extermination through disease, starvation and
> summary execution. So have many thousands already perished,
> and few, if any, will survive unless we arouse ourselves into
> a more dynamic military aid policy.

Roosevelt recalled the many conversations he'd had with his former naval aide, William Mott, and his ill-concealed anxiety about his brother Barton, one of those very prisoners in the Philippines. The president had always extended words of sympathy and encouragement to Mott; at the time, it was all he could do.

But now, God help him, with the burden of this new and terrible information on the treatment of these men, here was a letter from Mott's mother! What could he possibly say to comfort her, given what he now knew? Helen Cross's maternal tenacity was not so different from that of Roosevelt's own late mother, Sara—legendary for her fierce protectiveness and involvement in all matters relating to Franklin.

When the president was deep in thought ahead of dictation, he would pause and tap his fingers on the arms of his wheelchair. His secretary knew that dictation would usually begin when he stretched out his arms and placed his hands flat on the top of his desk. He would then push back his chair a bit, grab hold of a trouser leg at the knee, swing the leg over the other knee, and fold his hands. This was the familiar series of gestures he repeated before dictating the following:

The Citadel

Quebec

August 24, 1943.

My dear Mrs. Cross,

Mrs. Roosevelt and I have read your letter of August
10th and we want to assure you that the subject of American
prisoner of war, their treatment and the distress and
anxiety of their relatives, is among our many grave

concerns. Having in mind the character of our enemies, it
seems improbable that repeated declarations of that anxiety
or concern would help the prisoners or improve their
condition.

The most effective step at this time appears to be
through the good offices of the Red Cross with the help of
the benevolent neutrals.

Every effort is being strained to end the war at the
earliest possible date and one of the most urgent reasons
for that haste is the desire to release our prisoners. I
know that your sons understand how anxiously all our
country look forward to their day of release.

At the White House we miss your son, William, and I am
sure you must feel equal satisfaction for the fine work of
your other sons and your daughter in the Service.

> With all good wishes,
> Sincerely yours,
> Franklin D. Roosevelt

When the freshly typed letter was handed back to him, he read it
through. He then slowly unscrewed the cap of his fountain pen. First, he
scrawled an *s* after "prisoner" in the opening paragraph, correcting it to
reflect the grim plural that it was. Plural in the tens of thousands, he knew
too well. Then, pressing hard on his fountain pen nib, he scratched his signature.

He had answered a mother's lament as best he could. Never far from
his mind were his own four children, also in uniform and in harm's way. In
that, the parental anguish of Helen Cross and Franklin Roosevelt were one
and the same.

Soon thereafter, the president received an effusive response:

Lilac Hedges
Oceanport, New Jersey

September 9, 1943

To the President and Mrs. Roosevelt,

Dear Friends,

How can I consider you other than friends when you were good enough to give me time out of your busy lives? Time to say a few words to assuage a mother's real and protracted anxiety! Your letter must have brought good luck, for the next day a postcard arrived from Barton, from Military Prison Camp Number Two in the Philippines. It bore his dear signature in a firm hand and the information checked that things are not too bad.

Thank you also for your kind words about William. I am proud also of his brother, Commander E. Bertram Mott of the "workhorse of the Pacific"... and our Ensign Rosemary Cross of the Brooklyn Navy Yard.

God bless you in your wise and single hearted direction of our land!

Sincerely Yours,
Helen Cross

In time, however, the tone and content of Helen's correspondence with President Roosevelt would change dramatically.

22

★ ★ ★

REVENGE ON THE INNOCENT
AND A COVERT PLAN

AFTER CROUCHING FOR THIRTY days in feces strewn wire hutches and in constant dread of summary execution, the fellow tenants of the four escape-party-occupied barracks were let out of their cages and ordered to line up outside their isolated compound. A weakened Barton Cross and a subdued Charles Armour fell in with their fellow prisoners. It appeared their deaths were near, in keeping with the Japanese ten-for-one shooting squad rule on prisoner escape.

In his immaculate uniform and shiny boots, Major Maeda twitched his riding crop as he paced up and down the nervous, hollow-eyed assembly. His demeanor betrayed a mix of contempt and disgust—but also something else: Was it resignation? Maeda began his address to the prisoners. When the interpreter translated the remarks into broken English, the men could barely maintain their fixed expressions.

They had been "bad boys," the interpreter delivered, for having allowed their barrack mates to escape, and they were ungrateful to the benevolent

Japanese for having spared their lives. Their punishment, therefore, would be severe: the prisoners would lose all the monies they had "earned" during their imprisonment, which, Maeda asserted, had been deposited on their behalf in Japanese postal savings accounts.

The comedy of the punishment was lost on none of its recipients. That they might have ever received such funds—and this was the first they'd heard of their existence—was not a prospect they could even contemplate. A dead man can't spend a penny, and all they could think when the interpreter finished was that, incredibly, they were not going to be executed.

Resisting the urge to throw his head back and laugh out loud had to be difficult for Barton. But as sure as he stood unsteadily on his filthy bare feet listening to Maeda's dispensation from the harshest rule of prison life, he believed the worst was over. If they could survive this, he would say later, they could survive anything.

Still, when the sequestered prisoners were returned to the main camp, they found a changed attitude among their captors, even among the previously friendly guards. Lieutenant Yuki, once compassionate and understanding, barely spoke to the ensigns after their return, indicating only that he felt betrayed for his previous kindnesses.

Reduced rations were now the new norm, and random beatings increased. Not surprisingly, unguarded work details were also a thing of the past—which drastically reduced the prisoners' ability to supplement paltry rations with food skimmed during farmwork. Some had lived this long only by snatching from these sources to supplement their starvation diet. To those men, this was the worst consequence of the escape.

Barton was among a small faction of prisoners who did not begrudge the escapees: to survive in the jungle and reach safety (if indeed they had; nobody knew) seemed a feat larger than life itself. Perhaps they felt this way because the navy man, McCoy, and the marine, Austin Conner Shoffner, had been respected as men of conscience. Surely these men would get word back to their families, let them know they were alive, tell them where they were; surely they would do at least that on behalf of the prisoners left behind.

This prospect was especially keen to Barton. Here it was summer 1943, and he still had not received a single piece of mail from his family. Nor did he know whether they had received the cards he had written them. He agonized over the possible reasons. For all Barton knew, his family had given him up for dead. *Maybe those escaped men will get word about us to the outside world*, Barton hoped. *That would make it all worth it.*

Such had been his ruminations during those long nights in the rabbit hutch. Some good might very well come of this.

But the majority of prisoners were bitter about the escape and ensuing crackdown. They could barely speak the escapees' names without modifying epithets. In their minds, those ten men had willfully inflicted mass punishment on nearly two thousand innocents. To the majority of prisoners at Davao, this was unforgivable.

IN SEPTEMBER 1943, AFTER lengthy hospitalization in Brisbane, Steve Mellnik and the other escapees flew thirty-six hours across nine time zones to Washington, DC. Their debriefings at the Pentagon, the State Department, and other relevant agencies went on for weeks. Throughout the process, he was reminded repeatedly that his experiences were a military secret. Like his fellow escapees, Mellnik was under strict orders not to divulge, even to his family, any detail of what he had been through. It was a new and cruel form of incarceration for all of them, especially because these men believed their escape would be justified—and their guilt assuaged—*only* by exposing what the Japanese were doing to Allied prisoners.

Mellnik took particular offense at disdainful bureaucrats who intimated he had lost sight of the greater war because of his singular concern for the prisoners he had left behind. Others, however, listened respectfully. Once Mellnik realized the degree to which a calm and professional demeanor improved his credibility, he conducted himself with special care.

The combined stress of the debriefings and forced repression landed Mell-nik back at Walter Reed Hospital for recuperation from a vicious recurrence of malaria. But the respite gave him an opportunity to refine his plan.

The idea had first come to him during the escapees' Brisbane debriefing. Mellnik's detailed description of the strengths of Mindanao's guerrillas was met with intense interest by MacArthur and his colleagues. What he had de-scribed wasn't an underground resistance with a few shortwave radios but a broad, deep, and sophisticated military network that included an island-wide supply, defense, and communications system. The guerrillas also commanded the deep respect and loyalty of virtually every island resident—thanks to their reliable enforcement of law and order and their ruthless treatment of the hated Japanese occupiers.

The original and core purpose of the guerrilla organizations—on Min-danao, in particular—had been to restore civil order when local authority crumbled at the war's outbreak. This function expanded rapidly to include harassment of enemy garrisons across the island. Word of their brutal and highly efficient ambushes spread fast, and the Japanese increasingly feared them.

How did they accomplish these feats with so few resources? At Bris-bane's GHQ and later at the Pentagon, Mellnik quoted the words of one guerrilla leader over and over: "What we don't have, we make, what we can't make, we steal, what we can't steal, we do without and still get the job done."

Brass curtain rods were melted down to make bullets, gunpowder was extracted from firecrackers, and the jungle was so laced with trip wires, sharpened bamboo spikes, and other death traps that the Japa-nese were afraid to stray from the main roads. And they stayed well away from the guerrilla strongholds dotting the island. The guerrillas had some natural advantages as well. They knew Mindanao's treacherous ter-rain intimately and navigated easily through even its most inhospitable areas. They had adapted and formalized military protocols to jungle life and abided by them. The American escapees—all professionally trained military officers—had been suitably impressed by the guerrillas' twenty-four-hour combat readiness.

Just as he had at Brisbane, Mellnik methodically spread the Mindanao guerrilla gospel throughout the warrens of the Pentagon, detailing the operation's leadership, breadth, size, and sheer gutsiness. He fascinated every interviewer with the guerrillas' methods and astonishing effectiveness.

Mellnik always began by differentiating Mindanao from Luzon, which was heavily garrisoned and controlled by the Japanese. The guerrillas controlled 95 percent of Mindanao, with enemy activity limited to patrols on major highways. In fact, Japanese soldiers were terrified of the jungle—home to both the guerrillas and the legendary head-hunting Moro tribes. "The possibility that the Japanese will send a strong force to Mindanao to neutralize this resistance does . . . not . . . exist." Mellnik would repeat the last three words slowly and succinctly.

Perhaps Mellnik's most important Washington meeting was with Lieutenant Harold Rosenquist, an officer with MIS-X, an unpublicized section of the army's G-2 (Military Intelligence) branch. MIS-X was an ultrasecret POW communication, support, and supply program operating with vaunted success in the European theater. Mellnik was stunned to learn that such an organization existed. So clandestine was MIS-X, code-named "1142" for the box number at which it received top secret correspondence, that relatively few within the military establishment had even heard of it.

Rosenquist was entranced by Mellnik's story and responded with a description of what MIS-X did to assist men trapped behind German lines. Its primary purpose there, he explained, was to rescue downed airmen as well as maintain communications with those inside German POW camps. Monopoly game boards and checkerboards loaded with real currency and forged documents were smuggled into camps throughout Germany. Chess pieces, shaving brushes, and other hollow items were packed with compasses, tools, and money. Decks of playing cards, when stripped of their backs and laid out, became full-color silk maps of Europe. Cribbage boards were actually radios, and rubber shoe heels were carved with the word "Visa" and other official stamps that could be inked and imprinted on forged papers.

Mellnik could barely contain himself.

"Why aren't you operating on Mindanao?" he asked, incredulous.

"Many reasons," replied Rosenquist. "First off, we're not bombing the Philippines—yet—so there's no urgent escape-and-evasion training required. Second, we had no information about conditions on the islands; your group was the first to bring back any solid data. Third and last, we had no way of getting to you! Darwin, Australia, our closest base, is twelve hundred miles from Davao."

Mellnik then outlined the very new Seventh Fleet submarine operation that was ferrying supplies to the guerrillas from Australia. Rosenquist responded with the confident tone of a man accustomed to overcoming the difficult and dangerous: "Well, then," he said, "we could reach the Mindanao prisoners by that means."

An elated Mellnik agreed. And, he ventured, there was one particular guerrilla unit on the island, headed by a Lieutenant Colonel Claro Lauretta, that already had the manpower to storm DAPECOL and rescue the prisoners. "All Lauretta needs," Mellnik said, "are supplies and guidance. I know that springing two thousand prisoners sounds like a major undertaking, but if you could see how well they function in that jungle area, you'd agree with me. I have it in mind to persuade GHQ to do something along those lines."

"I'll volunteer for that rescue operation," said Rosenquist. "I've had training in escape-and-evasion techniques. I'd like to put it to practical use."

"Well, if you do go in," Mellnik said, "it will have to be under MacArthur and GHQ's auspices; no one can operate for long without guerrilla support, and the guerrillas look to General MacArthur."

"I wouldn't have it any other way."

While jubilant at this turn of events, Mellnik felt it only fair to disclose the difficulties of the jungle—its intrinsic dangers to health and life, and the near certainty that a mistake or moment of carelessness would mean certain death.

"I'll chance it," said Rosenquist. "You people took worse risks when you made your break. I'll have GHQ and the guerrillas at my side."

Shortly afterward, Mellnik was contacted by General Richard K. Sutherland, MacArthur's Brisbane-based chief of staff, who was then in Washington at a war planning conference. With Pacific strategy beginning to crystallize, MacArthur had tapped Sutherland to negotiate his priorities with the War Department. In fact, Sutherland traveled between Brisbane and Washington extensively for this purpose. When he heard that Mellnik was in town, he requested a meeting with his old colleague from prewar Manila days.

"Sorry I couldn't welcome you in Brisbane, Steve," Sutherland said when they got together. "But I read your entire report with great interest— it has caused comment at the highest level of government! Tell me, what are your plans for the future?"

Mellnik said that General Willoughby had requested he return to Brisbane to work on guerrilla matters at GHQ. Sutherland nodded approvingly. "Excellent. It's about time we beefed up that new Philippine Guerrilla Section."

Remembering the contentiousness between Willoughby and Whitney on this point, Mellnik carefully pivoted the conversation back to rescuing the POWs at the Davao Penal Colony. He again described to an attentive General Sutherland the island's tough and well-organized guerrilla assets, with specific praise for Colonel Lauretta's unit that had controlled the Davao region so effectively since the fall of the Philippine government. Mellnik then repeated, nearly word for word, what Lauretta had told him one night regarding a possible POW rescue:

"'Steve,' he said, 'we've been operating effectively against the Japs without support for sixteen months. We are an agricultural island, so we have plenty of food, and some of the best-known physicians and trained nurses in the Philippines are operating clinics in the hills for guerrillas and civilians alike.

" 'My headquarters are about seven miles from the penal colony. The heavily jungled area in between is under absolute guerrilla control. So we could easily raid the colony, which has garrisoned, at most, two hundred and fifty Japanese soldiers—mostly low-ranking guards. But we cannot do it without more ammunition.

" 'It's a matter of simple arithmetic,' Lauretta said. 'So you see, I have four times the manpower of the Japs at the penal colony, and control the entire area between the prison camp and my headquarters, but I have only one hundred and fifty rifles. If I had a thousand rifles, we could overrun the colony and move the POWs to the mountains, where we have the resources to protect and feed them. The Japs simply don't have the troop numbers or knowledge of the terrain to challenge that.' "

A rapt Sutherland did not interrupt, and Mellnik continued full steam ahead: "Lauretta said they could take rifle and supply delivery from a surfaced navy submarine after sunset. It's already been done many times and works beautifully," he said. "His men wait in nearby *bancas*"—a canoe-shaped boat indigenous to the Philippines—"exchange recognition signals, load the supplies onto the *bancas*, and get them ashore. The sub is exposed only briefly, and the guerrillas have hours of darkness to move the supplies to safety."

Mellnik emphasized the guerrillas' unique dominion over Mindanao, as opposed to other islands in the Philippines. To curtail guerrilla control on Mindanao, the Japanese would have to send ten times as many men as they now had. He then told Sutherland about his meeting with Lieutenant Harold Rosenquist and MIS-X—about which, to Mellnik's surprise, even Sutherland knew little.

He explained MIS-X's capability for supporting behind-the-lines resistance. Not only could they arm and train the guerrillas in the art of rescue, escape, and evasion, he said, but also they could help map out multiple prisoner escape routes. Mellnik then related Rosenquist's offer to lead this very mission. "General," he concluded, "I think we have the ingredients for a successful jailbreak."

Sutherland had heard more than enough to be convinced. Mellnik's knowledge was detailed, and the information well presented, eliminating any concern that the former POW was pursuing the rescue plan out of guilt or outsized rage at his former captors. He had made a strong and persuasive case.

"It's a wonderful idea," Sutherland said, "and Harold Rosenquist sounds like the right man for the job. But don't underestimate the difficulties. It's a long way to Mindanao, transportation is limited, and our buildup is just beginning. But with those cargo subs the navy is lending us, we can send a hundred tons of cargo over at a time—and carry out a hundred passengers."

Steve Mellnik nearly skipped out of General Sutherland's Pentagon office. If General MacArthur's chief of staff—one of the most powerful men in the US Army—had viewed his rescue plan as wishful, impractical, or of secondary importance, he most certainly would have said so. Instead, Sutherland *approved* it.

The cargo subs that Sutherland mentioned referred to GHQ's recent agreement with the US Navy to commit a pair of Seventh Fleet submarines to supply the Philippine guerrillas. As agreed previously, the navy counterpart in the clandestine supply and intelligence operation would be naval reserve officer Commander Chick Parsons.

The army-navy negotiations over the subs had been delicate. Parsons's boss, Captain Arthur McCollum, and McCollum's boss, Seventh Fleet Commander Admiral Arthur S. Carpender (a vocal MacArthur detractor), had wanted a few things in exchange for lending from their precious submarine supply, particularly for fateful missions into enemy-controlled waters. Could MacArthur deliver coast-watcher reports of the navy's hit-and-run strikes against Japanese shipping in Philippine waters? The navy was sure that it was having measurable success with these raids, but its subs did not stick around to see if the ships it hit actually sank. They could get credit for these "kills" only with confirmed reports from coastwatchers in the Philippines—who reported directly to MacArthur.

When Whitney agreed to forward the coast-watcher reports to the navy, a deal on loaning its submarines was struck. That final detail also resolved Mellnik's one remaining logistical question regarding the Davao prisoner rescue. The freed men could be rotated out of Mindanao in these very submarines. With this, he immediately began devising a detailed rescue plan to present for General Sutherland's approval.

23

★　★　★

SECRETS INSIDE THE
OXYGEN TENT

DECEMBER 1943· EVEN IN his miserable, pneumococcal state, Bill entertained a feverish reverie inside an oxygen tent at the Naval War College infirmary. *A prisoner rescue mission? Is it too good to be true?* The dreamy vision came and went as if regulated by his wildly fluctuating body temperature. How hot he was, how cold now! The monotonous *whirrrr-tap-tap* of the oxygen pump, the beads of moisture on the plastic windows, the dampness of the sheets, the din inside the rubber enclosure—all combined to challenge his tether to reality as the monstrous double pneumonia fought to take over his lungs.

At a series of Pentagon briefings during Bill's brief Thanksgiving trip home—hardly a respite from the long hours of coursework and drills at the War College—he was stunned to learn from the Seventh Fleet's intelligence officer, Mac McCollum, that a plan to rescue the prisoners at Davao Penal Colony on Mindanao was in the works. Ever since March 1943, when Helen and Arthur were notified of the change in Barton's status from missing in action to prisoner of war, Bill had sought to triangulate his precise location by every possible means. When Barton's first, electrifying postcard subsequently arrived at Lilac Hedges from "Military Prison Camp Number Two," he confirmed this meant Davao Penal Colony on Mindanao.

Captain McCollum had also been elated to learn of the plan, for both personal and professional reasons. He too had a family member—his favorite first cousin, Shivers McCollum—being held at Davao. Bill's first question was inevitable: "After they're rescued from the prison camp, how the hell are they getting them out of the Philippines?"

"By navy submarine," came the answer, as though from the breath of an angel.

McCollum explained the arrangement that he and Admiral Carpender had negotiated with MacArthur's staff regarding GHQ delivery of coastwatcher confirmations of enemy ships sunk by US Navy submarines lurking in Philippine waters. With this proof, the navy would finally get due credit for its serial successes eliminating Japanese vessels. And besides, the two submarines McCollum had offered, *Narwhal* and *Nautilus*, weren't useful for combat: their torpedo capacity was limited, and their diving time slow. But with significant interior capacity, they were ideal for ferrying guerrilla supplies in—and men out.

McCollum had nothing but praise for the subs' covert trial missions under Commander Chick Parsons. Bill remembered Chick from his astonishing arrival in Washington from occupied Manila the previous fall. He was now back in Australia working to supply the Filipino guerrillas. It was Parsons who had arranged sub passage out of Mindanao for the ten escaped prisoners from Barton's camp.

McCollum explained the now-standard operating procedure: After unloading supplies, Americans who had been trapped behind enemy lines since the fall of the Philippines were boarded onto the empty subs. First evacuated were those of political or military significance, followed by American civilians, and, finally, other asylum seekers. As many as possible, as quickly as possible—that was the imperative. Parsons had been given significant leeway to save as many American lives as he could. McCollum had said they wanted to save these prisoners. "Not just Shivers—all of them."

The news had seemed incredible to Bill at the time, and now, in his oxygen-tent delirium, even more so. He liked—no, cherished—the fact that the navy would play a role in the covert operation. And what luck that the rescue was to be of prisoners from Barton's camp! Of course, he could tell their mother nothing of this, not until Barton was out safely. Bill so looked forward to that moment.

When would it take place? Not sure, replied McCollum, but the mastermind of the operation, Lieutenant Harold Rosenquist from MIS-X, meant business—that much was clear. Rosenquist would depart for Australia in January, but he was already hard at work on the rescue plan, McCollum explained.

There were risks, of course. The escapees' sworn statements cast plenty of doubt on any prisoner's ability to survive his ordeal much longer. Could Rosenquist get to Davao in time? Get them out without a bloodbath? Every worry spiked a coughing fit and expulsion of phlegm into the sputum cup.

Bill had paid close attention to any mention of MacArthur's GHQ during the Washington briefings he'd attended over Thanksgiving. For each section in Brisbane—G-1 (Personnel), G-2 (Intelligence), and so on— there was a corresponding oversight unit at the War Department. Useful information on developments in Brisbane could be extracted from these Washington counterparts.

Clouding matters right now was the fact that Courtney Whitney—no longer General Willoughby, who, Bill understood, had greater sympathy for the prisoners of war—had total control over Chick Parsons and his submarine supply missions. Rosenquist couldn't execute a rescue operation without access to those subs. It was no secret that "Colonel" Whitney was more MacArthur loyalist than military professional, one of a select circle of GHQ insiders that had fled Corregidor with the general—as well as partaken of enormous last-minute payments by the Philippine government to exiting US Army leadership before the doomed command was abandoned. Wealthy civilian Whitney had also been MacArthur's prewar Manila attorney, and the general placed considerable trust in him.

Of all the general's aides, Whitney seemed the most focused on ensuring the success of MacArthur's all-consuming objective: returning to the Philippines in a reputation-restoring blaze of glory, forever removing the humiliating blot of defeat.

Given Whitney's narrow objective and bewildering power at GHQ, it was unclear how MacArthur's overriding objective of retaking the Philippines squared with Washington-based Rosenquist's orders to rescue these prisoners—from the very island where the general planned to make his initial landing. Maybe it wouldn't matter. After all, Sutherland, MacArthur's chief of staff, had already approved the mission, hadn't he?

Still, there was cause for worry, especially given GHQ's obsession with interference from Washington. Normally Bill didn't concern himself with the army's petty rivalries or gnarled bureaucracy; there was plenty in the navy to keep him busy. But the question begged an answer: How would Brisbane's complicated office politics affect the rescue plan?

He remembered MacArthur's early and emphatic refusal of OSS intelligence support from Washington; it would be inefficient, the general had said. But everyone knew the real reason: MacArthur wanted complete control of intelligence gathering and distribution within his command area, *especially* with respect to the Philippines.

THE SEVERE BOUT OF pneumonia had Bill alternately gasping for air and coughing up blood-stained phlegm, prompting his transfer to Newport Naval Hospital. Even Eleanor Roosevelt's anxious phone calls to the night nurses ("Yes, this is Mrs. Roosevelt calling again. Can you tell me, please, how is Billy Mott?") did little to buoy his spirits or condition. He'd been lying there for three days, teetering on the edge of delirium as his fever climbed and plummeted, climbed and plummeted.

Bill could see the nurse through the tent's rubber-seamed windows, periodically checking the oxygen-ration meter, the pumping apparatus, and the tent's temperature readings. What a hell of a time to get sick. For now, all he could do was dream of this rescue plan's success and a Pacific reunion for Bill, Benny, and Barton.

24

★ ★ ★

HERO OF BATAAN VERSUS
THE WAR DEPARTMENT

IN THE FALL AND winter of 1943, the Davao escapees, especially Major William Dyess, continued to chafe under the government's gag order forbidding them from divulging any details of their imprisonment and escape. Dyess had become so outraged that he requested a meeting with General "Hap" Arnold, chief of the army air forces, to appeal for his help. While sympathetic, Arnold told Major Dyess there was nothing he could do. The Joint Chiefs of Staff had not changed their official position: the matter remained classified at the highest level of national security. Arnold could arrange a flight command in Europe for Dyess, but he was powerless to help the hero of Bataan get his story aired.

But the war censors were worried about Dyess, and for good reason. Possessed of the Silver Star, Legion of Merit, and Distinguished Service Cross with an Oak Leaf Cluster, Major William Edwin Dyess was already well known to the American public. The tough Texan's daring exploits against the Japanese had been splashed across every newspaper's front page throughout the slow, agonizing fall of the Philippines.

Stories abounded about his daring seaborne raid against Japanese amphibious landings. He had personally led twenty of his men and wiped out an entire enemy battalion. Then, with one of the few remaining airplanes on the Bataan Peninsula, Dyess took to the skies, alone and incredibly outnumbered. Yet he succeeded in destroying an enemy supply dump and sinking a twelve-ton Japanese transport, a pair of hundred-ton motor launches, and several loaded barges in Subic Bay. In the same daring run, he also seriously damaged another six-thousand-ton Japanese vessel. One article dubbed him the "Red Baron of the Philippines."

Pressure to grant his story's release swelled like an untapped fire hose, due largely to Dyess's own efforts. Ever since his escape, he had used his name recognition for one high purpose: to reveal what was really happening to the tens of thousands of prisoners left behind in the Philippines. He was certain that the resulting outcry would become a force in itself —one powerful enough to elevate, once and for all, the subordinate status of the war with Japan.

Dyess was just as sure that the resulting publicity would shame the Japanese into improving treatment of their prisoners. He was astounded that official Washington was preventing him from going public—and even more astounded by the given reasons. The War Department was holding firm that publicizing the story would *further* endanger those still in captivity, as well as jeopardize the mission of the *Gripsholm*, the neutral Swedish merchant ship delivering the desperately needed Red Cross boxes to POWs throughout the enemy-controlled Pacific. Again, Dyess disagreed vehemently. The prisoners would fare better, he countered, because the Japanese hate nothing more than being shamed publicly.

While the War Department may have named these concerns, its true motive for muzzling the escapees was common knowledge in closed military circles: that releasing the story now would derail the Allied grand strategy of prioritizing the European war—just as plans for the seminal cross-Channel invasion were entering their final, climactic stages. The policy of defeating Germany first, and then Japan, had been born out of a consensus that the former was the more powerful and destabilizing opponent; final implementation of that strategy could not be jeopardized. General Marshall had cautioned repeatedly since Quebec that when the Japanese atrocities did come to light, the home front would be as outraged as it had been following the attack on Pearl Harbor. Their eyes would turn toward avenging the enemy in the Pacific, and the hand of war strategy would be forced to follow.

From the start, however, the War Department's attempts to silence the escapees—especially Dyess—had been flustered and ineffectual. First, it sent the feisty pilot to "recuperate" at the Greenbrier resort in West Virginia, which had been converted temporarily to an army hospital (named Ashford General) for recuperating soldiers returned from the front. Dyess was placed in the hospital's top-security wing. But the news media knew how to get to the Greenbrier, and whisking away the freshly escaped war hero only intensified their interest in breaking what was surely a headline-grabbing tale. Newspapermen from all over the country swarmed the coffee shops in nearby White Sulphur Springs, waiting for their chance.

Throughout the final months of 1943, conservative maverick Colonel McCormick—owner of the *Chicago Tribune* and long a thorn in Roosevelt's side—was adding First Amendment muscle to his quest for government clearance to publish Dyess's account. The War Department finally allowed veteran *Tribune* reporter Charles Leavelle to take down Dyess's story at the Greenbrier, but Leavelle was not given permission to publish it. Now his fourteen-part series was ready to go, but the War Department still declined to permit its release, repeating its national security concerns.

When the *Gripsholm* returned unmolested from the Pacific after completing its dispatch of Red Cross packages to Allied prisoners of war, the newspaper renewed its petition for release of the Dyess story. With the ship's humanitarian mission no longer at risk, the *Tribune* argued, it was the paper's constitutional right to report this important story.

Leaks were springing too, despite the blanket gag order, worrying the censors all the more. Horror stories from others repatriated from the Philippines had reached the Bataan Relief Organization chapters that had been created by POW families across the country and were hinted at in their newsletters. Now these groups were joining ranks with the *Tribune*'s growing band of advocates to ratchet up pressure on the government to allow release of the story.

Even Great Britain, which had plenty to lose by a radical change in American sentiment, now favored the story's publication. Why? The British had several times more prisoners in Japanese hands than the Americans did—caught when the former colonies Singapore and Malaya fell early in the war.

In a December 1943 memorandum to the Joint Chiefs of Staff, President Roosevelt himself revealed an increasing inclination to release the story. He requested a recommendation from the JCS as to when, not whether, the White House should permit its release. Then a tragic but galvanizing event occurred just before Christmas.

By this time, a fully recovered William Dyess—promoted again, to lieutenant colonel—was in California flying practice drills in preparation for his return to combat. On December 22 his P-38 Lightning caught fire while on a training mission over the heavily populated city of Burbank. In heroic Dyess fashion, he remained aloft in his burning aircraft—despite ample opportunities to bail out safely—in order to guide the crippled aircraft to a vacant lot on Myers Street. His action saved the lives of countless civilians on the ground.

His plane crashed, however, killing William Dyess on impact. The tragic event was the fatal blow to Washington's resolve to contain the POW story. Dyess's grieving—and media savvy—father, Judge Richard T. Dyess, as well as Colonel McCormick, was now threatening to have a member of Congress read the entire story into the *Congressional Record*.

After a final flurry of tense meetings and consultations in Washington, a compromise was reached: an official joint army-navy statement would first be made public regarding the sworn statements of the escapees. Following its release at midnight, January 28, 1944, Charles Leavelle's fourteen-part series would be published.

25

★ ★ ★

BAD TIDINGS

ON JANUARY 16, 1944, in New York City, Helen Cross made the following diary entry:

> *Rosemary came to see us tonight, a respite from her work for the*
> *Commandant at the Brooklyn Navy Yard. Her news was so disquieting*
> *that Arthur and I lay awake all night practically. The navy has struck*
> *us foul blows—I wish none of mine had put on their uniform.*

Helen was tense for the rest of Rosemary's visit, barely able to contain her anxiety. She and Arthur had hoped to distract themselves from their ceaseless worries by spending January in New York City—to escape the isolating snows at Lilac Hedges, visit friends, attend the theater. But with Benny back in the Pacific and Bill soon to be, and with no word from Barton since September—and little, at that—the unconfirmed rumors had Helen on edge.

The next few days passed slowly, cruelly. Her diary entries from January 17 to 21 recorded forced distractions, including her attendance at the Broadway performance of *The Duke in Darkness*, and Olympic gold medalist Sonja Henie's figure skating show at Madison Square Garden. She also went to Red Cross headquarters to again partake in packing boxes destined for Allied prisoners of the Japanese, hoping that she might overhear something there to refute for a day, an hour, Rosemary's troubling report.

ON JANUARY 25, 1944, Bill's train rolled into Grand Central's bustling track yard. Still recovering from his bout of pneumonia at the War College, he buttoned his long overcoat before shouldering into New York's damp, snowy streets. Bill was thinner from his hospitalization, and he still had a deep, raspy cough, but he wanted to say good-bye to Helen and Arthur before leaving for the war zone. He had another mission in coming to see them, too, and not a happy one.

Despite the icy wind tunneling up the avenues, he walked the several blocks to the Henry Hudson Hotel on West Fifty-Seventh Street. It would give him a little more time to decide exactly what he wanted to say, and how. Feeling compelled to prepare them, Bill had decided to come tell them in person about the coming publication of Dyess's account before the story broke in the newspapers. He wished he could share the counterbalancing good news, but of course that was out of the question. The risk of Helen Cross not keeping that secret was greater than the risks inherent in the rescue operation itself.

It was just past five o'clock in the evening, but blacked-out New York was winter-dark, chill, and comfortless. Still, the hotel was not difficult to spot: the boxy high-rise loomed over the aging brownstones on West Fifty-Seventh like a Nebraska grain elevator. Entering through its revolving door, Bill made for the lift. The lobby's music and conversation faded as the car creaked up the shaft, stopping several times before finally reaching the fifteenth floor, giving Bill a few more minutes to rehearse.

When the elevator operator called out "Fifteen!" and cranked open the lift's brass accordion door, Bill headed toward room 1547 in a state of half anticipation, half dread. When he reached their room, he put an end to his internal deliberations, took a deep breath, and gave three quick raps on the door.

His heart jumped when his mother answered, smiling up at him. She was quickly joined by Arthur, who took Bill's damp woolen coat from him but kept the other hand, for an overlong moment, on his stepson's shoulder. "Bourbon?" he offered, gesturing proudly to the makeshift bar he had set up in their small accomodation. Bill gladly accepted the drink offer.

As Arthur prepared the beverages, Bill couldn't help but notice how tired and careworn both he and his mother looked. What else did he sense? Something told him that their seeing him uniformed and ready to depart— even his new commander's bars—triggered more anxiety than pride.

They sat with their cocktails, uncomfortably close in the tiny quarters. Bill showed them recent photographs of Adam and baby Janie ("almost eight months old!") and exhausted every other possible family topic until Bill knew the time had come. He took two long draughts of his bourbon and water, more than half the glass, in preparation for the conversation's next phase.

"There are some other things I thought you should know," he started. At this, they sat still, listening expectantly.

"The Joint Chiefs of Staff," he said, choosing his words carefully, "met earlier this week and decided to recommend the release of a story about the Japanese and their"—he paused, thinking—"*treatment* of the prisoners of war in the Philippines." Helen leaned forward and clasped her hands, appearing to believe something good was coming. Here was Rosemary's rumor, debunked! Arthur sat back and crossed his legs, reserving judgment. They seemed to barely breathe.

"You remember," Bill resumed, "there was an escape from a prison camp on Mindanao in the Philippines last spring? Barton's camp?" They nodded silently, but their expressions registered *That had been good news, hadn't it?*

"Well, when those men got out, they gave sworn statements on every aspect of their . . ."—he paused again—"experiences. But the War Department would not allow them to divulge any of the details—not even to their own families—for fear the Japanese might retaliate against the prisoners still being held. Among other reasons, they did not want the revelations to get leaked and possibly interrupt delivery of those Red Cross boxes." On this last point, he gestured to his mother, knowing how much effort she had devoted to the packing project.

Helen and Arthur nodded again, but with visibly waning enthusiasm at the word "retaliate." Still, this was perfectly acceptable so far; they knew Barton was among the hopeful recipients of the boxes. Packing them had brought Helen almost as much satisfaction, she'd mused, as they likely would bring the prisoners themselves. Here had been something she could *do* to manage her pain.

"But now," Bill continued, "the Joint Chiefs think—and the president thinks—that it's time for the American people to know about these atrocities."

"Atrocities?" Arthur repeated in his proper British accent. He shifted in his chair. "What do you mean, atrocities?"

Bill fingered the rim of his glass before responding. He hadn't intended to put himself in this corner. "Well, actually, before I get into all *that*, I have some good news. Some very good news. Just this week past, I spoke with one of those escaped prisoners, the navy man. He knew Barton, and saw him in April, just before they got out."

"Was it as far back as April?" Arthur asked. "You do mean April of 1943, I assume?"

"Well, yes, but it took some time to get them back to the States," Bill said, trying not to sound defensive. "This fellow said that when they left,

Bart was alive and in pretty good shape, considering. In fact, he said that Barton had done real credit to himself under difficult circumstances. Other prisoners look up to him, he told me—the ensigns especially. I thought you would like to know that." Bill remembered his own flush of pride when he'd heard this about his brother.

Helen leaned back in her chair and let a moan escape her lips. Arthur, in an effort to check another of his wife's teary descents, jumped in. "Well, that *is* good news, Bill; let us pray it is still the case *now*." Bill nodded. That round had ended in a draw.

Helen and Arthur could tell by Bill's demeanor that something hard was coming. They had grown accustomed, over time, to Bill's method of breaking the sparing news he had gathered about Barton. First came the good news and reasons why they should be encouraged, updates from well-placed sources—after which came the less good news, often couched in maddeningly optimistic language.

Tonight was different, they detected; they were about to hear something from which even Bill couldn't protect them. Helen braced for affirmation of Rosemary's rumor (of tortured prisoners), which had plagued her since hearing it. Bill took another long draught of his drink, nearly empty now. He then started talking again, a little faster.

"So, anyway, back to the other. I thought you ought to know ahead of time that the story these prisoners had to tell about their experience in the Philippines is going to be published—in all the papers—sometime in the next week, I expect. And it's, well, I wanted you to be prepared that some of it is quite graphic."

He paused again and then said, "Frankly, you might be better off not even reading it." For several seconds—the seeming length of an eternity—the three of them said nothing. Bill broke the silence.

"Remember, the best information so far is that Barton has come through. And the thinking now is that when this story is made public, the

Japanese will be shamed into treating the remaining prisoners . . . better. They know they are losing right now. General MacArthur himself is preparing a stern warning to the Japanese that's going to be released with the government's statement.

"I just thought you should be prepared—for the media sensation around it all, too," he finished, wishing he had not used the word "sensation."

What registered on their faces when Bill stopped talking was that if Bill was willing to say to them words and phrases such as "atrocities" and "really bad," given his propensity to soft-pedal the negative to them, this must be *really* bad.

"Billy, dear, you must tell us, what exactly is this story going to say?" Helen entreated, almost in a whisper.

Worn down by the conflicting desire to both shield and inform them, Bill proceeded with mixed emotions to reveal the nature and content of the escapees' sworn statements, all of which he'd read several times. While omitting the most chilling details, he went as far as he did because he knew they *would* read the story—and would have lost their trust in him had he kept it from them.

What Bill did keep hidden was that he too was angry—very angry. He was in a pent-up, self-blaming, roiling rage for being the very person who had unwittingly put Barton, despite his best intentions, in harm's way. It had eaten at him day and night for weeks, months, and now years. Only getting on a ship and getting to the front—and eventually to the Philippines itself—would relieve the building pressure in his chest.

When he finished talking, Bill looked down at his hands and rubbed his Academy ring, a habit when he was nervous. "They will pay with their lives, Mother," he blurted out, feeling the color in his cheeks rise. "Their army hasn't just been lying to the International Red Cross; they've been lying to their own people. This story will—"

He stopped abruptly. His mother had buried her face in her hands and begun to sob. Arthur, who had sat pale and stoic throughout Bill's difficult revelations, moved only when Helen broke down—raising his right hand, trembling, as a signal to Bill to pause.

Her hair fell forward, thrown out of place by her shuddering. Bill saw streaks of gray that he had never noticed before and suddenly realized how Barton's removal from her life had utterly transformed their mother. It was as though a vital organ had been ripped from her core, and she could not get on without it.

Bill saw full force that no matter how hard he or Benny or even Rosemary tried to make her proud, to fight the good fight, this pain was deep and untouchable. There was no earthly remedy for it. He had never felt so helpless.

Bill said no more about the impending news story after that, except to again suggest tenderly that she avoid reading it. All he could muster was to repeat, "The Japanese will pay for what they've done, Mother; you can be sure of that." At this, Helen shored herself up and narrowed her eyes contemptuously.

"By the time *they* get around to it, it will be too late for Barton, I fear," she said angrily, her old imperiousness making a brief reappearance. "*They*," Bill knew, meant all the people he worked for, right to the top.

The visit did not last much longer. He embraced his mother and shook Arthur's hand after putting on his overcoat and reclaiming his cap from the end table. "I am doing the best I can, please know that at least," he said, his voice thick but the words forceful and clear. They nodded.

"Be careful, Billy dear," Helen said, regaining her composure. "I do need at least one son left to carry on." Bill was both touched and taken aback, just as he had always been by her brief spasms of warmth. This was the best he could hope for, he understood now.

THREE DAYS LATER, A Friday, Helen remained in her New York hotel room for the entire day with the dreaded copy of the *New York Times*. Her eyes welled with tears each time she reread the opening line of the front-page story. "A pent-up story of atrocities perpetrated by the Japanese army on the captured heroes of Bataan and Corregidor was released by the United States government today in sickening detail."

Contrary to Bill's advice, she pored obsessively over the article, alternately sobbing and lying down. Arthur was stricken, too, but by early afternoon, he implored his wife to get dressed and go for a walk with him. Getting some fresh air would help them both, he urged. But Helen declined, remaining in her bedclothes the entire day.

The story went on for pages, the details beyond the opening paragraphs so much worse than her worst expectations that Helen had to pause every few lines to absorb the shock. Before switching off the light and ending the day's misery, she opened her diary and unscrewed her fountain pen, hand shaking slightly:

> The Japanese atrocity stories are out. Oh God! They cannot be true!
>
> A million bayonets pierce my heart—my dear one, my lad of peace and kindliness—where are you? How fare you, beloved one? I die for you in your pain. No food, no solace in this life until Barton comes! If only I could bear each insult, torture, pain for him. I will not even call on the name of God again.

And the next day, written diagonally across the page, was only: "Sick, sick, in body and mind."

By the end of January, the story had been told and retold in thousands of newspapers and magazines across the country and around the world. It punched the public with predicted emotional force and the response was universally vengeful. At the Brooklyn Navy Yard's ceremonial christening of the USS *Missouri* the day after the story's release, a somber Vice President Harry S. Truman stated, "May this great ship be an avenger to the barbarians who wantonly slaughtered the heroes of Bataan."

Whether Helen saw the coverage of the *Missouri* ceremony in the New

York newspapers is unknown. There were no further entries in her diary until February 6, 1944. On that day, she wrote:

> For Arthur, I cannot go on this way. I must keep living in the slipping hope that my boy may come back. And Rosemary came by today too and said, coldly but logically, I suppose, "Either Bart returns or he doesn't. There is nothing you can do to alter that fate. But you can prevent it from killing all of us, Mother."
>
> I _must_, I _will_ face it.

26

★ ★ ★

POLITICS IN BRISBANE

HAROLD ROSENQUIST ARRIVED IN Brisbane in early December, and he and Steve Mellnik went right to work fleshing out the logistical details of the rescue proposal. Under General Willoughby's guidance, they crafted a staff study that covered every aspect of the mission. For comparison purposes, Mellnik also prepared a memorandum on the potential for escape from the Cabanatuan prison camp and the significantly greater logistical challenges it presented. Luzon was far more heavily garrisoned than Mindanao, and Cabanatuan significantly more so than Davao.

In a race against time, they focused primarily on the details of a Davao rescue, which had the greatest potential for success. Mellnik laid out the proposed timetable based on his own escape and knowledge of the island. First, he explained that Rosenquist's submarine would need to rendezvous with local guerrilla units in the waters off the Davao Gulf on the east coast of Mindanao. Once ashore, he would then have to make his way to Major Lauretta, whose Davao guerrilla unit would be central to the plan's implementation.

Under Lauretta's guidance, Rosenquist would then initiate contact with select Davao prisoners. Letters from Mellnik, written on GHQ stationery, would be passed to trusted prisoners inside the camp. This aspect of the operation was not as daunting as it might seem, Mellnik assured Rosenquist, as many locals came and went from the penal colony daily, and prisoner work details moved in and out of the compound frequently.

Once these clandestine contacts were established, the next priority would be to smuggle in vitamins, medicines, and badly needed quinine tablets to bring rampant malaria under control. The prisoners would have to regain as much strength as possible ahead of a mass evacuation.

Rosenquist assured Mellnik that this would be the least of his problems: his MIS-X expertise was camouflaging and smuggling such items past hostile parties. Compared with what his team of experts had concealed and smuggled into German prison camps—money, maps, radios, compasses, even weapons—vitamins, medicine, and quinine tablets would be a cakewalk.

The men spent countless hours refining the elements of the rescue itself, including the logistics of the predawn raid and the distribution of prisoners to multiple safe havens within the Mindanao hill and jungle communities and other outposts under guerrilla control. Sophisticated escape-and-evasion maps, complete with topographical data, were prepared, in addition to "Plan B" maps detailing alternative escape routes to the sea.

Ultimately, the men would be rotated off Mindanao by submarine. *Nautilus* and *Narwhal*, and additional navy submarines as they became available, would provide the conveyance. In the cover memo of the detailed Staff Study submitted for General Sutherland's approval, Mellnik wrote:

"Recommend that Lieutenant Rosenquist, MIS-X, be authorized to proceed immediately to Mindanao and that Colonel Fertig be directed to make arrangements for his trip to Major Claro Lauretta's headquarters. Its proximity to the POW camp . . . makes it the logical point of contact from which active assistance to the POWs can be initiated. It is further recommended that Lieutenant Rosenquist work directly under the auspices of G-2."

General Willoughby signed off on the Staff Study on December 11, 1943, and immediately forwarded it to General Sutherland for final approval. Mellnik and Rosenquist were jubilant when the plan came back in January with General Sutherland's consent, after which he departed Brisbane for Washington for an indeterminate length of time to promote General MacArthur's control of the entire Pacific theater. Rosenquist prepared to depart on the very next Mindanao-bound submarine scheduled for February 16, 1944.

But from the moment Courtney Whitney got Rosenquist's dispatch request and learned the details of the rescue plan, he raised loud and continuous objections. Thus was launched the GHQ battle royal over control of the Philippine theater. The rescue plan—placed under G-2 auspices—had been specifically designed to bypass Whitney and his new Philippine Regional Section, with the exception of his control over its use of the submarines. Rosenquist would need to be transported to Mindanao by submarine, and the freed prisoners evacuated in them.

Whitney objected that the rescue operation would endanger the Mindanao guerrillas' primary goal: the eventual facilitation of MacArthur's return—the principal reason, he argued, that PRS had been supplying the guerrillas in the first place. He further objected that the plan rendered Colonel Wendell Fertig—GHQ's anointed Mindanao guerrilla leader—subordinate to Rosenquist's orders, and by extension, General Willoughby's. Whitney adamantly opposed Rosenquist's "unwarranted" authority over Fertig.

Lacking veto authority, Whitney's tactic was to delay the operation, at which he proved very effective. Each new delay was cleverly disguised as a "concern." As the lives of Davao's prison population hung in the balance, dueling memoranda between PRS's Whitney and G-2's Willoughby locked Australia's army headquarters into inaction. With General Sutherland on a possibly months-long mission to Washington, he was unavailable to break the tie. General Richard Marshall, acting chief of staff during Sutherland's absence, declined to mediate. "I'm staying out of this . . . brawl," he said flatly. "Take the problem up with Sutherland when he returns."

And so, on February 16, 1944, Courtney Whitney's cargo list for the Mindanao-bound USS *Narwhal* emphatically excluded one Lieutenant Harold Rosenquist.

27

★　★　★

"PROCEED TO KWAJALEIN"

IT HAD BEEN A long time coming. Bill slung his duffel over his shoulder and stepped onto the gangway of the USS *Rocky Mount*, the Fifth Fleet's amphibious flagship. Anchored in the central lagoon at Kwajalein, in the heart of the Marshall Islands, "the Rock" had just completed a victorious sweep of the southern half of the Kwajalein chain, the world's largest coral atoll. The operation had been supported by two naval task forces—one, the new, hard-hitting "Fast Carrier Force" (TF 58), and the other led by the battle-hardened *Enterprise* and her screening vessels.

Bill was to report to Admiral Richmond Kelly Turner, Allied commander of the Fifth Fleet's new Joint Expeditionary Force—responsible for the seizing of designated Japanese-held islands across the Central Pacific, and for all naval, air, and landed troops in each operation. Bill's new position was flag secretary to Admiral Turner. He was also designated the fleet's legal officer. Turner desperately needed a new flag secretary; many had already been chewed up and spit out by the famously abrasive admiral.

As head of the Navy Department's War Plans Division in the crisis-ridden years of 1940 to 1942, Turner recalled young Lieutenant Mott as one of the few people there that he hadn't fought with and also that Bill had been quite helpful to him on occasion. In his note requesting Bill's services, Turner wrote:

> Between 1940 and 1942, I was the Director of War Plans in the
> Office of the Chief of Naval Operations. During this period,
> Lt. Commander Mott was on duty in the Office of Naval Intel-
> ligence and very frequently came under my close observation.
> I observed his great energy and attentiveness to duty during
> long hours and well in excess of prescribed hours, including
> most Sundays. I would welcome his attachment to my personal
> staff.

In the exponentially expanded US Navy of 1944, résumés for top staff positions requiring both amphibious and code-and communications backgrounds were "as scarce as glassy seas in the Bay of Biscay," one admiral mused; those selected would require a strong work ethic and hard, on-the-job training. Bill Mott amply satisfied both requirements, and with the rare quality of never having previously crossed hairs with Admiral Turner, his orders to *Rocky Mount* were drawn up.

He was needed immediately. With completion of the Allied occupation of Kwajalein—relatively lightly defended but valuable for its large and deep natural harbor and sturdy, coral-surfaced airfield—Turner's forces had begun planning their next series of amphibious assaults: Eniwetok, followed by Truk and then Saipan, the most prized of the inner protectorates of the Japanese islands. A continuation of the amphibians' thrust across the mid-Pacific, this next phase was designed to pierce the enemy's perimeterisland defensive arc that protected mainland Japan itself.

★   ★   ★

HIS NEW HOME, FLAGSHIP USS *Rocky Mount,* was unlike any ship Bill had ever boarded. Its superstructure was dominated by a geometric tangle of radar and radio gear. Above the bridge was another curious gnarl of transmitters of various shapes, sizes, and heights, all positioned next to a phalanx of receivers. In most other respects, *Rocky Mount* resembled little more than an old supply transport—a purposeful disguise. Experience had shown that enemy bombers went after this sort of ship last.

Rocky Mount was not only the Amphibious Force Command head-quarters; it was home to its Combat Information Center (CIC), the fleet's electronic nerve hub, and served as the floating residence for top brass from every service taking part in each island offensive. The Rock was to Pacific amphibious campaigns what the Map Room was to the world war: the decision-making epicenter for all commands. In sight of all action at all times, it was the lead vessel in every action. The monumental challenge of coordinating combined amphibious operations, among the most demand-ing of military missions, was soon to become Bill's life—heart, soul, body, and mind.

For the three months prior to Bill's arrival at Kwajalein, Admiral Turner and the amphibians had been busy seizing Makin and Tarawa Is-lands and gaining a toehold in the Gilberts and Marshalls. But personnel losses from those operations had numbered in the several thousands due to stiff enemy resistance, inadequate resources, and flaws in their advance reconnaissance—as well as in planning and execution. This was especially the case with Tarawa.

The objective had been narrow: seize Tarawa's strategic mid-Pacific airfield. But the losses were staggering and caused a storm of stateside pro-test. Was that seven-hundred-yard-wide scrap of mid-Pacific coral and sand, smaller than New York's Central Park, really worth the lives of a thousand marines, and twice that wounded? MacArthur wasted no time pouncing:

he placed square and very public blame on the navy for Tarawa's "tragic and unnecessary massacre of American lives."

Kelly Turner was not taking time off to celebrate his recent promotion to vice admiral; the next objective was imminent, and lessons from Tarawa needed to be understood and applied. First of all, four million pounds of explosives dropped on the island ahead of the landings had not made a dent in enemy positions. Unmolested, 4,600 Japanese ambushed the landing marines. Another ugly surprise had been the dual effect of Tarawa's jagged coral reefs and a lower-than-hoped-for tide—a deadly combination of landing conditions that exposed wave after wave of marines to murderous artillery fire as they struggled toward shore through wide stretches of razor-sharp coral.

Admiral Turner wasted no time applying these hard-won lessons to future planning. Naval and air pre-bombardment was revised following grim proof of its ineffectiveness at Tarawa. Henceforward, pre-invasion firepower would focus on destroying specific enemy capabilities, not neutralization. More amphibious landing vehicles (amtracs) with better armor were also ordered, as well as side armor for the marines. And underwater demolition teams were created to search out and clear all natural and artificial beach obstacles ahead of future landings.

And so it was that one of Bill's first reading assignments was to memorize his new boss's post-Tarawa memorandum, "Recommendations for Changes and Improvements in Tactics, Techniques, Existing Instructions and Material," as well as that of Turner's senior amphibious subordinate: Rear Admiral Harry Hill's sobering "Lessons from Tarawa."

According to Bill's position description, he was to "supervise and direct production plans and execution of major amphibious operations." This meant coordinating among a myriad of constituents the logistics and battle plans that make up an expeditionary force invasion: naval support groups; underwater demolition teams; meteorologists; beachhead organization (beachmasters); the amphibious corps; marine personnel; medical personnel; and the strategists who determined the timing and disposition of the multiple landing forces and whether they were variously supplied with rations, water, ammunition, tourniquets, and morphine in advance of battle. And, of course, there would have to be major contingency plans to all the above—for according to naval doctrine, "No battle plan survives contact with the enemy."

Bill read his orders with the appropriate humility of one whose longest prior ship duty was his post-plebe midshipman cruise more than a decade earlier. He was terrified and thrilled in unequal parts by the enormity of the challenge. But the home front had done its part. Turner's Joint Expeditionary Force encompassed 634 ships and more than 300,000 navy, marine, and army personnel. With the country's industrial might ramped up to full war footing, the sailors' joke now was that they could walk for miles across Pacific anchorages without getting wet: the ocean was paved with steel.

BEFORE SETTLING INTO HIS duties aboard *Rocky Mount*, Bill requested permission to board the *Enterprise*, lying astride recently annexed Kwajalein. Time was short: *Enterprise* was preparing to depart for its next enemy raid of Truk. Benny had been cautiously optimistic that he and Bill would intersect at Kwajalein, but he had avoided setting his heart on it, given the potential for snafus in the navy generally and in the middle of a war zone specifically.

So when Bill came through the heavy door of *Enterprise*'s Sky Control, Benny let out a howl of delight. One proud introduction followed another, Benny making great hay out of Bill's new job as "Terrible Turner's" latest flag secretary.

The brothers' reunion was brief but upbeat—until the end, when Bill shared the difficult details of his January visit in New York. He didn't need to brief Benny on the Japanese atrocity story; it had reached the farthest Pacific outposts in no time, smacking Allied forces like a rogue wave. With each printed word, every man on the front lines seethed for revenge.

Bill told Benny of his exchange with one of the Davao escapees while he was recuperating at Walter Reed in Washington. And that "positive developments" had him hoping for a three-brother reunion. When it was time for Benny to share his own news, he wished he had told Bill sooner. But perhaps it was obvious. The toll of alternating days, months, and years of high alert, worry, and fatigue had gathered in darkening ditches beneath Benny's normally bright eyes.

"Bill, I've been on this ship for four years, and I'm proud of the work we've done, what we've accomplished. But I'm exhausted. My marriage is in shambles, and I've only seen Jeanne Marie once in eighteen months. I have put in for a transfer to Washington. I can really help those desk captains there in Ordnance—they need an experienced hand from the field. So I guess that means it's up to you now to see the rest of the way through to Barton."

Bill took in Benny's every word without interrupting. He was a combination of sad and relieved at Benny's news, but not surprised. Remembering his own anxiety during engagement after engagement, wondering if Benny was dead or alive—if it had left *him* emotionally whipsawed, he could only imagine its effect on Benny. Bill knew he would find out soon enough.

They stood together for a few more minutes, having no idea when—or if—they would see each other again. No more was said about Barton, but they did agree that Benny's reassignment was a wise move for their mother's sake, not to mention his own.

Benny fought welling emotion as he watched Bill make his way toward the idling launch that would take him back to *Rocky Mount*. With forced cheerfulness, he called out to his brother, "Just remember, Bill, hell, be *careful*. It can get dicey out here!"

PART
THREE

28

★ ★ ★

THE BEST-LAID PLANS

IN APRIL, 1944, GENERAL Sutherland finally returned to Brisbane. He left behind the bitter scrum in Washington over whose military strategy would dominate the balance of the Pacific War—only to step into the GHQ turf war that had been simmering in his absence. The widening scope of Courtney Whitney's PRS and its control over the submarine missions had become the sorest of points to G-2 generally and to General Willoughby specifically.

As PRS activities had expanded—adding more coastwatchers, clandestine radio receivers, and Filipino agent nets, plus stepped-up supply and support of the guerrillas—so had Whitney's free agency and access to MacArthur. Severely irritated by his rival's increasing stature and erosion of his own authority over Philippine affairs, Willoughby greeted General Sutherland with a formal recommendation for a GHQ reorganization regarding the handling of Philippine affairs. They should be split among staff sections, Willoughby argued, and, as head of G-2 for SWPA, the majority of Philippine activity should be returned to his purview. Willoughby also

asked Sutherland to immediately re-approve the Rosenquist prisoner rescue mission, which had been inexcusably thwarted by Whitney during his
long absence.

For the previous twelve weeks, Willoughby, Mellnik, and Rosenquist
had all tried to placate Whitney with revision after revision of the rescue
plan so that Rosenquist could depart for Mindanao. After Whitney scuttled
his February departure, Rosenquist made a brief diary entry: "Ready to go
on mission, but Whitney's influence too strong." He had begun to fear privately that they were running out of time.

Tensions were exacerbated further by the media sensation over the
Davao escapee story. Whitney and Willoughby had quarreled endlessly
over whether the story's publication had likely worsened (Whitney) or improved (Willoughby) the Japanese captors' treatment of Allied prisoners.
Inevitably, the argument expanded to include their respective opinions on
whether or not this had a bearing on Rosenquist's incipient mission.

When General Sutherland returned to GHQ, Whitney fired off a memo
justifying his actions:

```
My objection to [the plan] lay in the:


(a)  Status given Lieutenant Rosenquist rendering him
     subject only to the direction of G-2, GHQ [Willoughby];

(b)  Rosenquist's unrestricted right to call upon the local
     commander [Fertig] for such personnel, supplies,
     communication and transport facilities and other
     assistance as may be necessary to accomplish his
     mission;

(c)  Establishment of an intelligence system within the POW
     camp by written directive from this Headquarters to
     certain officer prisoners and;

(d)  Plan for mass evacuation or escape of prisoners.
```

```
    . . . I believe that we should but ask these prisoners
to continue to show the fortitude that alone will make it
possible to survive the difficult and trying ordeal which
yet lies ahead.


                        C. W.
```

Sutherland was unmoved by Whitney's arguments, and General Sutherland had the final say—always with MacArthur's presumptive authority. He was MacArthur's top confidant at the time and widely regarded as his full and equal partner. In fact, it was an open secret that General MacArthur was positioning Sutherland for the highest office in the army, one that he himself had held: army chief of staff. As popular as "Court" Whitney was with General MacArthur, Sutherland's power trumped any amount of shameless flattery Whitney could pour on.

RICHARD KERENS SUTHERLAND HAD been unwavering in his endorsement of the Davao prisoner rescue mission from the start—despite the risks it might pose for MacArthur's planned Mindanao landing, for the Mindanao guerrillas, or for the prisoners themselves. To Sutherland, its potential rewards outweighed all imagined downsides.

But to say that General Sutherland had a complicated relationship with the whole idea of POWs would be a serious understatement. For eighteen months, he had been conducting an intense and surprisingly public affair with one Elaine Bessemer Clarke, the Australian wife of a British captain whom the Japanese had taken prisoner at the fall of Singapore.

The married Sutherland had met Clarke and her infant son in Melbourne, Australia, in March 1942, shortly after he, MacArthur, and other senior MacArthur staff had fled the Philippines. According to sources present, Sutherland and Clarke were attracted to each other from the moment they met. The new couple quickly became the subject of endless staff gossip.

When MacArthur's headquarters moved offices from Melbourne to Brisbane, eyebrows rose further as Clarke, her toddler son, the nanny, and their cocker spaniel packed up and made the six-hundred-mile journey with them. And they rose all the more when Sutherland pulled strings and appointed the Australian Clarke a captain in the American Women's Army Corps (WAC), making her the first non-American woman to join those proud ranks. Captain Clarke became the receptionist at GHQ's new Brisbane headquarters at the AMP Building on Queen Street.

The couple's bold intimacy became increasingly apparent over time, with Sutherland playing father to Clarke's young son. All the while, the uncomfortable subject of her POW husband reportedly weighed heavily on them both. It is unknowable whether Sutherland and Clarke's intense relationship propelled his support of the Davao prisoner rescue plan. Was he allaying his guilt by supporting the rescue of an unrelated group of war prisoners? What if the plan had been to rescue the British prisoners in Singapore?

Sutherland's relationship with Clarke would eventually put him in an untenable position with MacArthur, but at the time, Sutherland still had his mentor's full support. So in April 1944, when Sutherland overruled all objections and reasserted his earlier approvals of the rescue mission, even Court Whitney had to accept it. Lieutenant Rosenquist would depart for Mindanao on the next available submarine.

Whitney conceded defeat reluctantly; this was the *third* time Sutherland had ruled in favor of the Rosenquist plan. Yet even as he agreed to arrange Rosenquist's submarine conveyance to Mindanao, Whitney continued deploying delay tactics. In his capacity as head of PRS, he had the final say on *when* submarines could be dispatched to the Philippines. On the April night of Sutherland's latest ruling, Rosenquist confided to his diary, "Okay again by General Sutherland, but again, delays."

Rosenquist did not board the USS *Narwhal* until May 10, 1944, but with cautious optimism, he wrote his boss at MIS-X's secret headquarters in Virginia. Both men understood each and every carefully veiled reference in the letter, including its high praise for Steve Mellnik:

> Lt. Colonel John H. Starr
> P.O. Box 1142
> Alexandria, Virginia
>
>
> May 10, 1944
>
>
> Dear Colonel Starr:
>
>
> At last! After much fussing around, I can write you that my mission is now set and I'm going shortly. The good news came quite unexpectedly after many trying months of nursing the project.
>
> Eventually and without question . . . everything hoped for should materialize. You can be certain, Colonel . . . my designation is fixed and reachable . . .
>
> Knowing the responsibility of this job, perhaps more than people realize, makes enthusiasm secondary to firm patience. I realize the big opportunity to save lives and the joy my presence will bring people who have untiringly waited for word of encouragement.
>
> I pray God I can completely execute the job you have assigned me, through the untiring efforts of one who for so many months has pushed this assignment . . . in the face of many obstacles. For him, and you know of whom I speak, I have the highest admiration and respect. Knowing he will be on the job here is of great consolation to me . . . and I

know that reports will get through to you as he finds them
possible.

My best regards to all at PO Box 1142. I sincerely hope I
can do the job with credit to our Section.

H. A. R.

Rosenquist was delayed another five days at the Darwin rendezvous point without explanation. On May 15, 1944, he confided to his diary: "At last . . . after eleven months, on our way." He estimated that the voyage would take ten days, putting him in Davao by early June.

But on May 27 and 28, a dismayed Rosenquist was still aboard *Narwhal*. He wrote, "We are way off course . . . no contact . . . disappointed . . . navigation lousy . . ." Then again, on May 30: "Marking time . . ." On the thirty-first of May, he reported: "Sight of land through periscope."

That faint outline of land, however, was the *southwest* coast of Mindanao, hundreds of kilometers (hundreds of miles) from Rosenquist's explicitly planned debarkation point near Davao, on the island's *southeast* coast. But Rosenquist had no alternative. He and the other *Narwhal* passengers, weather observers carrying a supply of weapons, pistols, daggers, emergency rations, and numerous thermometers, were told they must debark and make the best of it.

The disoriented party paddled ashore in a rubber boat and, fortunately, was intercepted by local guerrillas instead of the Japanese. Colonel Robert Bowler, the senior-most guerrilla in that part of Mindanao, questioned the group, but Rosenquist declined to disclose his mission. When Bowler told him that Wendell Fertig insisted on seeing him personally before he could proceed, Rosenquist reluctantly agreed. Fertig's Tenth Military District headquarters in the Agusan Valley, however, was even farther from Colonel Lauretta and the Davao Penal Colony than the submarine's erroneous landing point, causing Rosenquist still more costly delays.

The guerrilla-guided journey, however, confirmed everything Mellnik had told him about Mindanao's skilled and fleet-footed guerrilla population. Rosenquist's journey across miles of jungle, enemy-infested mountains, and treacherous inland waterways was made possible only by his seamless conveyance from one guerrilla unit to the next. They fed, housed, and protected him every step of the way, and even arranged for a dentist and barber en route. Rosenquist was impressed.

The orders he carried from GHQ explicitly sanctioned his mission and ordered the guerrillas to fulfill it. They also made clear that Rosenquist reported directly to General MacArthur's command, not Wendell Fertig's:

```
"Captain Harold Rosenquist, O-278037, has been placed
on temporary duty . . . for the purpose of acting as advisor
in the planning of assistance to prisoners of war in your
military area. Such matters will be conducted in accordance
with the policies of [General MacArthur] as communicated
to you from time to time."
```

In addition, he carried letters from Steve Mellnik to specific trusted individuals inside Davao Penal Colony, men who could be relied on to facilitate the escape from the inside. One letter, dated February 10, 1944, was written after the broad publication of the atrocity stories. It was addressed to Lieutenant Colonel Memory "Doc" Cain:

```
                         General Headquarters,
                         Southwest Pacific


Dear Doc,

    It's been almost a year since we talked about things
at Barracks Number 8. I pray you are still there to read
this . . . The country has just heard the news. Congress
```

and the people have sent up a cry that's echoing around
the world. Things are afoot to do things. I won't give
any "target dates." This letter, written from General
MacArthur's headquarters, is sufficient proof of what is
happening. He is taking a great and active interest--I
should know.

Much has to be done, Doc. I'm depending on you to do it. The
source of this message was sent by me to you. Trust him. He is
H. A. R. He will get in touch with you. You've got to consider
yourself C.O. of the camp with this. Mobilize all of [his]
activities. Exercise extreme security precautions . . . Take
your time, be awfully careful, and remember all of this is
being done to speed up the DAY. I cannot reiterate too strongly
that the success of our plans depends on 100% secrecy.

Steve Mellnik

En route to Wendell Fertig's headquarters, Rosenquist encoded a preliminary report for relay to Brisbane once he reached Fertig's radio station.
Despite the serial setbacks and detours, the indefatigable Rosenquist remained optimistic:

Guards and outposts covering trails, roads, and rivers
everywhere; one rifle, fifteen rounds of ammunition per two
men of front line units, who are familiar with respective
sectors. Plan formulated for roadblocks, bridge construction,
trail coverage, and delaying enemy action . . . Troop and
civilian morale high. Our trip untold value.

BUT WENDELL FERTIG—WEARING locally crafted silver stars of
a brigadier general on his collar despite his actual US Army Reserve rank

of lieutenant colonel—was of another mind when Colonel Bowler radioed him that an unannounced submarine had surfaced off the coast of southwestern Mindanao and unloaded five surprise guests: four enlisted weather observers, and one highly ranked intelligence officer on an undisclosed mission "of great importance."

Fertig said to his aide de camp, Commander Wheeler (no relation to Ken), who had delivered the dispatch, "You send a message back to Bowler. Tell him to disarm those weather people and turn their stuff over to people who can use it . . . Make clear," he added sarcastically, "we won't interfere with their basic mission of wetting their fingers to detect which way the wind is blowing."

Fertig was just getting warmed up. "And tell Bowler," he continued, "to make sure these people understand that all persons reporting to Mindanao *must* come under my direct command, and that all activities will be directed by *me*. And Bowler is to tell this Rosenquist that as far as we're concerned, he is a visiting staff officer without authority. Until I find out what his mission is and *I* approve it, he is not to issue orders to any of our men. I need to find out from Headquarters what the hell is going on."

Then Fertig gave Wheeler a second order. "Send a message to GHQ asking them what the hell is going on with Rosenquist. Tell them all activities on the island of Mindanao *must* be controlled by me." Then he muttered, "Thickheads." A bewildered Wheeler left to carry out the orders.

Fertig sat back, absorbing what he had just learned. Weathermen were one thing; hopefully their presence presaged an increase in US air reconnaissance, which hopefully presaged an imminent landing by MacArthur on Mindanao, a moment he had been savoring for some time. But a highranked intelligence officer on a secret mission? That was something else entirely.

Fertig's disposition did not improve when Wheeler returned with a response from Brisbane. "Headquarters," he reported, "says we are to furnish Rosenquist with any aid and assistance he may require."

Fertig spun around, eyes wide. "What is his mission?"

"They won't say," Wheeler said, "just that it's of the 'greatest importance' and that all we have to do is follow orders."

Fertig then spat, "I haven't stayed alive here for over two years by allowing a crowd of dreamers fifteen hundred miles away to tell me what I have to do. And, by God, I'm not going to start now. I'm not going to have them sending special missions in here that could get my tail in a crack without my knowing what's happening until it's too late. Therefore, you will tell Bowler to send this Rosenquist to me, and *I'll* decide whether we'll help him or not."

Since late May, Fertig had been hearing the distinctive drone of US Navy carrier aircraft strafing in the distance. He had interpreted this as further corroboration that MacArthur planned to make his first strike at Mindanao—*his* military district—meaning, hopefully, his place in history would soon be secured. After that first landing, or so he had heard, Allied troops would slog their way north to Leyte, and then Luzon—and its prize, Manila. Both Fertig and the Japanese were expecting this scenario to unfold in the coming weeks.

So when Rosenquist finally arrived at Wendell Fertig's headquarters, the colonel's guard was up. Whatever this stranger was up to, Fertig was determined that it not derail his grand plan at the last minute.

Rosenquist shook Fertig's hand enthusiastically. "It won't be long now," he told the guerrilla leader at their introduction. "I don't know when it's going to be, but it's an open secret it's going to be soon."

He then complimented Fertig on his work of the past two years, adding that GHQ thought that he'd "done one hell of a fine job."

"My instructions are to give you any assistance I can," replied Fertig, in a tone of one unaffected by compliments. "Whether I do depends on whether I decide your mission is practical. I want to make that clear."

Rosenquist replied that it was. He had great confidence in his mission, he said, and the potential for its success had been confirmed by everything he had seen in his smooth guerrilla passage across the island.

Fertig listened without expression, and then replied flatly, "If I decide not to help you, you will remain in this area as a staff officer without command authority, subject to a letter of instruction that will be furnished to you."

Rosenquist was taken aback. Ever since the first mention of this proposed mission, back in Washington the previous summer, he had maintained a singular focus on freeing some two thousand systematically beaten, tortured, and starved Americans. After surviving General Whitney's serial delays, he thought the only remaining obstacle was the enemy.

"I don't mean to be abrupt," Fertig continued. "I just want you to understand that I will be the judge of any operations within my area. Now, just what do you intend to do?"

It was a shocking moment for Rosenquist. Armed with orders from General MacArthur's chief of staff, as well as other weighty documentation from Brisbane's SWPA Headquarters, Rosenquist had imagined that all he needed to do was direct Fertig to put men under his command, no questions asked. To surrender any classified information to Fertig violated everything this intelligence officer—trained and experienced in top secret missions—held dear.

But Rosenquist realized there was no way out: Fertig would have to know if he was to proceed. Moreover, precious time was slipping away. "We intend to free the American prisoners from Davao Penal Colony before they can be moved," he said.

"I have no information that they're about to be moved," replied Fertig, genuinely startled by Rosenquist's confident pronouncement. "When are they going, and *where* are they going?"

Rosenquist answered the question with a question. "Do you think it's impossible to get them out of there?"

"Certainly not," Fertig said. "The prison camp is not heavily guarded. Twelve of my men have already escaped from it. They were working on a road gang under one Japanese guard. One day they rushed the guard, beat him with shovels, and walked away."

Relieved, Rosenquist felt his old enthusiasm return. "How many men do you think I'll need?" he said eagerly.

"Tell me this," Fertig said. "Is headquarters going to supply a hospital ship to pick up the prisoners as soon as they're freed?" The look on Rosenquist's face supplied the answer.

"I know what's going on in that camp," Fertig said. "Some of those men are friends of mine. But can you imagine anything more stupid than releasing two thousand weak and sick men on an overburdened local economy? You'll attempt no such rescue. Headquarters can call my refusal to cooperate with you any damn thing it likes."

Rosenquist was stunned. Fertig's response constituted willful disobedience of a direct order from high command—surely the man knew its potential consequences. Fertig had no trouble reading the disbelief on his face. "You go to Davao and see for yourself," the colonel said, ending the conversation. "But you are to make *no* attempt to get those men out of there."

29

★ ★ ★

INITIATION AT SAIPAN

IN MARCH 1944, WASHINGTON military planners decided the next amphibious operation would be to seize the primary islands of the Mariana atoll. The trifecta conquest of Saipan, Tinian, and the former American base at Guam would be the Allies' bold first strike at Japan's inner defense perimeter. Preparation for a fanatical resistance began immediately.

Operation Forager had two overarching goals: to sever the enemy's north-south supply and communications route, and to secure mid-Pacific bases for the Superfortress of the air, the B-29 bomber. From the Marianas, B-29s could easily reach Japan's home islands and begin fire bombing, a tactic designed to shake the country's resolve and hasten surrender.

The decision to strike the Marianas next was made despite unrelenting pressure from Douglas MacArthur to do something entirely different with the naval forces in the Pacific. He wanted those forces to report to him as soon as possible to support his advance on the Philippines—and sooner rather than later. MacArthur had proposed seizing Rabaul, New Guinea, and then basing the Fifth Fleet there. From that vantage point, the navy could assist him in retaking the Philippines. In a dispatch to General Marshall in Washington, MacArthur wrote:

"I propose that with the completion of the operations in the Marshalls [Kwajalein, et al.], the maximum force from all sources in the Pacific be concentrated [to assist] my drive up to Mindanao."

But the vote taken by the Combined Allied Chiefs of Staff at Cairo, Egypt (Sextant conference) the previous December, concurred with the US Joint Chiefs' recommendation: that whenever there was a conflict over resources, the US Navy's crucial thrust across the Central Pacific would take priority over MacArthur's objectives. Undeterred, MacArthur continued to lobby for a strategy shift in his favor. This was the reason he had dispatched General Sutherland to Pearl Harbor in January 1944: to negotiate this revision with Admiral Nimitz. When that effort failed, Sutherland pushed on to Washington to make the case.

Admiral King had one word for the proposal to divert the bulk of the Pacific Fleet to MacArthur's command—*absurd*. King's negative opinion of MacArthur had been formed early in the war by Admiral Hart's highly charged eyewitness account of the general's role in the disastrous fall of the Philippines. But King's mistrust of MacArthur wasn't the only reason for his opposition. He was convinced that the Central Pacific thrust—which included seizure of the Marianas and additional islands to their west—was the key to dominion over Japan because of their B-29 base potential. Not surprisingly, King had the full backing of Army Air Forces Chief General Hap Arnold.

Furious that the "navy cabal" had won again, MacArthur reacted bitterly to what he viewed as a barely concealed plot to prevent him from taking overall command of the Pacific War. "The navy fails to understand the strategy in the Pacific," MacArthur scolded. But the Joint Chiefs held firm. MacArthur's Mindanao landings would be allowed to proceed only after the Central Pacific forward areas were secured.

★   ★   ★

THANKS TO A COMBINATION of factors, the war in the Pacific was finally getting its share of resources. Admiral King's relentless push for a stepped-up Pacific offensive was key, but so also was home front outrage over the widely publicized accounts of Japanese atrocities against American prisoners. All that was needed now were the right men to lead the effort.

Admirals Nimitz and King had easily agreed that Raymond Spruance, now a vice admiral, should be placed in overall command of the Central Pacific sweep. King, Nimitz, and Spruance had also been unanimous in their choice of Kelly Turner as the Central Pacific's amphibious assault commander. He was bold and brilliant, if exceedingly profane—even by US Navy standards. But in their view, Turner alone had the unique combination of talents and skills to seize the target assets and lead the navy's vast armada of ships and troops all the way to Japan's doorstep.

The amphibians had their work cut out for them. Operation Forager would be their biggest operation so far, by orders of magnitude. Saipan was sacred ground to the Japanese, and a full-blooded samurai defense was expected. Nor was it a tiny islet bluff measurable in yardage. Saipan's seventy-two-kilometer-wide terrain was a hellish montage of coral-aproned beaches, high plateaus, rolling hills, jagged ridges, blind ravines, sheer cliffs, and an extinct volcano—plus a new logistical nightmare for amphibian planners: a vast network of caves.

Saipan's human defenses were also formidable. In addition to a Bushido-stout army, it was home port to Pearl Harbor villain Admiral Chuichi Nagumo and his fleet. It was also home to tens of thousands of Japanese civilians. The stakes were sky-high for both sides, just as they had been at Guadalcanal, but in that action, the navy had snuck into Japan's side yard. At Saipan, they would be breaking into their house. Forager would be an assault of unprecedented scale, and Bill Mott wasted no time immersing himself in the planning.

If he was going to keep this job, he needed to learn quickly, perform optimally, and make Admiral Turner happy. Many of his predecessors had succeeded at the first two but failed at the third. But Bill was optimistic. Hard work had always propelled him toward his goals, and this would be no exception. In this case, he had two aspirations. One was career advancement—stellar performance in this job would ensure his dream of transferring from the naval reserves to the regular navy. The other was to advance toward the Philippines and Barton. Some days he wasn't sure which was the greater motivator.

The planning process itself was byzantine. Fine-tuned sequencing of every land, sea, and air offensive was essential, and a daunting mobile logistics force had to be assembled. Avoiding the sorts of horrific and costly errors that had unfolded at Tarawa was always uppermost in his mind.

He rose well before dawn each morning to analyze documents, maps, memos, manifests, intelligence estimates, and massive to-do lists—and then create his own. He marshaled every scintilla of his accumulated knowledge of complex communications and radio transmission codes and distribution networks among and between the services, in order to build a largely unprecedented mastery of multiservice amphibious assault operations. It was the toughest task he'd ever undertaken, and his new boss was a living, fire-breathing homing device for the slightest human error. President Roosevelt himself had been easier to please.

Battle plans were drafted and redrafted with continuous input from a vast orchestra of individuals from all the services, from Generals Marshall and Arnold to Admirals King and Nimitz. Updated intelligence was layered in daily, requiring more drafting and redrafting. Operation Forager planning was then put to the test, repeatedly, with rigorous landing rehearsals at Maui. After each multiday rehearsal, plans were revised and more rehearsals were conducted.

At Turner's behest, Bill marshaled the preparation of inventories, indexes, and execution orders. The logistics of long-distance provisioning alone seemed infinite. With Saipan 3,500 miles from Pearl Harbor, the closest full supply depot, 120 days' worth of everything was needed for more than three hundred ships' companies. All combatant and auxiliary ships required capacity stores of ammunition, fuel, lubricants, fresh provisions, dry goods, clothing, and medical supplies. An additional 60-day supply was required for the landing forces—some one hundred thousand men in all.

Compounding these dizzying logistics were the complications of fueling hundreds of vessels at sea, with each class of vessel having different protocols. There were also the details of aircraft replacement, repair facilities, salvage operations, and coordination of the four hospital ships to move wounded from the beaches to the ships—with the added consideration that all the above would likely take place in the heat of air and sea battle and in the vicinity of torpedo-bristling enemy submarines.

Coordinating the multiple services' contributions to this quadrille of an assault plan—designed to put eight thousand men ashore every twenty minutes—was another herculean undertaking, alone requiring thousands of man-hours. And, of course, there had to be contingency plans for each one of these carefully laid plans, because battles rarely go according to plan. As samurai warrior Sun Tsu had observed centuries earlier, "Many calculations lead to victory and few calculations to defeat."

Successful amphibious operations also required reliable intelligence estimates of the number and types of enemy forces and the location of fixed artillery and other equipment, as well as anything else that might improve assessment of enemy potential. After collecting such intelligence, the estimates then needed to be scrutinized, questioned, and revised over and over and *over* again. Admiral Turner—in a style that overwhelmed and terrorized nearly everyone around him—demanded it all at his fingertips, funneled to and from him through his fledgling aide and flag secretary.

In addition to these duties, Bill was also the ship's legal and personnel officer, in which capacity he was responsible for issues ranging from promotion and decoration recommendations, to dereliction of duty, drunkenness, and assault. He was also the ship's media censor: he had to read and approve all copy written by the dozens of war correspondents aboard before it could be transmitted from *Rocky Mount*'s communications center. Despite the other demands on his time, Bill attached no small importance to this task. He had witnessed firsthand how one errant news report had the potential to derail the war effort.

Lastly, he was to see that a discreet group of Navajo Indians aboard— whose assignment was the synchronous transmission of radio messages between the flagship and landed parties in their little-known Native American tongue—coordinated properly with their multiple constituents in the amphibious force's complex communications chain. The Navajo code system was valued for its unique ability to transmit real-time battle-status updates to and among units onshore and to and from the fleet without time-consuming enciphering and deciphering.

All this planning was for a landing nearly the size and complexity of the impending Normandy invasion (deferred from May to June, 1944, due to weather)—but which had to be assembled in a fraction of the time. It was the busiest Bill Mott had been in his life. Admiral Turner arose each morning at 0430, and by 0700, the admiral's orderly would have made several trips to Bill's quarters with instructions relating to the full range of matters listed above. So many notes from Turner's personalized notepad would arrive before breakfast each day that Bill came to refer to them as "snowflakes." Like his own boss, Admiral Spruance, Turner famously believed in delegating authority. Bill felt the full brunt of this management style early on.

The only way to become an accepted member of Kelly Turner's rarified inner circle was to be able to interpret and respond to his orders intelligently and on the double, as well as to have the physical capacity to remain alert and quick on the uptake at all hours. One also had to accept the occasional "spit in the eye," by way of the admiral's famously foul mouth, bad temper, and general dearth of charm. His transport commanders were said to fear Kelly Turner more than they did the Japanese.

But Bill got on well with his new boss. In fact, a bond formed between the two men, just as had been the case with virtually all of Bill's previous mentors and bosses—sequential father figures so lacking in his early childhood. After Bill's relatively mild trial by fire at Eniwetok (at the end of the Marshall Islands campaign), Admiral Turner made clear he was impressed with his new charge. For one thing, Bill never seemed to fall behind on the formidable list of tasks assigned him. For another, the irascible Turner observed, Bill was "unfailingly courteous." Even the admiral understood this challenge.

FOLLOWING ONE LAST DRESS rehearsal in late May 1944, Admiral Turner approved the plan for Operation Forager. The volume dwarfed all previous Pacific assault directives. Including the 163-page executive order issued by CINCPAC Admiral Spruance, Turner's master plan ran 800 pages; it had been assembled and tested to the teeth in an impressive three months. Saipan would be invaded on June 15, followed quickly by Guam on June 19, and Tinian last.

Between May 29 and June 6, 1944, the various contingents of the huge invasion fleet sortied from multiple ports for convergence off Saipan. As the world's eyes fastened on events unfolding on the beaches of northwest France, the largest naval convoy ever assembled in the Pacific set sail in 550 ships, auxiliary vessels, and landing crafts; 128,000 troops with 75,000 tons of supplies were in tow. Fanned out ahead of them were dozens of armed, prowling submarines, primed for the kill.

On the long voyage to Saipan, Bill began to feel ill. Initially, he wrote it off as seasickness, but in time, he knew it was something more serious. He wondered if departing for the Pacific the previous January before fully recovering from double pneumonia was the cause. But these were different symptoms. He could barely keep down food, and coffee, critical sustenance for months of long days and short nights, burned into his stomach and intestines like battery acid. Bill returned to his cabin each night doubled over in pain.

When the ship's doctor, Captain Gillette, suggested he take to Sick Bay, Bill declined. After years of scheming and countless setbacks, he was finally at sea on the eve of battle; surely he could make it through Operation Forager. Instead, he requested a hefty supply of magnesium hydroxide for its antacid properties, and aspirin. The latter, it turned out, would only make matters worse.

One night, during a break in the earsplitting pre-invasion shore bombardment of Saipan, Bill mixed a rounded spoonful of magnesium hydroxide in a metal cup of water and swallowed it with two gulps and a wince; this usually kept the symptoms at bay for a few hours. He then left his cabin for the deck. At the forecastle rail, he beheld a sight as spectacular as the one that spread out before him on the sea. The star Sirius—the brightest in the night sky and crucial to nautical navigation—was the centerpiece of a celestial light show of shooting stars and crystal-clear constellations. These jewels of the night backlit a dark and quiet Saipan.

The vast waters surrounding *Rocky Mount* were studded, too: hundreds of ships reached beyond the horizon in every direction. The prodigious fruits of America's war industries were arrayed before him like a feast. In fact, the exponentially expanded United States Navy of mid-1944 was about to surpass the size of all the navies in history combined.

Bill allowed a measure of relief to mingle with his physical discomfort. So far he had delivered fully on each task required of him. He'd grown confident in this daunting new role. Despite the initial—and steep—nautical learning curve, his sea legs now stood firm. Battle would be quite another thing; he would find that out soon enough. This moment, he knew, was a rare snatch of tranquility.

Enterprise was visible in the middle distance. With Benny now in Washington, Bill was grateful that perpetual worry over his safety, if not his happiness, was behind him. He also indulged in a deep sense of optimism about reaching Barton. He had measured in centimeters the shrinking distance on the map more than once over the past few weeks. In Washington, he had been some 14,000 miles away; now Mindanao lay less than 1,500 miles to the west.

Unable to sleep after retiring to his quarters, Bill switched on the tiny light over his bunk. He had always enjoyed penning spontaneous verse when the muse called, and tonight its bid would not be ignored. He turned over a spare map and scratched the following lines across the back:

At Sea, off the Marianas
June, 1944

Peace at War
Through many a year I've failed to dream
And soothe my heart and soul with fancy,
Too long a slave to life's routine
And none of nature's necromancy.

But now by Ares' paradox
My mind is free; no longer chained,
And damned up worry burst its locks
To loose those cares which long have reigned.

How easy here it is to dwell
On beauties dead and long forgot,
On stars and birds and ocean swells
And other charms that God hath wrought.

My ship for me a castle fair
And all around the sea, a moat
The drawbridge up; no stranger dare
Invade my world with boresome rote.

Time was the clouds could never be
Much more than shadows passing by;
But now they are the world to me,
And here, my other self, is why:

Confess, in all these years, to you
A cloud has been a cloud, naught more;
No towering castle in the blue –
Or tufted rug on heaven's floor.

The sea, alas, has seemed but water
And salt, at that, your dull mind said,
Because poor fool, you never sought her
And only stared while beauty bled.

Now the truth burns through at last
And you, the light from dark can sift
Away the worry of the past
And in mind's cup pure beauty lift.

Drink in the ocean's white nip'd breasts
Pay court to her in all her moods
Come skip from cloud to flowing crests
And fill your mind with fancy's foods.

See how the west wind comes a' prancing
And slices wavelets at their crest,
To spin and swirl them off a' dancing
Like Spanish Capes to castanets.

Thrill with the east wind's vicious strafe
Which cleaves the billows through and through;

A pure white counterpane to make—
The spread for Neptune's bed of blue.

And mark the ocean's face when still,
An image of the clouds and sky,
No song do breaking waves then spill,
A breathless beauty to the eye.

Save when the south wind's zephyrs trace,
The mirrored surface with design,
As water striders in a race
Or school fish airing in a line.

Seek out these beauties for, each day
The guns and falling death ignore
But if they speak, as soon they may,
Remember peace can come with war.

Naval bombardment of Saipan resumed the following morning: loud, lurid, and violent. Overhead, US planes circled and strafed. At 0400 tens of thousands of marines were served a princely breakfast of steak and eggs. For an unknown number of them, it would be their last meal. Chaplains were on hand to hear confessions and offer last-minute prayers.

At 0542 Admiral Turner's voice bellowed through the ship's loudspeakers: "Land the landing forces!" As rehearsed, the first marine-laden amtracs kicked up their wakes and churned toward the beaches of Saipan.

Rocky Mount's flag staff watched from the ship's rail as the battle, its blueprint so long in the making, unfolded before them. The plan had called for the simultaneous landing of two marine divisions on a beachfront spanning six thousand yards. Eight thousand marines were to go ashore in the initial wave; another twelve thousand would follow shortly thereafter.

But from the first hour forward, Operation Forager did not go according to plan.

The initial sign of trouble was a crescendo of murderous artillery fire when the leading line of amtracs reached the outer lip of Saipan's coral reef. Death rained down as their ramps splashed into the surf and marines hurtled out, only to slog toward the beach through heavier than predicted surf and larger than anticipated hummocks of coral.

Almost immediately, a chorus of desperate wails competed with the deafening artillery barrages. "Corpsman! Corpsman, Corpsman!" rose up from men cut down all along the shoreline. The less fortunate floated voicelessly in the seaweed, lapping to and fro in the reddening tide.

Three days of brutal cannonade ahead of the landings—165,000 large shells and another 2,400 sixteen-inch shells—had done little to dislodge well-concealed Japanese blockhouses and gun emplacements. The fleet's new, fast battleships had been trained for sea battle, not routing out hidden land targets. And they had fired their volleys from ten thousand yards offshore to protect the ships from return fire, too far for any real measure of accuracy. These errors would be grimly noted for future campaigns, as those at Tarawa had been.

Navajo radiomen positioned onshore sent their first chilling message back to anxious receivers in *Rocky Mount*'s communications center: "They're being killed all around us." There would be two thousand American casualties in the first hundred hours of the battle for Saipan, and it would get worse. Transports overflowing with the wounded rushed men from the beaches to the hospital ships throughout the day. Every sailor and officer who could donate blood did so.

Then came another staggering piece of news.

When Bill returned to the flagship's communications center after giving blood, it was buzzing with excitement. A cryptic piece of radio traffic originating from a coastwatcher in the Philippines had been picked up by

San Francisco's KFS Radio and beamed to the fleet. If the stunning report could be verified, the largest amphibious campaign of the Pacific War—now under way and not going particularly well—was about to become its largest sea battle as well.

ON THE MORNING OF June 15, 1944, twenty-three-year-old coast-watcher Gerald Chapman picked his way barefoot up a craggy path to his lookout post: a sea cliff overlooking the San Bernardino Strait on the southern tip of Luzon. Lieutenant Chapman had previously covered the strait from the island of Samar as part of the expanding coastwatcher network in the Philippines. On Luzon, Chapman had a much better view of both the strait and surrounding waters, but heavy Japanese presence made his current operation much more difficult and dangerous. Here he had to keep well hidden and limit his airtime to avoid enemy triangulation of his position. Detection would result in his instant execution.

On that morning, Chapman sat down and prepared for another hot, solitary day. But no sooner was he in position than he scrambled back to his feet. Undernourished and weak from malaria and tropical ulcers, he didn't trust the initial report of his naked eye. Chapman grabbed his binoculars and adjusted the focus, blinked, and adjusted it again.

Training the magnified field on the top of the waterway, he was sure now. Ships! No, an entire fleet! My God, such a fleet as he had never seen in his life! First, the outline of slim gray destroyers, and then the broader beams of cruisers, and then a phalanx of flat, boxy aircraft carriers hove into view. Soon there was no need for binoculars; he could see Japanese sailors all along the rails of an endless parade of vessels; they were looking out at both sides of the Strait, laughing and talking among themselves. Chapman ducked down as shadows of aircraft, their engines grinding, swept over his cliff outpost and fanned out eastward ahead of the flotilla, toward the Pacific Ocean.

When the last ship had passed, Chapman raced back to his low-slung, brush-covered radio shack. He cranked up his set with its meager 4-watt output and tapped out the message to Wendell Fertig's Mindanao station, call letters KUS, praying that his rusty instrument would not fail him now. Optimally, his urgent message would move from Fertig along the flash line engirdling the Philippines and then beam south to Australia and east across the Pacific, alerting likely Allied recipients of the surprise armada's approach:

```
Going east northeast . . . Jap Naval Fleet consisting of
two small patrol boats, eleven destroyers, ten cruisers, three
battleships, and nine aircraft carriers, last ship passed two
four degrees nine min lat one from west.
```

The Japanese immediately blasted Chapman's already weak transmission with intense jamming signals. But Chapman persisted, sending out the same message over and over again.

Bob Stahl, another coastwatcher posted on Samar, picked up Chapman's repeated relay attempts. He noticed that the enemy's jamming was unusually intense and that Chapman was struggling to get his message through. Stahl also knew how vulnerable Chapman's lookout post was and that he was supposed to limit his airtime—and that Chapman was fully aware of the swift and gruesome fate that befell apprehended coastwatchers. Yet he doggedly repeated his relay attempts.

The intensity of the jamming, Chapman's audacious persistence, and gut instinct told Stahl that this transmission must be of special significance. Without knowing its contents, he copied the entire message code and sent it out himself from his sturdier 12-watt radio. For hours, he received no response, even as Chapman boldly continued to relay.

Finally, Stahl received a response from KFS in San Francisco, directing him to move to a higher frequency. He complied, and resent Chapman's message, still unaware of its contents.

After what seemed an interminable wait, a coded response from KFS chirped through Stahl's headset:

```
Message received.
```

Then, later:

```
Well done.
```

Stahl's relay had also been picked up by navy submarine USS *Flying Fish*, lying off the Philippines. Her skipper corroborated what Chapman had observed:

```
Large enemy fleet headed east from San Bernardino Strait
at 20 knots.
```

What Chapman reported was the gathering strength of the entire Imperial Fleet en route to prevent the US Navy's seizure of Saipan. Its plan was to attack the Fifth Fleet—standing off Saipan in support of the marine landings—by a sneak attack from the rear. It was the same surprise strategy that had been deployed by Admiral Spruance at Midway—only applied in reverse. If the Japanese flotilla could take the Americans by surprise and strike a swift and decisive blow, it could save the hallowed Saipan.

AS THE BATTLE RAGED ashore, Admiral Spruance convened his commanders in the *Indianapolis* wardroom following receipt of Chapman's relay. "Well, gentlemen, the Japanese are coming after us," he said calmly, and then delivered another of his thoroughly risk-assessed decisions. Despite pressure to dispatch the bulk of his force as far west as necessary to obliterate the Japanese Fleet—a thrilling temptation with realistic potential—Admiral Spruance had concluded that his primary mission was to protect the vulnerable landings at all costs and to capture Saipan. He was also mindful of the Japanese penchant for diversionary lures, as well as the painful lessons from the first landings at Guadalcanal when the navy pulled back its ships prematurely—with nearly disastrous results for the marines ashore.

So, in this instance, Spruance decided to both protect the Saipan beachhead *and* sortie to meet the Japanese Fleet. He ordered Admiral Marc Mitscher and his powerful Task Force 58—comprised of fifteen new Essex and Independence-class aircraft carriers (with a total of 956 planes), as well as fast battleships, cruisers, and destroyers, all of which could sail at an impressive thirty knots—to ply northwest to meet the approaching armada. But also, guided by his primary mission of guarding the beachhead, he ordered a disappointed Mitscher to restrict his foray to a two-hundred-mile radius of Saipan. This was so the carriers could return quickly in case of a Japanese end run on the vulnerable island. Spruance further ordered a small but sturdy staple of escorts and carriers to remain in the immediate waters to provide continued bombardment and air cover to the beachhead—reassuring a visibly relieved Turner. "I'm going to join up with Mitscher and TF 58, but I'm also going to keep the Japs off your neck," Spruance told him.

For the next thirty-six hours, Mitscher's task force and the Japanese Fleet raced toward each other across the reaches of the Philippine Sea—the section of the Pacific Ocean between the Marianas and the Philippines. Finally, the location of the enemy fleet was confirmed: two hundred miles west of Saipan and on the move. Admiral Jisaburo Ozawa, in command of the Imperial Fleet—large, but inferior in airpower to the Fifth Fleet—had mistakenly assumed he could advance so close because he would be supported by five hundred land-based planes on nearby Japanese-held Guam. Unbeknownst to Ozawa, however, those planes had been dispatched elsewhere.

On the morning of June 19, Mitscher launched his planes to greet Ozawa's first wave of 545 aircraft, to deadly effect. Three hundred and sixty-six were shot down by American planes. Another nineteen were downed by antiaircraft fire. The sinking of three Japanese carriers, the *Shokaku*, the *Taiho*, and the *Hitaka*, as well as a destroyer and a fleet tanker, soon followed, along with the downing of hundreds more enemy aircraft. An *additional* three carriers, a battleship, three cruisers, and three fleet tankers were also maimed. So lopsided was the aerial battle that a pilot from the new USS *Lexington*, a Texan, said it reminded him of a good old turkey shoot at home. The Battle of the Philippine Sea was thereafter nicknamed the Great Marianas Turkey Shoot.

Admiral Spruance's measured strategy not only broke enemy hopes of saving Saipan and destroying the Fifth Fleet, but it diminished forever their remaining carrier strength: they were floating airfields without aircraft. The engagement would rank into the twenty-first century as the biggest aerial battle in American history.

GERALD CHAPMAN'S RELAYS MEANT abrupt alterations to Forager's timetables, which meant that Bill Mott would not see his bunk for nearly seventy-two hours. With fleet adjustments and battle plans in rapid flux, he loped from cabin to deck to transport to wardroom and back to *Rocky Mount*'s CIC to relay real-time updates to Admiral Nimitz at Pearl Harbor, Admiral King at the Navy Department, and his former staff in the White House Map Room—waiting anxiously, he well knew, for battle news.

Meanwhile, mounting marine casualties quickly overwhelmed the fleet's hospital ships, and scores were diverted to *Rocky Mount* for treatment. Stretcher after stretcher was handed up the gangway as Bill raced by. Many had limbs blown off. Others had bloodied bandages covering gruesome trunk wounds. Still others wore stained strips of cloth over their skulls or empty eye sockets. The ship's surgeons, dentists, and medical corpsmen worked around the clock, in both sick bays and wardrooms. The latter had been hastily converted to emergency dressing stations outfitted with plasma, morphine, whole blood, dressings, instruments, splints, litters, and an ample supply of body bags.

The first of several Japanese prisoners was brought aboard as well—for medical treatment and questioning. Though he had known to expect it, Bill was taken aback by his first encounter—face to face and in the flesh—with an enemy who had so inflamed his passions over the previous thirty months. He had been more prepared for a defiant, insolent soldier than this frightened, bloodied teenager before him. The prisoner glanced nervously between Bill and the interpreter as he answered the basic questions: name, rank, division. The boy was hardly the embodiment of evil Bill had conjured so fully in his mind.

By sunset on June 19, the battle outlook on Saipan had improved. The ships composing Spruance's ad hoc shore defense were doing their job and the marines had established a beachhead and were advancing inland. The US Army's Twenty-Seventh Infantry Division, which had been standing in reserve, had also joined the fight. Saipan's all-important airfield passed into American hands the next day, and the Fourth Marine Division reached the sea on the opposite side, bisecting the island. Given these positive developments, Admiral Turner handed over complete control of the landed forces to USMC general Holland "Howlin' Mad" Smith. And with the return of Mitscher's task force following the "Turkey Shoot," the tempo of the invasion was stepped up.

But two days later, a new kind of trouble started simmering—between the marines and the Twenty-Seventh Infantry Division. Here Bill found himself in familiar territory: in a bitter war of words between the army and the navy. He might just as well have been walking the halls of the Pentagon.

On June 22, USMC's Holland Smith had positioned the Twenty-Seventh Infantry Division between the Second and Fourth Marine Divisions in preparation for a broad sweep across the island. The two marine divisions advanced on schedule, but the army division did not. By nightfall on the twenty-third, instead of a straight line of advancing troops, the line had taken on an ominously concave U shape. On June 24, the army infantry division was still bogged down, threatening momentum and dangerously exposing marine flanks on both sides.

A jowly bulldog of a man, Howlin' Mad Smith stormed aboard *Rocky Mount* clutching his battle maps. He'd had enough. In an invective-laced conversation with Turner, the marine general lived up to his nickname, conveying in no uncertain terms his opinion of the Twenty-Seventh and its relatively young commanding officer, Army General Ralph Smith (no relation). Holland Smith had drafted a letter for Turner's signature removing Ralph Smith from his Saipan command. But Admiral Turner—while never noted for his tenderness toward the opposite service—wasn't going to relieve an army general at the height of battle without some flank of his own. Good reasons notwithstanding, there would be hell to pay between the services.

So Admiral Turner, Holland Smith, and a handful of hastily summoned aides, including Bill Mott, took *Rocky Mount*'s launch over to *Indianapolis* to confer with Admiral Spruance. Could Spruance fix this problem with Ralph Smith and the Twenty-Seventh Army Division? Spruance listened to his Forager commanders present their complaint and then asked what, precisely, they recommended he do. Both men advised that Ralph Smith be replaced by the more seasoned army general, Sanderford Jarman, who had already been designated to take over the Twenty-Seventh once Saipan was declared secure.

Spruance rightly paused before answering. Yes, there would be hell to pay: the open firing of an army general by a navy admiral on the joint recommendation of another navy admiral and a Marine Corps general? But lacking better alternatives—and with the faltering army line becoming dire—Spruance concurred. He issued the following order to Holland Smith:

```
You are authorized and directed to relieve Major General
Ralph Smith from command of the Twenty-Seventh Division,
US Army, and place Major General Jarman in command of this
division. This action is taken in order that the offensive on
Saipan may proceed in accordance with the plans and orders
of the Commander, Northern Troops and Landing Force.
```

When General Jarman stepped in, the line advance dilemma resolved quickly, but a furious reaction by army brass ensued. The long-simmering interservice rivalry in the Pacific—rooted in the struggle for theater primacy between Admiral Nimitz and General MacArthur—roared into public view. Bill admonished war correspondents aboard that this was a strictly military matter and not fodder for newspaper reports. He then shuttled endlessly between *Rocky Mount* and *Indianapolis* as part of an attempt to contain the firestorm.

But it was too late, thanks to reporters in Pearl Harbor who had somehow sniffed out the story. The controversy was lustily played out by the largest newspaper chain in the country. Strong coverage of the "navy scandal" story gave its owner, conservative William Randolph Hearst, an ideal opportunity to advance his political agenda in support of MacArthur. Hearst editorials spewed blame at the marines for excessive loss of life in the Pacific and called for General MacArthur, whose leadership resulted "in little loss of life, in most cases," to be named supreme commander of the Pacific.

MacArthur's abject failure and subsequent personnel losses in the Philippines, and the fact that he hadn't had much enemy contact since, factored little in the press accounts. Scandalous headlines dominated: Holland Smith was the butcher he had been declared to be after Tarawa, and he fired gallant Ralph Smith for refusing to send his men into certain slaughter. The precipitating facts and factors in the Smith vs. Smith contretemps faded into the background. Another press account competed unsuccessfully for attention: that Ralph Smith was not sufficiently battle tested and/or lacked the requisite training and discipline necessary to advance men under fire.

On July 9, Admiral Turner declared the island of Saipan securely in Allied hands. The final carnage was staggering: the Americans suffered 16,000 casualties (dead, wounded, and missing). Japanese losses were worse: at least 24,000 dead and 3,612 missing. Enemy casualties climbed sharply toward the end when defenders launched a series of final banzai charges, and Japanese-born civilians by the thousands rushed to the island's steep cliffs and jumped to their deaths. When the battle outcome was certain, Admiral Nagumo, General Saito, and their senior commanders all committed ritual suicide rather than surrender. The loss of Saipan also prompted the once-powerful prime minister, Hideki Tojo, to resign his cabinet—all proof of how catastrophic the sacred island's loss was to the Japanese.

Turner and the amphibians went on to prevail at Tinian and Guam as well, and on August 9, the Marianas conquest was complete. But Operation Forager had taken its own toll on Bill Mott. Over the two-month campaign, he had progressed steadily from unwell to seriously ill. On August 10, the day after Guam was secured, he collapsed on the bridge.

When Bill regained consciousness, he was on a stretcher alongside numerous battle casualties awaiting airlift to Pearl Harbor's Aiea Heights Naval Hospital. Humiliated that he hadn't kept the pace he demanded of himself and further embarrassed to be evacuated alongside gruesomely wounded marines who'd given nearly their all, Bill sank into despondency. Not only did it likely mean back to a desk job, but it also meant he had failed in his quest to reach Barton—a possibility he had never even considered until now.

It was in this morose frame of mind that Bill, waiting for trans-Pacific air transport, looked up to see Admiral Turner standing over him, holding an Armed Services paperback edition of *The Razor's Edge*. He'd been looking all over for him, the admiral said cheerfully. He thought Bill might like to read W. Somerset Maugham's brand-new novel while recovering. Even at this zenith of self-loathing, Bill thanked and then apologized to Turner, who he was sure was about to become his ex-boss.

But Turner seemed to miss none of the turmoil that was clawing holes in Bill's stomach. "You've done a fine job, Commander," said the admiral, a man not given to flattery. "If you can get yourself well by the time the ship returns to Pearl, consider your job as my flag secretary and legal officer a permanent assignment."

30

★   ★   ★

DECAMPMENT

AS EARLY AS MAY 1944, changes in guard behavior and camp routine at Davao augured another mass prisoner move. Agitated by yet another successful escape, camp administrators had been further spooked by rumors that local guerrillas, whom they believed to be greater in size and strength than their own tiny garrison, were planning to storm the camp and free the remaining prisoners.

Nearly all productive work details had stopped. Rice paddies and vegetable gardens were not replanted, and tools and equipment were being crated and shipped out. In addition, all prisoners were given dysentery tests, presaging the dreaded possibility of shipment to Japan.

The most recent escape had taken place in March. An eleven-man work detail, armed with heavy shovels, had left the camp to reinforce fences around a cucumber field near the jungle perimeter. Following a work break, one of them clubbed the head guard to death. Another prisoner struck the second guard, but not hard enough to kill him. The group then fled into the rain forest. Six of the escapees survived the jungle trek, met up with the guerrillas, and joined their forces.

Not long afterward, guards overseeing another work detail discovered a cache of vitamins, chocolates wrapped in papers with "I Shall Return" stamped on them, and a copy of *Free Philippines*, the Filipino resistance publication printed by the US Army, all compliments of Courtney Whitney's PRS advancement efforts. Reprisals, including further food curtailment, fell once again on the innocent.

But the point of having nothing left to withhold was fast approaching; the Japanese needed a new strategy to prevent escape. Each day some action by camp administrators or a comment by the despised hunchback interpreter, Shusuke Wada, increased prisoner suspicion that they were going to be moved. The men had long feared being sent to Japan, but now even more so; thanks to contraband radio reports, they knew that the war had turned decisively in their favor and that liberation of the Philippines was approaching.

In late April, 750 prisoners had been trucked off-site with orders to finish constructing two nearby airfields. The sudden urgency to accelerate completion of the airstrips—one near Barrio Lasang and the other near Davao City—was yet another sign the Japanese feared that the Allies were closing in. Communications were severed between the airfield detail and the prisoners that remained at DAPECOL—another precaution taken by the increasingly uneasy prison administration.

Speculation finally came to an end on June 5, 1944, when a fleet of empty flatbed trucks rolled in and parked across from the camp compound. The prisoners were told at *tenko* that evening to prepare for an early-morning departure; they were leaving Mindanao for good. Each was handed an ominous-looking thirty-six-inch strip of white cloth and told to bring it with him the following morning, along with any remaining personal belongings.

At first, the men were oddly nostalgic, remembering their initial elation upon arriving at Davao nineteen months earlier. Then an almost festive

mood swept the camp. Charles and Barton, their surnames near the beginning of the alphabet, would be in the first echelon to move out. They wasted
no time organizing activities for their final night, of which the guards were
surprisingly tolerant. After a moment of hesitation at the thought of his precious spaniels Jasper and Sable back home, Barton joined Charles and Ken
Wheeler in the sacrifice of the protein component of the last supper, the
camp's stray dogs and Susie the cat and her offspring. Barton's motive was
pure: to live long enough to see Sable and Jasper again at Lilac Hedges, at
which time he would somehow make it up to them.

The ensigns stripped all remaining edibles from individual gardens and
the prison kitchen—mostly cassavas and squash—rounding out the final
Davao repast. Against the din of screaming scarlet macaws and raucous parrot
chatter, the men talked and even laughed as the unfortunate animals sizzled on
spits and the potpourri of residual victuals simmered in a pot over a campfire.

In an unexpected act of clemency, the Japanese distributed several bags
of mail that evening that they had inexplicably been holding back. It was on
this occasion that Barton Cross received his first letter from home, from his
mother, dated a full year earlier—June 1943. He was overjoyed. Written in
her familiar, sweeping hand, it included family news, greetings from neighbors, and photos of her, Arthur, and Rosemary. Bill's and Benny's activities
were not mentioned, perhaps because of their military positions and combat activities.

Barton was euphoric, and the photos made numerous rounds during
the festivities. While the prisoners indulged themselves under the stars that
night, they speculated endlessly on their destination, about which camp administrators had been tight lipped. The men suspected and hoped for Manila, but, as ever, they worried about being shipped to Japan.

The next morning, the first group was ordered to assemble at 0400.
Barton and Charles rousted themselves from their hard bunks and took
one last look around. At each juncture of their now two-and-a-half-year
imprisonment, hope had vied with apprehension as to how their next set

of living conditions would compare with the last. But with the amulet of a letter from home tucked into a tiny satchel, Barton radiated optimism that things were on the upswing.

ON THE MORNING OF June 6, 1944, as the epic cross-Channel invasion of Western Europe—D-day—unfolded continents away, 1,239 war prisoners were marched to the awaiting trucks outside the Davao Penal Colony. Those who still had shoes were ordered to remove them and tie them around their necks. Any prisoner who failed to follow orders exactly received a rifle butt reminder. The guards' generous demeanor of the previous evening had vaporized; they were visibly nervous and determined to prevent another escape.

The twenty-two truck beds were loaded to overcapacity. Thirty men were jammed into each, tight against one another, then ordered to remain standing even though the slatted sides were barely eighteen inches high. A guard with a long rope then boarded each truck bed. Beginning in the right forward corner, he tied the rope around the waist of the first prisoner, and successively tied him to the man on his right and left, or to the person in front of him if he was at the end of the row. This continued until all thirty men on each truck bed were tethered together with a single piece of rope.

As the truck engines growled to life, the men were ordered to blindfold themselves with the strips of white cloth they'd been issued the previous evening. With these tasks complete, two armed guards boarded each truck, and the convoy rumbled out of Davao in the semidarkness.

It was a difficult trip. The men lurched and reeled; they couldn't brace for stops, acceleration, turns, or cavities in the rutted road that they couldn't see. Slowing jammed them forward, accelerating swung them backward, and turns pitched them outward. More than once, an entire truckload nearly toppled over the low railing.

When the tethers and blindfolds were finally removed, the prisoners found themselves at the Lasang dock, not far from where the *Erie Maru* had

first off-loaded them in October 1942. Once on the docks, the men were
ordered to sit in the hot sun for hours while the trucks left to collect the
rest of the prisoners. Anchored out in the harbor was a single ship: a rusted
freighter with *Yashu Maru* painted on its side.

With signature adjectives, Charles Armour noted that the ship did not
carry any markings indicating that it would be carrying prisoners of war.
They all knew Allied submarines lurked in nearby waters. How would the
submariners know to let them pass? "Maybe they should just paint a big
bull's-eye on her," Charles remarked, but in a tone less defiant than in the
past.

When the second group of prisoners arrived, those that were removed
from Davao in April to work on the airfield were not among them. When
questioned, Mr. Wada declined to disclose their whereabouts. Speculation
on the fate of these many friends rippled through the group as they waited.

In the peak afternoon heat, the prisoners were ferried out by launch
to *Yashu Maru*, and the dreaded boarding began. Barton and Charles were
among the first to descend the ladder into the dark, steaming hold; al
phabetical loading made their very surnames a curse. The first group was
jammed so tightly into the hull's canted rear that they couldn't sit, much less
lie down. The men girded themselves for a miserable trip. No reminder was
necessary that their voyage to Mindanao had taken eleven days.

Ominously, the Japanese guards began removing all life jackets from
the hold's storage area. But just when it seemed things were going from bad
to worse, they distributed Red Cross parcels to every prisoner—for which
any prisoner would have happily traded a life jacket if given the option.
Such was the unpredictability of their captors. Spirits gradually declined
again as *Yashu Maru* languished in the harbor for an impossible six days.
Some prisoners became so agitated after crouching so long in the airless
hold, they had to be tied up like dogs.

Finally, on June 12, the engine sputtered to life. A cheer went up as the
movement generated a subtle flow of air belowdecks. *Yashu Maru* departed

its prolonged anchorage in a small convoy, and the captain steered a careful northward course. Fearful of attacks from above and below, he hugged the coast so closely it seemed at times the ship might run aground.

Once under way, the men were allowed to rotate to the deck for rations and to relieve themselves. To ease the crowding below, a few lucky ones, including Barton and Ken Wheeler, were allowed to sleep on the deck, a tremendous reprieve. However, that privilege ended after only a few days when two prisoners, army officers John McGee and Don Wills, jumped over the rail into the ocean. This time the hatch was bolted shut.

Defiant and hopeful that McGee and Wills had made good on their escapes—despite the thirty-foot drop to the water and the hail of gunfire that followed their overboard leaps—the locked-down prisoners began to sing. Hoarse, repeated strains of "God Bless America" drifted up through the floorboards. A visibly irritated Mr. Wada finally opened the hatch and glared down at them. "You crazy Americans," he spat, and slammed it shut again.

Misery below mounted as the convoy plied glacially north for three more days. Then suddenly the prisoners lurched as the ship turned abruptly, accelerated, and headed toward land. It seemed they were making an unscheduled stop at the island of Cebu, south of the San Bernardino Strait. The date was June 15.

To the prisoners' relief, the hatch opened, and they were ordered to exit the ship. The guards yelled, *"Speedo! Speedo!"* as the 1,237 men struggled up the ladder. Squinting out into Cebu Harbor, they were taken aback by an enormous formation of Japanese warships.

The bewildered prisoners were herded ashore and marched to an old American bastion, Fort San Pedro. The building, which still bore the sign "USAFFE Headquarters," had been heavily bombed, but its shell was intact. The interior was a heap of stones, dirt, and coal ash.

The men were held here, without explanation, for five days. Eventually a local Filipino tipped them off as to the cause of their detour: the

Americans had landed at Saipan, and the Japanese Fleet that they had seen in the harbor was now battling the US Navy in the Philippine Sea. The thrill of hearing that their countrymen were so close shot through the group like an electric current. The outcome of the engagement was not yet known, but to the prisoners, the Allies were hard by and on the offensive, nourishing their hopes of imminent liberation.

On June 21 the prisoners were rousted off the fort's floor and marched back to the docks. Smudged black from the coal ash, they drew sympathetic stares from Filipinos all along the route. At the dock, their guards were testy and brusque, leading to upbeat prisoner speculation on the winner of the naval clash. But the grins soon vanished.

Crammed belowdeck on an even smaller ship, they braced for another stretch of misery. The prisoners murmured prayers and clung to their sanity for five more days inside a hold normally used for coal storage. A collective sigh went up at the clank and grind of an anchor chain followed by a splash. They were back in Manila Harbor.

The psychological relief this brought was short-lived as the desperate men remained in the hold for another four days in the scorching June heat. They fretted and cursed. Why had they not disembarked? Was this just a stopover en route to Japan? The uncertainty was as maddening as the dim and increasingly fouled quarters.

On the afternoon of June 26, three weeks since departing Davao, an unfamiliar guard finally opened the hatch and called down, "All men go now!" The body of a prisoner who had died of heat exhaustion was lifted out first, followed by a long queue of litters. The hold's rear echelon, including Barton and Charles—badly depleted but able to walk—were the last to emerge.

In stark contrast to his appearance and present circumstances—and the emotional state of many of the others—Barton's morale was "sky-high." The news at Cebu surely meant that the US Navy was on the way! Armored in optimism, he gulped the harbor air and lined up for the march back to

Bilibid Prison. Given the range of lesser alternatives, all the prisoners were encouraged by this development. Here was a place they could walk around, breathe fresh air, and even lie down—if on a cement floor. And also reunite with old friends.

The Davao returnees were greeted warmly by several familiar faces, including some of the original navy doctors and medics from Canacao Naval Hospital. These were the men who had cared for Barton and so many other wounded during and after the attack on Cavite. But the doctors were shocked by what they saw.

After examining their group, Surgeon Thomas Hayes confided to his journal, "1,234 prisoners arrived from Davao after 21 days in route . . . A horrible, miserable lot, many officers, both Army and Navy, among them. A wild eyed, dirty mob, many changed almost beyond recognition."

The resident prisoners at Bilibid must have made similar observations; they showed extraordinary sympathy toward the returnees, despite their own privations. Miraculously, they produced a tub of ice water to welcome them. *Ice* water? From where in all of war-torn Manila was there ice to be found, the Davao group marveled—much less at Bilibid Prison? Many described feeling the most grateful they had felt in their entire lives at that sole gesture.

But the reprieve was brief. After four days at Bilibid, some of the Davao draft received bad news; others worse. Nine hundred were to go back to Cabanatuan. The rest would be shipped to Japan.

31

★ ★ ★

SEPTEMBER 1944,
LILAC HEDGES

ON EVERY SEPTEMBER FIRST in memory, Helen Cross had launched her autumn garden preparations as if prompted by the same lunar pull that stirs birds to journey south. Just as winged migrants detect a scent in the wind, a shift in the stars, or the changed direction of a late-summer breeze, something tugged at Helen's soul when the calendar page turned to September. The first day of that month always marked the start of a weeks-long autumn gardening ritual.

The summer of 1944 had been unusually hot and dry in New Jersey, killing some of her plants outright, despite Helen's vain attempts to keep them hydrated. To her diary, she complained:

*Pretty hot, diary mine! Rainless for over a month. I have visions of
a nice stand of hay where lawns used to be! Jupiter Pluvius must
be on some Olympian holiday. The flowers and bushes droop for his*

attention—the expected thunderstorms seem to pass right out to sea—
poor garden!

Barton's twelve-year-old spaniel, Sable, trailed behind her during this autumn's garden rounds at a noticeably slower clip. Helen lamented:

I think this may have been his last summer—he is very feeble, yet he
follows me slowly and faithfully all over the yard. He's now blind and
deaf to all but my whistle. Queer, but he seemed to fail fast once Barton
went away. I remember him sharp as a trigger years ago, cute as a fox,
and fast on his little feet. He is Barton's dog, and I hope he lives for his
homecoming.

As usual, Helen began her fall inspection at the outer-perimeter beds and worked her way in toward the house. She would set out each morning in the early-autumn cool, wearing sensible shoes and her favorite apron, with its wide band of pockets, home to a notepad, trowels, and other gardening implements. Her auburn hair was tucked under a broad straw hat the color of sunflower petals.

She noted first that the plants in the unshaded southwest corner of the property were parched and wilted; they must be dug up and replanted. ("It will look nice, I think, for Barton to see," she wrote that evening.) Moving on, she decided to plant a new bed of yellow tulips and relocate the red ones to the side lawn.

She would then address the routine tasks: dig up and divide her daylilies, which had come back crowded that summer, barely able to breathe. Her rosebushes needed cutting back, too, after which she must lay down a protective winter blanket of good straw. The next job would be an all-day project: fertilizing her dozens of precious lilacs from the lovingly tended compost pile behind the shed. But first, some fall adornment to cheer her as she worked:

Geraniums came for the beds—a blaze of scarlet glory!

As skeins of southbound geese passed over Lilac Hedges in military-like V formations, Helen worked her trowel with the same focus and passion that she did her pen. And for nearly nine months out of the year, the glorious gardens at Lilac Hedges repaid her with pendulous blooms of every description—one of her few remaining sources of pleasure.

But on the fifteenth day of that September, Helen's hopes, plans, and gardens were fouled—like so many other events of late—by circumstances beyond her control. What would go down in history as the Great Atlantic Hurricane of 1944 slammed into coastal New Jersey.

Sixty-foot trees toppled like sticks, pulling down wires and telephone poles with them. Whipping winds dashed a 250-ton freighter onto the shore like a toy boat. Atlantic City's iconic boardwalk and Steel Pier were laid to waste, and hundreds of homes were reduced to rubble. Lilac Hedges—and Helen's gardens—were not spared:

> *Last night the house shook, windows rattled, and trees bent before the onslaught . . . And oh! Never can I forget the sight which met our eyes this morning. Trees crashed through the garage, all smaller trees bent to 45 degrees, the lilacs—as though beaten nearly to death by some sinister force.*
>
> *Sick at heart as we survey the damage, try to straighten small trees and tie up plants. Every one of the Jap lilac trees on our western border is devastated, huge centre haunches broken off at the base . . .*
>
> *The horror at the shore is terrific—everywhere trees through rooftops—wild demonic destruction—worst storm in 75 years and it must come now?*
>
> *God in heaven, isn't war's anguish enough?*

For the next two weeks, Helen cleaned up from nature's vicious attack. She stumbled through fallen boughs and heaps of brush as she worked, wringing her hands over the destruction. The wreckage that surrounded them, she mused to Arthur, matched the wreckage in her heart.

SOME RELIEF ARRIVED WHEN Benny, now stationed in Washington, arrived by train. It was only his second visit to Lilac Hedges since his orders to the Pentagon. There had been little respite from his work as the harried new chief of Ship Characteristics and Fleet Requirements—or from vexing negotiations with his estranged wife.

Over a rare home-cooked meal with Helen and Arthur—prepared lovingly by William and Nelly in his honor—Benny covered many topics, including Bill's recovery. He was much better and had finally been released from Aiea Heights Naval Hospital at Pearl Harbor, Benny reported. He hoped to be back in the fight soon. But Helen's focus never wavered. To her diary that evening, she confided:

> Benny had news of Bill, healing from ulcers of the stomach. But he
> [Bill] had apparently done nothing to get news of Barton. I had asked
> him to call on the Provost Marshall.

Benny's visit to New Jersey was actually official business. He was scheduled to honor the workers at a converted sewing-machine factory in Elizabethtown for their extraordinary productivity. He had hoped a respite at Lilac Hedges would restore his flagging spirits, but the arrival of bad news the following morning foiled that plan.

> A letter came today from a Bataan Relief correspondent confirming the
> Japs' report to International Red Cross of the sinking by an American
> submarine of an American prison ship. It was said to be carrying
> hundreds of American prisoners of war, and was off the coast of
> Mindanao . . .